THE BEGINNINGS OF POLITICAL DEMOCRACY
IN JAPAN

THE BEGINNINGS OF POLITICAL DEMOCRACY IN JAPAN

BY

NOBUTAKA IKE

*Issued Under the Auspices of the International Secretariat,
Institute of Pacific Relations
and
The Hoover Institute and Library
On War, Revolution, and Peace*

GREENWOOD PRESS, PUBLISHERS
NEW YORK

Copyright © 1950 by the Johns Hopkins Press

Reprinted by permission of the Johns Hopkins Press

First Greenwood Reprinting, 1969

Library of Congress Catalogue Card Number 69-13946

SBN 8371-1802-5

PRINTED IN UNITED STATES OF AMERICA

The Institute of Pacific Relations is an unofficial and non-partisan body, founded in 1925 to facilitate the scientific study of the social, economic and political problems of the Pacific area. It is composed of National Councils in twelve countries.

The Institute as such and the National Councils of which it is composed are precluded from expressing an opinion on any aspect of national or international affairs; opinions expressed in this study are, therefore, entirely those of the author.

TO
TAI AND LINDA

CONTENTS

PART FOUR:

THE ABSOLUTE STATE

PART FIVE:

EPILOGUE

PREFACE

In preparing this study the author received the assistance of many people. To Mr. Owen Lattimore, who directed the work from beginning to end, the author owes a heavy debt. It is a pleasure to acknowledge gratefully the invaluable guidance and constant encouragement which he so generously provided. Professor V. O. Key, Jr. read the entire manuscript, as did Dr. Edwin Reischauer, of Harvard University, and Dr. Thomas C. Smith, of Stanford University. For their help the author is most grateful. Dr. John M. Maki, of the University of Washington, and Dr. Robert Ward, of the University of Michigan read portions of the manuscript and made important suggestions. The author is indebted to Dr. E. Herbert Norman for suggesting the topic, and, for his pioneering studies of the Meiji era. It should be made clear, of course, that the author is solely responsible for all errors and inadequacies.

The major portion of the material used in the preparation of this study was obtained from the Library of Congress. Thanks are due to Dr. Edwin Beal, Mr. Andrew Kuroda, and Mrs. T. Takeshita, all of the Division of Orientalia of the Library, for their courteous cooperation.

The author wishes to thank the Social Science Research Council for financial assistance in the form of two Demobilization Awards granted in 1946 and 1947.

Publication of the book is sponsored and supported by the International Secretariat of the Institute of Pacific Relations and by the Hoover Institute and Library. For their support, the author wishes to thank Mr. William L. Holland, of the Institute of Pacific Relations, and Dr. Harold H. Fisher, and Dr. C. Easton Rothwell, of the Hoover Institute and Library.

Finally, the author is indebted to his wife for help in preparing the manuscript.

N. I.

Stanford, California
February, 1950

xi

INTRODUCTION

THE conception of Japan as a tightly knit and well integrated totalitarian state became well fixed in the American mind during the war and was carried over into the post war era. It was widely anticipated that the Japanese people would be politically apathetic and that a long interval of tutelage would be required to implant in them a desire for democratic government. Yet hardly had the military government removed the restrictive laws that had been acting as a political straitjacket than there emerged a popular movement, the vigor and scope of which surprised the occupation authorities.

Such a development, however, need not have occasioned surprise, for it was not exactly without precedent. There were occasions in earlier years when liberal sentiment seemed to eclipse the authoritarian tendencies which characterized Japanese history as a whole. One of the most noteworthy of such liberal periods was the several decades preceding the promulgation of the Meiji constitution in 1889. Although it is not generally known, at that time the Japanese endeavored to attain democratic institutions much in the same manner as they are doing today. Unlike the current experiment in democracy, which in the main was initiated and encouraged from above by the occupation, the earlier attempt was essentially an indigenous movement. As such it deserves the serious attention of students of Japanese politics.

The main purpose of the present study is to trace and to explain the origins, growth, and decline of this liberal movement. In the Japanese literature on the subject, it is known as the *Jiyu minken undo* or the "Movement for liberty and popular rights," but throughout this work it has been described as the democratic movement.

Because the word democracy often implies different things to different people, it is perhaps well to attempt at the outset a brief definition. The author understands democracy to refer to a form of government in which the governing minority is more or less accountable to the majority in the conduct of public affairs. This is achieved largely by the requirement that those who rule must compete at regular intervals for the vote of the electorate. In order that there may be competition, the group in power must tolerate the dissemination of views which may be at variance with its own views; and, moreover, it must not attempt to eliminate political competition by the use of force. If this definition is acceptable, then the question arises as to whether the " Movement for liberty and popular rights " had as its objective the creation of a government fulfulling the above requirements. Although this anticipates the material presented in the main body of this study, it may be stated somewhat dogmatically at this point that the answer appears to be in the affirmative.

Basically, the present study is a historical analysis of a political movement. But because the democratic movement represented an important phase in the transformation of Japan into a modern state, its ramifications are rather broad. It is in one way or another related to such phenomena as the development of Japanese capitalism, the growth of modern political parties, and the impact of Western influences on Japanese politics. For this reason, the scope of the work has been extended beyond the narrow limits of the democratic movement proper. Accordingly, excursions have been made, on occasion, into matters which, strictly speaking, belong more in the realm of economic history, constitutional history, and political theory.

Thus, although the movement itself did not begin until the early 1870's, the present treatment takes as its starting point the closing days of Tokugawa rule. This makes it possible to examine, for instance, the historical position of the landowner—small industrialists who formed one of the most important elements within the democratic movement. It also enables us to trace, from its early beginnings, the expanding influence of certain Western political concepts like parliamentary government on the structure and operation of Japanese government.

This paves the way for the discussion and analysis of the formation of political parties, of the powerful drive to petition the government to establish representative institutions, and of the spread of Western political theory that provided the movement with its intellectual underpinnings. Then the economic depression of the early 1880's and the local revolts which largely found their origins in this depression are treated in some detail in order to examine the causes behind the collapse of the movement. To round out the picture, the reaction of the government to the growing demands for democracy and civil rights is considered. This is followed by a brief account of the drafting of the constitution of 1889, which symbolized the final failure of the struggle to obtain a democratic government in Japan. The concluding chapter attempts to assess briefly some implications of the movement to the present political situation in Japan.

Implicit, also, in this study of the Japanese democratic movement is the question of its relation to political movements in general and to liberal middle class movements in particular. Since the main focus of the present study was to make, as it were, a case study of a single movement, nowhere has the author specifically addressed himself to these questions at any length. It is hoped, however, that the material contained herein will prove to be of some value to those interested in the general problem of the sociology of political movements.

LIST OF ABBREVIATIONS

CK	Chuo Koron
Emergence	Japan's Emergence as a Modern State
Feudal Background	Feudal Background of Japanese Politics
JGD	Japanese Government Documents
JS	Jiyuto Shi
KSK	Keizai Shi Kenkyu
KUER	Kyoto University Economic Review
MBK	Meiji Bunka Kenkyu
MBZ	Meiji Bunka Zenshu
MJR	Minken Jiyu Ron
NKST	Nihon Kensei Shi Taiko
NSHSK	Nihon Shihonshugi Hattatsu Shi Koza
Political History	A Political History of Japan During the Meiji Era, 1867-1912
RGK	Rekishi Gaku Kenkyu
SKS	Shakai Keizai Shigaku
SNST	Sogo Nihon Shi Taikei: Meiji Jidai
SSMHS	Shimbun Shusei Meiji Hennen Shi
TASJ	Transactions of the Asiatic Society of Japan
TJB	Tempu Jinken Ben

NOTE

Japanese personal names are given in the conventional form with the family name preceding the given name. However, in the case of a few Japanese authors whose works were published in English, Western usage has been followed.

Japanese words have been italicized except for a few common words like samurai which are listed in the Webster's Collegiate Dictionary.

Unless otherwise noted, all translations from the Japanese were made by the author.

Part One:

THE RESTORATION PERIOD

CHAPTER I

COUP D'ÉTAT

DARKNESS gradually shrouded the beautiful and historic city of Kyoto. Outwardly it was no different from the myriad nights that had descended on the Imperial capital in the past. But on this day of January 3, 1868, the approach of night symbolized the end of an era.

The sprawling Imperial palace, situated in the heart of the city, was the scene of unusual activity. Earlier in the day when the regular guards appeared to take their places at the six gates that cut the roofed wall of earth and plaster surrounding the palace, they found them already in the possession of strange soldiers. On being told that they were relieved of their duties, they sullenly withdrew.[1]

The change in the guards did not augur well for the Tokugawa house which had ruled the country for more than two and a half centuries. The regular guards consisted of men from Aidzu and Kuwano, two fiefs, or to use a more common term, clans (*Han*) [2] allied with the Tokugawa family. The newcomers, in contrast, were drawn from five clans openly hostile to the Tokugawa and were commanded by a cunning leader and conspirator, Saigo Takamori, of whom we shall have occasion to speak again later.

The newly-appointed guardians of the palace gates presently admitted a small group of men, many of whom were destined to become the leaders of a new Japan. Only a few hours had elapsed since an unexpected Imperial decree proclaimed the end of Tokugawa rule. A new provisional government, replacing the defunct Shogunate or *Bakufu*,[3] was established; and now these men, ap-

[1] James Murdoch, *A History of Japan* (London, 1926), III, 773.

[2] *Han*, originally meaning "military frontier," is usually translated "clan," but it signifies merely a territorial division ruled by a feudal noble and has no reference to a group related by blood.

[3] *Bakufu*, literally "Tent Government," was originally used for the army headquarters in the feudal period. It is usually applied to the military dictatorship under the Tokugawa family.

3

pointed to important posts in the new government, were proceeding
to their first conference.

The men were ushered into the section of the palace known as
the *Kogosho* or Little Palace, which was reserved, as a rule, for
minor functions. But this occasion was far from minor. In fact,
owing to the importance of the subject to be discussed, the meeting
was being held in the presence of the sixteen-year-old Emperor.
The participants were arranged according to rank. The Imperial
princes and Court nobles or *Kuge* sat facing the west. Opposite
them sat five feudal nobles. In the middle section were seated a
number of low-ranking samurai.[4] These samurai had won the right
to participate in the discussions by virtue of their daring and
ceaseless efforts to undermine the foundations of the old regime.

The big question to be decided by the assembled notables was
the disposition of the former Shogun.[5] Ever since the beginning of
the seventeenth century, the Shogun had ruled the country as
virtual military dictators. But in November, 1867 the reigning
Shogun, Tokugawa Keiki (or Yoshinobu), took an unprecedented
step. He resigned and " returned " the rule to the Emperor, who
at that time lived in seclusion in Kyoto. However, in his letter of
resignation, the Shogun was conspicuously silent about the surrender of the vast resources possessed by the Tokugawa family.
As head of the Tokugawa house, Keiki still controlled an area
equal to about one-fourth of the realm. He remained, therefore,
the most powerful political figure in the country, despite his resignation as Shogun.

Such an arrangement was understandably looked upon with dis-
favor by most of his traditional enemies. Having plotted for years
to destroy the Tokugawa house, they were in no mood to permit
Keiki to retain any semblance of power. On the other hand, there
were a few who took a more moderate position. Although they
approved of the abolition of the Shogunate, they felt that the
former Shogun should be given an important position in the
provisional government.

[4] Fujii Jintaro and Moriya Hidesuke, *Sogo Nihon Shi Taikei: Meiji Jidai* [A
Synthesis of Japanese History: The Meiji Period] (Tokyo, 1934), p. 91. (Hereafter this work will be cited as *SNST*).

[5] The full title is *Sei-i-tai-Shogun* or " Barbarian Quelling Generalissimo," and it
was an office originally established in the campaigns against the Ainu. From 1603
to 1868 the Shogun was always a Tokugawa.

The meeting was opened by Yamanouchi Yodo, the Lord of Tosa, a fief located on the island of Shikoku. He stated frankly that there was, in his opinion, something highly suspicious about the whole affair. He expressed fear that someone was planning to seize power by taking possession of the young Emperor. He was adamant in his plea that the former Shogun be invited to the meeting.[6] Quite obviously he still felt some loyalty to the Tokugawa house. It is believed that he sided with the Tokugawa on this occasion because in the seventeenth century, an ancestor of his had been treated liberally by Iyeyasu, the founder of the Tokugawa Shogunate.

A Court noble, Iwakura Tomomi, rose to reply to Yamanouchi's accusations. A master of political intrigue, Iwakura was no mean foe. He was well informed because of his connections with the anti-Tokugawa underground movement.[7] Furthermore, he came well prepared, having earlier held a caucus at his residence with a few samurai from Satsuma and Choshu, the two clans most hostile to the Tokugawa.[8] Iwakura, in answer to Yamanouchi's accusations, asserted that the decision to call the meeting had been made by the Emperor himself. He strongly urged that the Imperial court order the former Shogun to surrender all of his land holdings and revenues.

The two protagonists exchanged sharp words. Since both had factions backing them, neither would give in, and the meeting was deadlocked. At this point, the Emperor called a recess. In the meantime, Iwakura apparently came to the conclusion that the situation necessitated drastic action. Putting a dagger in the bosom of his *kimono*, he summoned one of the feudal lords and through him let it be known to Yamanouchi that if the latter " persisted in his attitude he would be invited to an ante-chamber where he and Iwakura would poniard each other." [9]

[6] *SNST*, p. 91.

[7] A brief sketch of Iwakura may be found in Yosaburo Takekoshi, *The Economic Aspects of the History of the Civilization of Japan* (New York: The MacMillan and Company, 1930), III, 373-375.

[8] *SNST*, p. 88.

[9] Murdoch, III, 774. See also Sashihara Yasuzo, *Meiji Seishi* [Meiji Political History] reprinted in Yoshino Sakuzo (editor), *Meiji Bunka Zenshu* [Collected Works on Meiji Culture] (Tokyo, 1930), II, 13-14. (Hereafter the *Meiji Bunka Zenshu* will be cited as *MBZ*).

Presently the meeting was resumed. A long debate followed, lasting until the early hours of the morning. Apparently the threat had produced the desired effect, for in the end Iwakura emerged victorious. The Lords of Echizen and Owari, two clans once friendly to the Tokugawa family, were deputed to call on Keiki and inform him that his resignation was accepted and that he was to surrender his land holdings and revenues therefrom to the Imperial court.

For Keiki this was an unexpected turn of events. Understandably, he was reluctant to accede to such demands. Moreover, even if he personally was willing, there was little likelihood that his retainers and allies would permit him to surrender so easily. There followed a series of informal discussions and negotiations, in the course of which the moderates regained some power and managed to reduce the severity of the original demands.[10] But the breach was too wide to be bridged successfully. On January 6, Keiki slipped out of Kyoto under cover of darkness and rallied his forces in the nearby city of Osaka.

Soon civil war broke out. Keiki's forces were pitted against those of the new provisional government consisting chiefly of troops from the Satsuma and Choshu clans. For eighteen months the Tokugawa armies, having retreated into the northern sections of the country, managed to remain in the field. But eventually they were forced to acknowledge the supremacy of the new government.

The coming of peace marked the end of the Tokugawa regime and the beginning of a new era in the political history of modern Japan. And as if to emphasize the new spirit which permeated it, the new era was called "Meiji" or "Enlightened Government." Just how "enlightened" it was, we shall see in the succeeding chapters.

[10] For a brief account of these negotiations, see SNST, pp. 99 ff.

Chapter II

THE BACKGROUND OF THE MEIJI RESTORATION

THE Meiji Restoration, as the emergence of the new government described in the previous chapter is called, was the product of complex changes which had been at work for a number of decades. These changes—economic, intellectual, and political—had emasculated the once powerful Shogunate and reduced it to a shadow of its former self. Thus the way was paved for the final seizure of power by a handful of able and determined young samurai who, together with their allies, deposed the Shogun to set up a new and modern regime.

I.

Of the various corroding influences contributing to the collapse of the Shogunate, the economic factor was of first-rate importance. It lay at the very root of the grave problems which plagued the Tokugawa administration in its last days. Taken alone these economic difficulties would have been serious enough; but since they had far-reaching political and social implications, the failure to provide a satisfactory solution proved to be fatal.

It is one of the ironies of Tokugawa history that these economic ills originated in no small measure from the policies of the Shogunate itself. The early Shoguns, moved by an overwhelming passion to perpetuate the hegemony of the Tokugawa family, devised an ingenious system of checks and balances. They hoped to arrest, by the application of sundry devices, the processes of change and thereby maintain themselves in power.

Territorially this system involved the division of the country between the Shogun and the feudal lords or *daimyo* (literally, great name), numbering more than two hundred and fifty. The Tokugawa family ruled directly through its bureaucracy an area comprising about one-fourth of the realm, including all of the important cities. The remainder of the country was parcelled out

7

among the feudal nobles, who were divided into two classes—the
" hereditary nobles " or *fudai* who had allied themselves with the
first Shogun during his rise to power, and the "outside nobles"
or *tozama* who had opposed him. The latter, especially powerful in
western Japan, were watched very closely and excluded from posts
in the Tokugawa administration. Within their fiefs the lords
enjoyed considerable autonomy, but were subject to certain indirect controls. These controls took several forms. The *daimyo*
were not allowed to fortify their castles nor conclude marriage
alliances without the consent of the Shogun. In order to prevent
the *daimyo* from accumulating excessive wealth, the Shogunate
made them contribute heavily towards the construction of public
works. In assigning the fiefs, the Shogun followed the principle
of placing trustworthy lords in areas of strategic importance. An
elaborate system of espionage kept him informed about the activities of his vassals. In addition a system of hostages known as the
sankin-kotai or alternate attendance was established. The more
important feudal nobles were obliged to reside a part of the year in
Edo (present-day Tokyo), the capital of the *Bakufu*, and when
they returned to their respective fiefs they left behind their families
as hostages.

Socially the system of checks and balances involved the continued division of the population into sharply defined classes. In
theory the Emperor was placed at the apex of the social pyramid;
in fact he was relegated to obscurity in Kyoto where he participated in innocuous ceremonial functions with the Court nobility.
Below the Shogun and the nobles were their followers, the samurai,
numbering about four hundred thousand households or roughly five
percent of the population. These samurai, for the most part,
resided in castle towns and subsisted on hereditary rice stipends
provided by their lords to whom they owed military service. There
were numerous sub-divisions among the samurai with marked differences in rank and income. As members of the governing class
privileged to wear swords and given legal immunities, the samurai
looked with contempt on the rest of the population consisting of
merchants, artisans, and peasants—the last named forming the
great bulk of the population.[1]

---

[1] For more detailed accounts of the Tokugawa political system see Murdoch, III,
Chap. 1, " The Social and Political Structure "; G. B. Sansom, *Japan, A Short*

The peasants were looked upon mainly as a source of dues and services. Honda Masanobu, a Machiavellian adviser to the first Shogun, epitomized the attitude of the military caste towards the peasantry when he wrote: " The peasants are the basis of the empire. There are ways of ruling them. First, clearly mark off the boundaries of each man's fields; then have each one estimate the portion of the crop necessary to feed him for a year and make him pay the rest as land tax." [2] Besides giving forty percent or more of the yield to the lord, the peasants paid countless dues assessed on windows, doors, female children and the like. They were also compelled to provide forced labor for public works and horses for courier and postal service.

Like the serfs in Europe, the Japanese peasants were bound by numerous restrictions. They were not supposed to migrate to the towns; they could not permanently alienate their fields nor divide their holdings among their heirs unless the plot was larger than one *cho* (2.45 acres) and yielded at least ten *koku* (1 *koku* = 5.12 bushels) of rice. In order to achieve the maximum in food production, the authorities prohibited the growing of crops like tobacco on rice land. Numerous sumptuary laws limited the peasants as to the type of clothing and the dwelling they could have. To facilitate social control the peasants were organized into the *gonin-gumi* or five-man groups. Through the *gonin-gumi*, collective responsibility for the collection of dues and the maintenance of law and order was achieved.[3]

At first the system described above proved rather effective. Not

Cultural History (Revised Edition) (New York: D. Appleton-Century Co., 1943), Chap. 21, " The Tokugawa Regime "; E. Herbert Norman, *Japan's Emergence as a Modern State* (New York: Institute of Pacific Relations, 1940), Chap. 2, " The Background of the Meiji Restoration." (Hereafter *Japan's Emergence as a Modern State* will be cited as *Emergence*).

[2] *Hon-Sa Roku* [The Record of Honda, Sado-no-Kami] reprinted in *Nihon Keizai Taiten* [A Cyclopedia of Japanese Political Economy], edited by Takimoto Seiichi (Tokyo, 1928), III, 21. Many writers characterize Honda as " Machiavellian," and Takimoto suggests that it was possible that Honda was influenced by Machiavelli's writings, although it is evident that he thinks it highly improbable. See his *Nihon Keizai Shiso Shi* [A History of Japanese Economic Thought] in *Dai Shiso Ensaikuropijia* [The Great Thought Encyclopedia] (Tokyo, 1928), XV, 197-207.

[3] The more important decrees on the control of the peasantry are given in Tokutomi Iichiro, *Kinsei Nihon Kokumin Shi: Tokugawa Bakufu Joki* [A History of the Japanese People in Modern Times: The Early Part of the Tokugawa Bakufu], (Tokyo, 1924), II, 512-530.

only were the feudal barons kept in line, but the *pax*-Tokugawa, following a long period of devastating civil wars, encouraged progress in the arts, learning, and not the least important, in commerce. Agricultural production appears to have increased; and for a time there was prosperity.

But in time the seeds of decay contained within the system began to germinate. The expenditures of both the Shogun and the nobles tended to outrun revenues. By the end of the seventeenth century the Shogunate experienced financial difficulties when famine relief, the rebuilding of Edo after fires, and added administrative expenses ate away the reserves which the crafty Iyeyasu, the first Shogun, had carefully built up. The *sankin-kotai* system, involving the maintenance of elaborate establishments in Edo and frequent travel accompanied by huge retinues, impoverished the feudal nobility. Chronic deficits made such unpopular expedients as the debasement of the currency and forced loans tempting to the governing groups.[4] The proud *daimyo* became increasingly dependent on lowly merchants and money lenders for loans to tide them over from year to year. So conspicuous was this phenomenon that a well-known scholar, Sato Shinen, wrote in 1838 that, " Even in the case of feudal nobles holding large fiefs, most of the money they handle is borrowed, as a rule, from wealthy people." [5]

The impoverishment of their overlords seriously affected the economic well being of the samurai. Under the guise of " loans " the lords often held back a part of the stipends payable to their retainers. Since their needs and wants tended to increase, the reduction in income worked a real hardship on the samurai, so that by the end of the eighteenth century they were faced with serious economic difficulties. The upshot was that they became heavily indebted to money lenders and rice brokers.

One consequence of continued poverty was the gradual weakening of the loyalty of the samurai to their masters. Unable to live on their stipends, some of them severed their ties and became *ronin* or masterless samurai. Wandering about engaging in banditry and terroristic activities, these *ronin* contributed to the turbu-

---

[4] See Tsuchiya Takao, " Nihon Zaisei Shi " [History of Japanese Public Finance] in *Keizaigaku Zenshu* [Collected Works on Economics] (Tokyo, 1930), XXXI, 464-473; Sawada Sho, " Financial Difficulties of the Edo Bakufu," translated by Hugh Borton in *Harvard Journal of Asiatic Studies*, I (November, 1936), 308-326.

[5] Quoted in Tsuchiya, p. 477.

lence of the times. Other samurai took up agriculture or engaged
in commerce, while still others became laborers and craftsmen.
Among the lower samurai class distinctions were no longer strictly
maintained. They swallowed their pride and arranged financially
profitable marriages with members of the merchant class, or, for a
price, adopted sons of wealthy merchants and peasants. At the
same time, ambitious men from the non-privileged classes joined
the ranks of the samurai by purchasing the right to wear swords.
The resultant partial fusion of the two classes helped to change
the outlook of many of the low-ranking samurai and also gave them
common interests with the commercial and industrial classes.

In contrast to the military caste, the lot of the merchants and
small industrialists was improved appreciably. The return of peace,
the movement of men and goods through the operation of the
sankin-kotai system, and the growth of towns and cities stimulated the development of commerce and the penetration of money
economy.[6] That the volume of trade was considerable is revealed
by the fact that rice and commodity exchanges dealing in futures
as well as spot transactions were organized in Edo and Osaka.[7]
Marked regional specialization in the production of commodities
became commonplace. Sugar from Satsuma, paper from Tosa,
indigo from Awa, and high-grade fabrics from Kyoto, to mention
a few products, found wide markets.

Although the exact amount is not known, it is certain that a
relatively large portion of these commodities was manufactured by
a system of production organized along capitalistic lines. As Professor Allen has said in a recent study, " a form of domestic system
was widespread in Tokugawa times." [8] As in Europe, local capitalists directed and controlled production. Among these capitalists
were merchants, wealthy peasants, weavers, cloth brokers, and
dyers who advanced materials to peasants and craftsmen, some-

[6] The best work in English on the effect of the spread of money economy is
Takizawa Matsuyo, *The Penetration of Money Economy in Japan* (New York:
Columbia University Press, 1927).
[7] N. Skene Smith, " Materials on Japanese Social and Economic History: Tokugawa Japan," *Transactions of the Asiatic Society of Japan*, Second series, XIV
(1937), 123-137. (Hereafter the *Transactions* will be cited as *TASJ*).
[8] G. C. Allen, *A Short Economic History of Modern Japan, 1867-1937* (London,
1946), p. 13.

times even supplied equipment like looms and marketed the finished goods.[9]

In some instances, industrial production had even progressed beyond the domestic system and had reached the point where a number of workers were concentrated under one roof. Although power machinery was seldom used, production was at times on a fairly large scale. Using a term borrowed from Karl Marx, Japanese economic historians have generally labelled this system " manufacture."

The degree to which " manufacture " characterized Tokugawa economy is a question which has been the subject of long and acrimonious controversy among Japanese scholars.[10] Sharp differences of opinion over problems of methodology and interpretation of data have divided scholars into various schools. The evidence is by no means conclusive, but the indications are that in certain areas at least this type of industrial production played a leading role. In the textile town of Kiryu (in Gumma prefecture), for example, there were in 1766 seven dormitories housing 700 textile workers, with the largest one accommodating 200 workers. In 1846 there were 267 establishments equipped with a total of five to six thousand looms.[11]

The rise of rural industry and the growth of large-scale commerce had the effect of transferring wealth from the military caste to the merchants and rural entrepreneurs. A contemporary writer esti-

[9] This was true, for example, in the Kiryu textile industries. Yanagigawa Noboru, "Kiryu Orimono Gyo ni okeru Maegashi Seido" [The Domestic System in the Kiryu Textile Industries], Keizaigaku Ronshu [Studies on Economics], I and II (November, 1931 and February, 1932); 1121-1169; 250-284.

[10] The controversy may be followed in the following works: Hattori Shiso, "Gemmitsuna Imi de no Manufakucha Jidai" [A Period of Manufacture in the Real Sense of the Word], Meiji Ishin Shi Kenkyu [A Study of the Meiji Restoration] (Tokyo, 1933), pp. 93-117; Tsuchiya Takao, "Tokugawa Jidai no Manufakucha" [Manufacture in the Tokugawa Period], Kaizo [Reconstruction], XV (September, 1933), 2-21; Hattori, "Hoho Oyobi Zairyo no Mondai," "[The Problem of Method and Materials], op. cit., pp. 163-184; Tsuchiya, "Ishin Shi Kenkyu no Chushin Ronten" [The Central Point of Dispute in Restoration History], Kaizo, XVI (January, 1934); Tsuchiya, "Nihon Manufakucha Zusetsu" [Illustrations of Japanese Manufacture], Rekishi Gaku Kenkyu [Studies in Historical Science] (Hereafter cited as RGK), I (February, 1934). More recent literature on the subject is analyzed in Hatori Takuya, "Bunsan Manufakucha Ron Hihán," [A Critique of the Theory of Dispersed Manufacture], RGK, No. 127 (May, 1947).

[11] Tsuchiya, "Tokugawa Jidai no Manufakucha," op. cit., pp. 11-12. Other examples may be found in the material cited in footnote 10.

mated that fifteen-sixteenths of the wealth of the country was in the possession of the merchant class; [12] and while we need not accept his estimate unquestioningly, it is nevertheless revealing as to the distribution of wealth in this period. The gradual transfer of wealth would not have been so serious had it not aggravated, in turn, the agrarian problem and brought the ruling authorities into conflict with a rising group of rural industrialists.

One of the methods used by the lords to escape from the morass of debt was to increase the pressure on the peasantry. The already heavily-burdened cultivator was now made to deliver sixty and sometimes seventy percent of the yield. Such measures, however, had the effect of reducing agricultural production, and hence state revenues. Finding life too unrewarding, the peasants could abandon their holdings and flee into the towns; or when goaded beyond endurance, rise up in revolt, as indeed they did on many hundreds of occasions.[13] These peasant revolts, although they did not lead directly to the destruction of the old regime, undoubtedly helped to undermine its stability.

The persistent rural poverty, intensified by increased exactions, served as an incentive for the peasants to turn to subsidiary industries such as sericulture, weaving, spinning, and indigo production. Eager to add to their income by any means, they joined the growing number of workers and craftsmen turning out commodities for local entrepreneurs, until the spread of subsidiary industries became nation wide.[14] At first the feudal authorities looked with favor on such a development since it helped to alleviate agrarian distress. But later they changed their attitude when these industries began to divert labor from agriculture which formed the basis of the state. Finding their interests running counter to those of the rural industrialists, the feudal lords issued edicts aimed to prevent the further depletion of agricultural workers. In 1842, for example, the following edict was proclaimed in Bizen-no-kuni:

In recent years there has been a great deal of *kokura sanada* [a kind of Japanese duck cloth and braid] produced in the villages. Agriculture has

---

[12] Tsuchiya, "Nihon Zaisei Shi," *op. cit.*, p. 476.

[13] For peasant revolts, see Hugh Borton, "Peasant Uprisings in Japan of the Tokugawa Period," *TASJ*, Second series, XVI (May, 1938).

[14] Kajinishi Mitsumi, "Nihon Shihonshugi Seiritsu Shi," [History of the Establishment of Japanese Capitalism], *Yuibutsu Shikan* [Historical Materialism], J (November, 1947), 49.

been neglected, and in some villages cultivation has been impeded. There-fore, a proclamation was issued sometime ago, yet this has continued. We hear that on numerous occasions impudent people have laid in a supply of *kokura* and have sent out materials to have them woven. This is the rumor that has spread over the *gori* [county].

One loom per household is allowed for use in intervals when one is free from agricultural pursuits. Families with many hands may be per-mitted two looms. But no more than that will be allowed. It goes without saying that sending work to other families is prohibited. Therefore looms must not be rented out. Even though men and women servants [meaning workers?] have been coming previously, those producing *kokura sanada* must not hire them. Since, as stated above, it has been reported that cultivation is hindered, weavers, both men and women, must not go as day workers to the towns, to say nothing of other provinces and counties.[15]

Further conflict between the feudal lords and the rural industrial-ists was precipitated by the extension of monopolies. In some of the clans, particularly those in Western Japan, the management of economic and political affairs had largely passed into the hands of a group of lower samurai.[16] In order to augment revenues and thereby stave off bankruptcy, these samurai organized official monopolies in manufacture and trade. An extreme example was sugar production in Satsuma, located in the southern part of Kyushu. In some sections both men and women were allotted plots of land and compelled to grow sugar cane for the benefit of the clan monopoly. The use of money and private trading among indivi-duals were forbidden. The cultivators were paid in cards which could be exchanged for commodities.[17] In Tosa, another prin-cipality in western Japan, monopolistic controls were imposed on the sale of paper. Producers of this important commodity, number-ing about fifteen thousand households, were obliged to sell assigned quotas of paper at fixed prices to official companies.[18] Naturally such practices were not popular among paper manufacturers. It is noteworthy that the ten peasant uprisings reported in Tosa

[15] Quoted in Hirano Yoshitaro, *Buruja Minshu Shugi Kakumei* [The Bourgeois-Democratic Revolution] (Tokyo, 1948), pp. 106-107.

[16] Norman, pp. 62-64.

[17] Tsuchiya Takao, *Hoken Shakai Hokai Katei no Kenkyu* [A Study of the Pro-cess of Decay of the Feudal Society] (Tokyo, 1927), pp. 460 ff.

[18] Matsuyoshi Sadao, "Tosa Han no Gokurashi Kaiage ni Tsuite," [On the Purchase of Paper by the Tosa Clan], *Keizai Shi Kenkyu* [Studies in Economic History], I (1929-1930), 163 ff. (Hereafter the *Keizai Shi Kenkyu* will be cited as *KSK*).

between 1603 and 1871 were "largely the result of the methods of monopolistic control of local products by the fief authorities with practically no demands on the part of the peasants that their taxes be reduced." [19]

The forcible opening of the country to foreign trade in 1858 tended to intensify economic dislocations. The export of raw materials, for example, led to a sharp rise in prices.[20] The cost of raw silk tripled, tea doubled, and silk worm eggs were up tenfold. Between 1860 and 1868, the price of rice rose about 660 percent.[21] Those living on fixed incomes, which included most of the samurai, were caught in an economic squeeze. Discontented samurai complained bitterly that the "barbarians bring useless luxuries and deprive us of our daily necessities, and by impoverishing us hope, in the end, to annex our country." [22]

The outflow of commodities like raw silk and raw cotton deprived native manufacturers of raw materials. The weaving industry in Kiryu was hit by unemployment. Accordingly spokesmen for the weavers repeatedly petitioned the Shogunate to stop the export of raw silk.[23] On the other hand, the importation of cheap machine-made goods forced small handicraft producers to the wall. Foreign competition compelled some producers to adopt machine production or switch to more profitable industries like sericulture.[24]

The resumption of foreign commerce also altered the organization of trade. For years wealthy merchants, organized into guilds and enjoying monopolistic privileges granted by the Shogun, held

---

[19] Borton, p. 179.

[20] The effects of foreign trade on the domestic situation are carefully traced in Tsuchiya Takao, "Bakumatsu Doran no Keizai-teki Bunseki" [An Economic Analysis of the Unrest During the Late Tokugawa Period], *Chuo Koron* [Central Review], XLVII (October, 1932), 75-91 (hereafter the *Chuo Koron* will be cited as *CK*); Ishii Takashi, "Bakumatsu Kaiko ni Yoru Kokunai Keizai no Konran to Bakufu no Boeki Tosei Keikaku" [Internal Economic Disorder due to Opening the Country and the Bakufu's Foreign Trade Control Plan], *RGK*, IV (May, 1935), 2-24; Ishii Takashi, "Bunkyu Nenkan ni Okeru Gaikoku Boeki no Hatten to Bakufu no Yokuatsu Seisaku" [The Development of Foreign Trade in the Bunkyu Era and the Suppression Policy of the Shogunate], *Shakai Keizai Shigaku* (hereafter cited as *SKS*), V (July, 1935), 393-424.

[21] Tsuchiya, *op. cit.*, p. 83.

[22] Shibuzawa Eiichi, *Tokugawa Keiki Ko Den* [The Biography of Prince Tokugawa Keiki] (Tokyo, 1917), I, 403.

[23] Ishii, "Bakumatsu Kaiko ni Yoru Kokunai Keizai no Konran to Bakufu no Boeki Tosei Keikaku," pp. 11-12.

[24] Norman, *Emergence*, p. 42n.

16   *POLITICAL DEMOCRACY IN JAPAN*

a strangle hold on trade.[25] This was brought to an end by the insistence of the foreign powers that trade be thrown open to all comers.[26] Small rural merchants and industrialists were quick to seize this long awaited opportunity to expand their operations. They eagerly moved into the treaty ports from the country towns.[27] Many of these men had deep roots in the capitalistic industry in the countryside, for among them were cocoon brokers, thread dealers, and rural industrialists. They combed the raw silk districts, buying up raw silk to supply their foreign buyers. It appears that some of them even advanced funds to peasants in order to stimulate production.[28]

The real temper of these rural merchants was brought out in their struggle with the old-line guild merchants. The interests of the latter were closely bound to the old order since they owed their wealth and position to the fact that they were closely associated with the feudal nobility. Hence it is not surprising that instead of taking advantage of new conditions engendered by the opening of the country, they appealed to the Shogunate to suspend the export trade, using as their pretext the rise in prices and the shortage of goods.[29] The tradesmen from the countryside, however, were not the kind to acquiesce. They protested, disclaiming responsibility for high prices which they correctly attributed to the disparity between supply and demand.[30] Moreover, as if to put teeth into their arguments, they hired *ronin* to terrorize the guild merchants.[31] Finally, when restrictions were imposed for a short

[25] See Takekoshi, pp. 1-5.

[26] A translation of a decree declaring trade open to all is printed in M. Paske-Smith, *Western Barbarians in Japan and Formosa, 1603-1868* (Kobe, 1930), p. 201.

[27] A biography of prominent men from Kozuke contains accounts of at least seven men who engaged in foreign trade. See Okabe Fukuzo (editor), *Kozuke Jimbutsu Shi* [Accounts of Men from Kozuke] (Tokyo, 1924), II, 287 ff.

[28] Ishii, " Bunkyu Nenkan ni Okeru Gaikoku Boeki no Hatten to Bakufu no Yokuatsu Seisaku," *op. cit.*, p. 412.

[29] Ishii, " Bakumatsu Kaiko ni Yoru Kokunai Keizai no Konran to Bakufu no Boeki Tosei Keikaku," pp. 15-19.

[30] For example, Kashima Mampei submitted a memorial which attributed the rise in prices to the unbalance between supply and demand. Tsuchiya Takao, " Takinogawa Kashima Bosekisho no Soritsu Keiei Jotai " [The Establishment and Management of the Kashima Cotton Spinning Mill at Takinogawa], *Keizaigaku Ronshu*, III (October, 1933), 1427.

[31] Ishii, " Bunkyu Nenkan ni Okeru Gaikoku Boeki no Hatten to Bakufu no Yokusei Seisaku," *op. cit.*, p. 574.

while in 1863, some of them refusing to abide by the regulations, took to smuggling.[32]

Perhaps the significance of this episode is to be found in the fact that it was symptomatic of the times. In a sense it epitomized the whole course of events leading up to the Restoration. The battle between the old and the new — here symbolized by the guild merchants with their timidity and attachment to the past, and the rural merchants with their aggressiveness and fresh outlook — was to be fought time and again on other fronts. And as was the case in this instance, almost everywhere the forces allied with the old order were in retreat.

II.

The widespread discontent produced by the economic crisis and fed by the inability of the Shogunate to cope with the Western powers provided the basis for a political movement directed against the Tokugawa regime. The movement was led by a small band of young, low-ranking samurai who felt deep hatred of the Shogunate. They were drawn mostly from the western clans of Satsuma, Choshu, Tosa and Hizen, which were far removed from the main center of Tokugawa strength, and which traditionally had been anti-Tokugawa in sentiment. In their campaign against Edo, these samurai enlisted the support of a number of Court nobles The latter were useful because they not only provided prestige, but, being to some extent shielded from the prying eyes of the ubiquitous secret police, served as handy contact agents for underground activities.[33]

The movement had as its rallying cry the slogan *sonno joi* or " revere the Emperor; expel the barbarians." As a slogan calculated to bring discomfort to the Shogun, it had much merit. The foreigners were highly unpopular among those adversely affected by the opening of the country, and among a large number of narrow-minded chauvanistic samurai to whom anything foreign was anathema. A suggestion to drive out the foreigners, therefore, had wide appeal. But at the same time it embarrassed the Shogunate because it was manifestly powerless to carry out a policy so drastic.

[32] Honjo Eijiro, *Bakumatsu no Shinseisaku* [New Policies at the End of the Tokugawa Period] (Tokyo, 1935), p. 101.

[33] For details of the anti-Tokugawa movement see Murdoch, III, Chap. XVIII, " The Fall of the Bakufu."

The cry " revere the Emperor " also struck a weak spot in the Tokugawa armor. Although for centuries the sovereign had been a virtual non-entity in politics, his prestige was now growing among the intellectuals. This was a consequence of the revival of learning in the eighteenth century. With the coming of peace, the samurai were encouraged to turn from martial exercises to scholarly pursuits. The fief of Mito, ruled by a branch of the Tokugawa family, became a celebrated center of historical studies. Here a group of scholars, including an exiled Chinese, compiled monumental works on Japanese history which showed obliquely that the Shogun was an usurper and that the Emperor was the rightful ruler.[34] About the same time there was a revival of Shinto, the native religion. A school of nationalistic Shinto scholars criticised the prevailing subservience to things Chinese and glorified the indigenous culture. In their philological, literary, and historical studies they raised the ancient myth of the divine origin of the Emperor to new heights. Gradually the Throne took on new importance, while the authority and prestige of the Shogunate was correspondingly diminished.[35]

That the pro-Emperor propaganda was very effective among the lower samurai and *ronin* is well known. What is not so well known is that the wealthier groups in the countryside were also affected by it. To understand this phenomenon it is well to examine briefly the social organization of the rural villages.

By the end of the Tokugawa period the social stratification in the rural communities had become fairly marked. The most numerous class were the small cultivators whose income from their holdings was so meager that usually they were forced to supplement it with earnings from subsidiary industries. Below them were the tenant farmers, who cultivated land either wholly or partially owned by others; and even further down the social scale were the landless peasants who hired themselves out as agricultural laborers.[36]

[34] Norman, *Emergence*, p. 28.

[35] E. M. Satow, "The Revival of Pure Shin-tau," *TASJ*, III (1884), appendix.

[36] The following statistics based on a survey made around 1845 in Choshu and Boshu gives us some idea of the extent of tenant farming.

Percentage of landowning peasants in a village	Number of villages
100%	18
90% or more	26
80% " "	20

At the other end of the social spectrum were found the relatively well-to-do families. Mostly landholders, they included peasants, who through luck or skillful management, had enlarged their holdings at the expense of their less fortunate neighbors [37] and the "new landlords" or merchants and usurers who reclaimed waste land in partnership with landless peasants.[38] An interesting feature of the landed class was the fact that they generally had their eggs in many baskets. It appears to have been the usual practice for them to be the village money lenders and proprietors of pawnshops. They also served, in many instances, as rural merchants, buying and shipping locally-produced commodities to distant towns and cities. Perhaps most important, they were often the owners and operators of small-scale rural industries which became so widespread. It was they who produced textiles under the domestic system, or owned workshops for reeling silk, or operated the local brewery.[39] In Shibuzawa Eiichi, who became one of the leading bankers of Meiji Japan, we have a historical example of the

Percentage of landowning peasants in a village	Number of villages
70% " "	32
60% " "	40
50% " "	46
40% " "	32
30% " "	31
20% " "	17
10% " "	17
10% or less	7
0%	5

See Shimomura Fujio, "Kinsei Noson no Kaikyu Kosei: Choshu Han no Baai," [Class Structure in Modern Farm Villages: The example of Choshu Clan], *RGK*, III (December, 1934).

[37] Eg., "The 16 families of the Homma clan [one of the largest landholding groups in Japan] own about 4,000 acres of choice rice fields in Yamagata Prefecture, accumulated over two-and-a-half centuries according to the pattern of purchase and foreclosure typical of most large Japanese estates. A large portion of the 5,142 tenants who cultivate these holdings are descendants of small farmers who lost their lands to the Homma families as a result of famine, depression and the feudal and post-Meiji tax exactions and usury practices." William M. Gilmartin and W. J. Ladejinsky, "The Promise of Agrarian Reform in Japan," *Foreign Affairs*, XXVI (January, 1948), 318.

[38] Norman, *Emergence*, p. 53.

[39] Eg., the family of Okubo Masaji in Iwashiro (present-day Fukushima prefecture) owned 1,000 *cho* of land, brewed sake and soy sauce and also produced cloth. Nishioka Toranosuke, "Nihon no Nogyo ni okeru Jikyu Keizai Seikatsu no Shi-teki Tenkai" [The Historical Evolution of the Self-Sufficient Farm Economy in Japan], RGK, No. 123 (August, 1946), pp. 18-19.

20   POLITICAL DEMOCRACY IN JAPAN

diversification of economic activities among the rural aristocracy. Shibuzawa came from Hanzawa-gori (in present-day Saitama prefecture), situated in a general area where the raw silk and textile industries were well developed. His family, the second wealthiest in the village, were landholders, and tilled the soil in the old family tradition. But in addition they also produced and sold indigo used extensively as a dyestuff. And finally, as one might expect, they acted as money lenders.[40]

It comes as no surprise that the upper strata played a leading role in local politics. As is true in all agrarian societies, tremendous social prestige and economic power accrued to those who controlled or owned land. Members of this class had the additional advantage of being among the few in the village who were not only literate but also had sufficient leisure to participate in politics. That they should provide most of the officials comprising the local administrative hierarchy was to be expected. As one writer has said, the village offices were as a rule " held by the old families, generally well-to-do, and, it might be said, the aristocracy of the local community, who, by their possessions and their social position were able to occupy the chief post often for generations." [41]

Now this local aristocracy was strongly affected by the new propaganda glorifying the Throne because of several reasons. The very fact that they were literate and had the means to purchase books and acquire libraries made them susceptible to new intellectual influences. Through the writings of the nationalist scholars they obtained new ideas on the relationship between the Throne and the Shogunate. Of greater importance were the opportunities they enjoyed for personal contact with scholars. On occasion some wealthy individuals acted as patrons to impoverished savants. Others opened their homes to learned men who travelled from village to village spreading their doctrines.[42] The importance of personal contracts of this kind ought not be overlooked. Between 1804 and 1843 one scholar alone, the well-known Hirata Atsutane, had more than 530 disciples. After his death these disciples trained

[40] Ono Takeo, " Hyakusho Ikki ya Kinno Gun ya " [Peasant Revolts or Pro-Emperor Armies?], *Shakai Keizai Shigaku* [Social and Economic History], VI (July 1936), 14-15.
[41] D. B. Simmons and John H. Wigmore, " Notes on Land Tenure and Local Institutions in Old Japan," *TASJ*, XIX (1891), 111.
[42] Ono, pp. 3-5.

another 3,700 students. It is said that there were 627 nationalist scholars in Shinshu alone.[43]

But why were they attracted to the pro-Emperor cause? The answer probably lies in the economic frustrations of the times, which put them in a receptive mood for political change. There is no question that there was a serious conflict between the feudal nobility and the rural capitalists over the utilization of the peasants. So long as the former looked upon the cultivators as " a machine to produce rice for the samurai to swallow," [44] they were bound to resist the development of industry based on labor and raw materials supplied by the peasants. This conflict was indicated in the edict, noted earlier, forbidding the migration of weavers into the towns. And we may be sure that restrictions of this kind, acting as a brake on the development of industrial enterprise, were resented by the rural entrepreneurs.[45]

No more welcome was the growth of monopolies. Staple monopolies organized by clan authorities, as was done in Tosa, meant the imposition of quotas and fixed prices with little protection against rising costs. Such practices had the effect of hindering trade, and indirectly production.

Finally there was the matter of forced loans — which were really levies since they were seldom repaid. To a group with well developed acquisitive instincts, being forced to part with their hard-earned wealth must have been painful to say the least. But what added insult to injury was the attitude of the officials. Men like Shibuzawa Eiichi were infuriated by the haughty airs and overbearing manner of officials seeking loans. They felt that such officials at least could show more humility when they approached their benefactors.[46]

As the fortunes of the Shogunate declined, many of the important local figures threw in their lot with the *sonno* or pro-

[43] *Ibid.*, p. 5.

[44] Sansom, *op. cit.*, p. 465.

[45] For example a well-known supporter of the Imperial cause was Yamanaka Shinjuro, of Akita prefecture, who was, among other things, a raw silk broker. See Hattori Shiso and Shinobu Seisaburo, *Nihon Manufakucha Shiron* [Historical Essays on Japanese Manufacture] (Tokyo, 1947), p. 53.

[46] For Shibuzawa's reaction to forced loans, see Tsuchiya Takao, " Sonno Tobaku Undo to Shomin Kaikyu " [The Pro-Emperor Anti-Tokugawa Movement and the Common People], *CK*, LII (September, 1937), 146.

Emperor movement. In several ways they actively supported the underground movement directed against the existing regime. They facilitated the work, for example, of the many *ronin* and samurai who travelled from locality to locality laying the foundations of revolt by providing them with lodgings. More notable, however, were their financial contributions. There were instances where they gave assistance to individual *ronin* who were without funds. They also provided relatively large sums for various illegal activities, including the purchase of arms to be used eventually against the Tokugawa.[47] Although the total amount contributed by the rural well-to-do during the several years preceding the Restoration is not known, it is likely that it was not small. In fact it seems fair to say that without this financial support the anti-Tokugawa *ronin* and samurai would have been severely handicapped.

Finally in 1867 the long conspiracy against the regime bore fruit when a coup d'etat deposed the reigning Shogun, Tokugawa Keiki. Almost immediately, it will be recalled, a civil war broke out. In view of the fact that they had long supported the pro-Emperor movement, it was natural that the rural aristocracy should lend aid to the anti-Tokugawa forces. Some like Matsuo Taseko, a well-known woman leader of the *sonno* movement in Ina province, journeyed to Kyoto to take part in the battles against the Shogun's armies.[48] Others organized or supported volunteer bands which helped to immobilize the Tokugawa armies by attacking their flanks and rear.[49]

One such band came from the long-established textile town of Ashikaga where Fujita Koshiro, son of Fujita Toko, the famous nationalist scholar from Mito, had numerous followers.[50] This band, led by an artist-patriot by the name of Tazaki Soun, distinguished itself in the battle of Kamata. The following excerpt from Tazaki's biography throws light on the character of the forces he led:

At that time (March, 1867) those citizens of Ashikaga who had con-

[47] Konishi Shiro, "Bakumatsu no Shishi to Kane" [Money and the Loyalists at the End of the Tokugawa Era], *Nihon Rekishi* [Japanese History], No. 11 (March, 1948), pp. 21-24.

[48] Tsuchiya, *op. cit.*, p. 149.

[49] Cf., E. Herbert Norman, *Soldier and Peasant in Japan, The Origins of Conscription* (New York: Institute of Pacific Relations, 1943), pp. 37-38.

[50] Ono, p. 6.

nections with Tazaki were inspired by his ideals and were deeply devoted to the cause of the Imperial family. Responding to his summons, they bought ammunition at their own expense, prepared military uniforms and undertook the expenses of drilling. . . . All the soldiers of his corps were treated as *samurai* and were given permission to wear swords and assume surnames and present themselves at the clan palace. . . . He (Tazaki) led his glorious band and defeated the rebels (i. e., the Bakufu forces) at Kamata. The Mimpei (People's Army), who complained that they had nothing to do, now exerted their efforts in struggle, and having abandoned the trades of ordinary times, they marched to battle.[51]

In the preceding pages the contributions of the rural aristocracy have been emphasized for two reasons. First, most historical accounts neglect to give them full credit for the part they played in the events leading up to the Restoration. Second, they are, in a sense, the precursors of those men who later hoisted the flag of opposition to the government in the name of democratic rights. As the late historian, Osatake Takeki, once said, the democratic movement was a continuation of the *sonno* movement of the late Tokugawa period.

But lest the reader get a distorted view, it should be stressed again that the rural gentry constituted but one of the several groups that combined forces to attack the Tokugawa citadel. The Restoration was too great an undertaking for any one group, and hence it called for a coalition of the anti-Tokugawa forces. Within this coalition the leadership was provided by the young samurai from the western clans, with the Court nobles from Kyoto and the rural aristocracy rendering valuable assistance. But there was yet another group whose aid was important. After the seizure of power in 1867 the new provisional government, sorely pressed for funds, appealed to the great urban merchants like the Mitsui, Ono, Shimada, and Konoike. From this source the government was able to raise about 3,800,000 *yen* or a little more than ten percent of the first budget.[52] It was this money which helped the new government press the campaigns against the Tokugawa armies and also begin the work of reconstruction.

[51] Translated in Norman, *op. cit.*, p. 25.
[52] Honjo Eijiro, "The Importance of 'Goyokin' or Forced Loans in the Meiji Restoration," *Kyoto University Economic Review* (hereafter cited as *KUER*), XVIII (July, 1933), p. 25; and also Tsuchiya Takao, "Ishin Henkaku no Keizai-teki Urazuke" [Economic Support for the Meiji Restoration], *CK*, LV (September, 1940), 168-185.

CHAPTER III

THE IMPACT OF WESTERN THOUGHT

AFTER the middle of the nineteenth century the Shogunate was shaken to its very foundations by a series of economic and political crises. Widespread discontent with Tokugawa rule found expression in angry outbursts of violence, including the assassination of high officials, murderous attacks on foreign residents, and peasant uprisings. Given the advantage of hindsight, we can see that these incidents heralded the approaching end of Tokugawa domination. To contemporaries, however, the drift of the tide was not always so obvious. Their vision was clouded by the fact that institutions have a way of persisting even after they have long outlived their usefulness. It was not easy for them to forget that for more than two centuries and a half, the political life of the nation had revolved around the Shogunate and that, moreover, few aspects of Japanese civilization had escaped its pervading influence. Clearly the times called for creative thinking about political problems, yet the lingering memories of the once-proud Shogunate tended to stifle intellectual endeavors.

It is understandable, under these circumstances, that for many years the thinking of most statesmen and political theorists was colored by the assumption that the Shogun's government would be a permanent fixture. Accordingly their attention was primarily directed towards reform measures calculated to infuse new life into the tottering Shogunate.

Of these measures perhaps the most noteworthy, in the long run, was the proposal to broaden the basis of government. It will be recalled that the early Tokugawa rulers had excluded potention rivals such as the Court nobles and the powerful " outside lords " from participation in the affairs of state. In the nineteenth century, however, the tight monopoly of power was gradually relaxed. When the Western powers demanded the abandonment of the policy of national isolation, the Shogun, in order to fortify his position,

24

consulted various nobles and sought their advice on the conduct of foreign relations. About this time, too, he broke precedent and began to make overtures to the Imperial court, soliciting its counsel and support on matters of national importance. This policy of fortifying one's position by retreat was carried to its extreme on the eve of the Restoration when the last Shogun resigned his position to make way for a coalition government.

It would be a mistake to assume that in relinquishing his power Tokugawa Keiki contemplated retirement from the political scene. From his point of view this was a strategic withdrawal designed to outmaneuver his enemies, then engaged in forging a strong coalition against him through a series of secret alliances. By giving formal power back to the Emperor, he hoped to placate his opponents. At the same time, he planned to occupy a strong position in the new government, probably a post analogous to that of a prime minister.

The pivotal point around which this strategy turned was the proposal to create a bicameral assembly which would provide representation for the more influential groups in Japanese society. It was obviously a conscious attempt to adapt Western techniques of government in order to alleviate the political crisis engulfing the Shogunate. The stratagem did not succeed; nevertheless it affords an interesting illustration of the influence of Western political thought on political change in Japan.

I.

The Tokugawa seclusion policy put into effect after 1640 did not completely seal off Japan from foreign influences. Perhaps by deliberate design, two avenues had been left open. The first of these was the Dutch trading station which, although strictly supervised and given only limited trading rights, was allowed to remain at Deshima in Nagasaki. As a source of information about European developments, the Dutch became important especially after the Shogun Yoshimune (1716-1745) repealed the ban on the reading and translation of European books other than those on religion. Although this new policy served as a stimulus for new interest in medicine and science, it did not lead to an immediate increase in speculation about politics. This was partly because the Shogunate put a premium on orthodoxy and kept a vigilant look-

out through its ubiquitous secret police for " dangerous thoughts."
It is not surprising, therefore, that those new political ideas that
did come in entered through the side door, so to speak, imbedded in
translations of Dutch books on world geography.

A good example of this is the *Yochi Shiryaku* (Abridged World) [1]
written by Aoji Rinso, a physician and student of Dutch studies.
Although earlier books, notably Arai Hakuseki's *Sairan Igen*
(Foreign Topography), [2] Kukichi Shoko's *Taisei Yochi Zusetsu*
(Explanatory Diagrams of the Western World), [3] and Yoshio Sen's
Anyakuria Jin Seijoshi (On the Character of the English) [4] contained brief descriptions of European governments, Aoji's study
was probably the first important work. A seven-volume study
abridged from an earlier work of sixty-five volumes, this book was
in essence a translation of a Dutch world geography. [5] In the
section on English politics Aoji used the word " parliament,"
describing it as an assembly consisting of two chambers. Although
he mentioned the composition of the two houses, he did not make
it clear that the members of the House of Commons were elected.
He noted that parliament met once a year or once in two years,
and that the king had the power to convene it. Lastly, he said that
the decisions of the parliament required the approval of the ruler
before becoming effective. [6]

In 1846 another geographer, Mitsukuri Shogo, published *Konyo
Zushiki-ho* (Supplement to a Diagram of the World) [7] in which he
said that the House of Lords dealt with matters pertaining to the
nobility, and the House of Commons with matters concerning cities
and villages. [8] Obviously he had confused the composition of parlia-

---

[1] Probably written in 1827, it was circulated in manuscript form. It is now
available in the *Bummei Genryu Sosho* [Library of the Origins of Civilization], 3
Volumes, (Tokyo, 1912-1914). See Hirose Bin, *Nihon Sosho Sakuin* [A Bibliography
of Japanese Books] (Tokyo, 1939), pp. 547, 557; Asai Kiyoshi, *Meiji Rikken Shiso
ni Okeru Eikoku Gikai Seido no Eikyo* [The Influence of the British Parliamentary
System on Meiji Constitutional Thought] (Tokyo, 1939), p. 84.

[2] A five-volume work said to have been completed five or six days before Arai's
death. *Shiseki Kaidai* [A Bibliography of History] (Tokyo, 1936), p. 89.

[3] Published in 1789. Asai, p. 80.

[4] Published in 1825. *Ibid.*, p. 81.

[5] *Ibid.*, pp. 78-83.

[6] *Ibid.*, pp. 83-87.

[7] Published in 1846, this was a supplement to his *Konyo Zushiki* [Diagram of the
World (1845). *Ibid.*, p. 87.

[8] *Ibid.*, pp. 87-88.

ment with its jurisdiction. His adoptive father, Mitsukuri Genpo, a physician and student of Dutch, published in 1851 and 1856 a work called *Hakko Tsushi* (An Account of Distant Lands).[9] In this the author said that parliament had power to establish laws, and that the king was a person in parliament, probably referring to the concept of the king-in-parliament.[10]

So long as the Japanese were limited to Dutch books, there was little likelihood that new political ideas would spread very rapidly since the number of men capable of reading Dutch was fairly limited. About the middle of the nineteenth century, however, a second source of knowledge, namely Chinese books on Western government, became increasingly important. This brought a far larger audience within reach, for most educated Japanese were able to read Chinese, owing to the fact that the Japanese had adopted Chinese ideographs.

There was a good reason for the increased interest in Chinese sources. China had suffered defeat in the Anglo-Chinese war (1839-1842), and as a consequence, a few Chinese scholars began to take an interest in learning more about their former adversary. The reaction, however, seems to have been even stronger among the Japanese, who were not only well informed about the war, but also realized its implications much better than the Chinese themselves.[11]

Of the Chinese studies which appeared after China's defeat, the *Hai-kuo t'u-chih* (Illustrated Record of the Maritime Nations) was perhaps one of the most significant. It was written by Wei Yüan who used as one of his sources the *Ssu-chou chih* (An Account of Four Continents), a work completed under the direction of Lin Tse-hsü, who gained fame for burning the opium just before the Anglo-Chinese war. The *Ssu-chou chih* included translations from Western periodicals as well as selections from a monthly journal published by Karl F. A. Gutzlaff in Canton and Singapore between the years 1833 and 1838. In 1854 and 1855 abridged editions of the *Hai-kuo t'u-chih* were reprinted in Japan.[12] The Japanese editions

---

[9] Three volumes were published in 1851 and another three in 1856. *Ibid.*, p. 89.
[10] *Ibid.*, pp. 89-91.
[11] See Norman's summary of Tsuchiya Takao's " Bakumatsu Shishi no Mita Shina Mondai " [The Problem of China as Seen by Loyalists at the End of the Bakufu] in *Emergence*, p. 38n; also R. H. van Gulik, " Kakkaron," *Monumenta Serica*, IV (1939-1940), pp. 478-545.
[12] The *Hai-kuo t'u-chih* was published in 1844 in 50 *chüan*, in 1847 in 60 *chüan*

attracted wide attention and were read by Sakuma Shozan, Yokoi Shonan, Hashimoto Sanai and others noted for their advanced views.[13]

Although the *Hai-kuo t'u-chih* was a book on geography, it included a section on the British parliament. The translation contained some errors, and it was on the whole difficult to understand; but it did make it clear that the authority of the ruler was not absolute and that his power was restricted by representative institutions.[14]

Following this various other Chinese treatises were either reprinted or translated in Japan. Two of them may be mentioned here by way of illustration. In 1859 there was reprinted a book called *Ti-li ch'uan-chih* (Complete Geography) written in Chinese by an Englishman, William Muirhead.[15] A book written by the famous sinologist, James Legge, *A Circle of Knowledge* was translated into Chinese and published in Hong Kong in 1856. It was imported into Nagasaki and published in Japan in 1866.[16] The section on the British government said: "The three countries England, Scotland, and Ireland form the British nation. They are governed by laws which are decided in the two houses of parliament. These houses are named the House of Lords and the House of Commons; they pass laws, which, however, must be assented to by the Sovereign before they are in force." [17]

After the opening of Japan in the 1850's a third source of information was made available. Now intellectuals and officials were able to travel abroad and study Western institutions at first hand. In the earlier period many of them toured Europe and America as members of diplomatic missions. For instance, Fukuzawa Yukichi, who probably did more than any other person to introduce Western civilization to Japan, came to the United States in 1860 as a member of a mission sent by the Shogunate. One day, after their arrival in Washington, the members of the group were invited to

and expanded into 100 *chüan* in 1852. See article on Wei Yüan in *Eminent Chinese of the Ch'ing Period*, edited by Arthur Hummel (Washington, 1944), II, 851.

[13] Osatake Takeki, *Nihon Kensei Shi Taiko* [An Outline of Japanese Constitutional History] (Tokyo, 1938), I, 16. (Hereafter cited as *NKST*).

[14] Asai, pp. 94-101.

[15] Osatake, p. 21. Osatake erroneously gives the author as B. William.

[16] It was published by the Edo Kaibutsu-sha. Other editions and translations were published during the following few years. Osatake, p. 20; Asai, p. 110.

[17] Osatake, pp. 20-21.

visit Congress. Muragaki Norimasa who recorded a description of
the visit in his diary seems mostly to have been impressed by the
speech making. "As we entered," he wrote, "a member was
making a speech at the top of his voice. When he sat down,
another stood up and talked in an excited manner. There was no
end to the speakers. One after another they rose, some speaking
quietly, and some wildly brandishing their arms as if they had
lost their tempers." [18]

During the ensuing years the government sent various other
missions abroad. The one which went to England and France in
1863 reported that " customs in foreign lands are unlike those in
Japan. The ruler and the people have equal rights in governing." [19]
Okada Setsu who accompanied another mission to England in
1865 wrote a book called *Kosei Shoki* (A Short Commentary on a
Trip to the West) which described the House of Commons as
follows:

As for the lower house, the common people assemble and discuss matters.
Those who are present at the proceedings come to the chamber as representatives of the people. For example, if the people of a village designate
a certain individual as their representative, he goes to the legislative
chamber and gets into discussions. Both natives and foreigners are allowed
to participate in the discussions. Everything that happens in England must
be deliberated upon in the chamber.[20]

From the few examples cited above, it is readily apparent that
some of the information was incorrect and that many of the problems inherent in representative government such as legislative
procedure, the control of the executive, the rôle of political parties
and similar matters had completely escaped the notice of Japanese
intellectuals. This, of course, was due to the fact that the political
heritage of the Japanese was vastly different from that of the
Europeans. It is interesting to note, however, that the one idea
which everyone grasped was that of establishing a bicameral
assembly. But this, after all, was to them but an extension of the
council of feudal nobles which the Shogun had summoned for
consultation after the arrival of Commodore Perry.

In addition, problems arose not only from the fact that the

---

[18] *The First Japanese Embassy to the United States of America* translated by
Shigehiko Miyoshi (Tokyo, 1920), p. 47.
[19] Osatake, p. 33.   [20] *Ibid.*, p. 34.

source materials were written in foreign languages, but also from the fact that the Japanese were dealing in new concepts of government. New terms, for instance, had to be created for words like " parliament," and " legislature." And even when they went beyond literary sources and travelled abroad to observe legislatures in action, they were still likely to see only the outward forms since the inner workings would not be visible to an outside observer. Fukuzawa Yukichi summed it up well when he complained that he found representative government a " perplexing institution." [21] If this was the experience of one of the keenest students of Western civilization, we can surmise that the majority had at best but a hazy idea of parliamentary government.

Nevertheless, this new knowledge acted as a ferment among the intellectuals and began to suggest to them ways of modifying the old political structure. Just when the Japanese first began to think of adapting Western forms of government is difficult to determine. We do know, however, that as early as the Bunkyu era (1861-1863) the adoption of a deliberative assembly was proposed in several quarters. A Frenchman, Comte de Montblanc, advised some samurai of Satsuma to establish an assembly with the upper house composed of Court nobles and feudal lords, and the lower house consisting of their retainers to deliberate on national affairs.[22] About the same time, Yokoi Shonan, who had a precocious grasp of political principles, submitted a memorial which said: " Since this is a time of great change, an assembly should be established. The Court nobles and samurai should sit in the upper house, and in the lower house, talented men from all over the land should be used." [23]

In 1862 a Tokugawa official, Okubo Ichio, submitted a memorial urging the establishment of a bicameral assembly. The upper house, to be located either in Kyoto or Osaka and made up of feudal lords, five of whom were permanent members, was to meet once in five years, or in times of emergency. The personnel and the time of meeting of the lower house were to be determined.[24]

A much more elaborate plan was presented in 1863 by Akamatsu Kosaburo, of the Ueda clan. According to this scheme, six ministers

[21] *The Autobiography of Fukuzawa Yukichi*, translated by Eiichi Kiyooka (Tokyo, 1934), p. 143.

[22] Shibuzawa, *op. cit.*, IV, 57.   [23] *Ibid.*   [24] Asai, *op. cit.*, pp. 192-194.

chosen from among the Shogun, Court nobles, feudal nobles, and *hatamoto* (direct vassals of the Tokugawa) were to advise the Emperor. About 130 "enlightened men" chosen by ballot in accordance with the size of the clan were to make up the lower house. The thirty members comprising the upper house were to be elected from among the Court nobles, feudal lords, and *hatamoto*. The two houses were to vote on national issues and then submit a memorial to the Throne. After Imperial assent, the laws were to be promulgated. In case the Emperor did not give his consent, the bill was to be deliberated on a second time, and when an "impartial view" was obtained, it was to be proclaimed by the assembly as the law of the land. The chief duties of the assembly were to reform the defects of the old customs, establish laws which were in accordance with those of other nations, supervise the selection of officials, make laws on foreign relations, and on the receipt and disbursement of funds, etc.[25] There was, however, no immediate response to these proposals.

Meanwhile, other reform measures were being advocated. For a time in the early 1860's a movement known as *Kobu Gattai* or Union of Court and Military gained some momentum. Supported by Court nobles and some powerful feudatories like Mori of Choshu, the movement was aimed to heal the breach between the Imperial court and the Shogunate which had been produced by differences in attitude towards the foreign powers. The Court had been insistent on the expulsion of the foreigners, while the Shogunate, being incapable of driving out the foreigners, was lukewarm to the idea. The movement gradually declined when political reforms within the various fiefs forced the lords into the background and brought young samurai into positions of power.[26] Unlike their lords, who hoped to work through the Shogunate, most of the young samurai aimed at nothing less than the overthrow of the *Bakufu*. They were the ones who urged that the Emperor be "restored" to power.

Finally out of the conflicting views there appeared a compromise plan. This plan was a formula for political action containing two elements: the creation of a deliberative assembly combined with the resignation of the Shogun. It was given the name *Kogi Seitai Ron* or Advocacy of Government by Open Discussion.

[25] Shibuzawa, *op. cit.*, pp. 57-58.   [26] Norman, *Emergence*, p. 26.

The chief advocates of the compromise plan were the leaders of the Tosa clan. Although within the Tosa clan there existed an anti-Tokugawa group led by Itagaki Taisuke, the clan chief, Yamanouchi Yodo was friendly to the Tokugawa house. Hence unlike the leaders of the Choshu and Satsuma clans who were intransigently anti-Tokugawa, Yamanouchi did not wish to see the Shogun eliminated from the political scene. In 1867 word reached Goto Shojiro, an able Tosa samurai, that Saigo Takamori, of Choshu, was determined to overthrow the Shogunate, even by resorting to arms. Thereupon, Goto consulted Sakamoto Ryuma, also of Tosa, and one of the leading statesmen of his time. The latter suggested that hostilities might be avoided if the Shogun could be induced to surrender his power voluntarily. Goto then drafted a memorial which urged the Shogun to restore the rule to the Emperor. This memorial, signed by Yamanouchi, Goto, and two other Tosa samurai, was presented to the Shogun on October 27, 1867.[27] Appended to this memorial was a rather long document suggesting future policy.[28] It contained, *inter alia*, the following significant clauses: (1) full power to administer the country lies in the Imperial court; (2) all matters, including the organization and laws of Japan must come from the legislature (*gisei-sho*) in Kyoto; (3) the legislature is to be divided into an upper and lower house; (4) as for the legislators, upright and uncorrupted men from the Court nobles down to the vassals and the common people are to be elected.[29]

Now this compromise plan continued several features which helped to make it palatable to the various factions. It did not, to begin with, call for the destruction of the feudal system. What was to be formed was a federation of clans bound together by an assembly to which representatives would be sent. Moreover, the proposal to create a deliberative assembly helped to allay fears among the mutually suspicious clans that one or two powerful clans might usurp power and simply replace the Tokugawa. And lastly, although the memorial did not outline in so many words the position of the Shogun in the proposed government, the latter, it would seem logical to assume, expected to be given considerable

[27] Murdoch, *op. cit.*, pp. 767-768.
[28] Murdoch mentions this document but does not go into its contents.
[29] The entire document is quoted in Shibuzawa, *op. cit.*, pp. 72-73.

power. We can get some hints along this line if we turn to the plan worked out by Nishi Amane.

Nishi, a scholar who had studied in the Netherlands, presented two drafts of a constitution to Keiki in November, 1867. His plan called for a federal state consisting of the Imperial court, the Shogunate, and the feudal clans. Among the powers granted to the Imperial court were the power to approve laws, maintain guard troops, and receive contributions from the feudal lords. The Shogunate, as might be expected, was allotted much more extensive power. It was to preside over the administration of the country and to control the Tokugawa domains. The Shogun, henceforth to be known as the *Taikun,* was to become the president of the upper house. He was, moreover, given the authority to dissolve the lower house. Lastly, he was given control of the bureaucracy, with the right to hire and dismiss officials.

As for the upper house, it was to consist of feudal lords with more than 10,000 *koku* in rice stipends. They were to deliberate on laws. Each clan was to send one representative to the lower house which was also given the power to discuss the laws. The representatives, however, were to be limited to the samurai class, since the peasants and merchants were " ignorant." [30]

A Japanese scholar, Professor K. Asai, argues that Nishi's scheme was not very important and says that it was not adopted because the Shogun was more interested in the British parliamentary system than in a federal scheme of government.[31] This may well be true. Yet, on the other hand, it seems reasonable to assume that Nishi's plan represented more or less what Keiki expected to get in the new government. If such an assumption is justified, then one might say that Yamanouchi's memorial came at a time when the Shogun himself was trying to work out a system whereby he could step down and appease those clamoring for a change, at the same time, retaining the maximum of power in the reconstituted government.[32] At any rate, one thing is certain, and that is that the Shogun's resignation was not unconditional. Keiki's statement bears witness to the fact that he resigned on the assumption that a bicameral assembly would be established:

[30] Asai, *op. cit.*, pp. 196-202.
[31] *Ibid.*, p. 203.
[32] Fujii and Moriya, *SNST*, p. 73.

I had decided on returning the rule to the Emperor long ago. Yet there was no concrete plan for achieving the return of the rule to the Emperor in actual practice. This was because things could not be run by the power of the Court nobles alone. The same was true of the feudal nobles; nor did it appear that the country could be governed by the samurai. It was something that troubled me. In short, since in both the Imperial court and the Shogunate there were capable men among the lower ranks, but not among the upper, I felt that all matters should be deliberated in open discussion. But with respect to the method, there was as yet no fixed opinion.

Matsudaira Yodo's [i. e., Yamanouchi Yodo] memorial was presented, and it said that a system consisting of an upper and lower house should be established. It was indeed an excellent idea. If we chose the Court nobles and the lords for the upper house and the samurai for the lower, and decided matters on the basis of open discussion, the return of the rule to the Emperor could be put into effect. Getting courage and self-confidence from this, I finally carried it out.[33]

On November 8, 1868 representatives from some forty clans were summoned to the Nijo castle in Kyoto to approve the proposed surrender of power. The following day the Shogun presented a memorial to the Imperial court, and on November 10, he was notified that it had been accepted.

There still remained, however, the final act to this drama. Keiki clearly had miscalculated the temper and determination of his foes. The young samurai from the western clans would take nothing less than the complete elimination of the Shogunate; and so Keiki's ingenious plan to become the leading figure in the new provisional government misfired. It will be remembered that in the Imperial conference, described in the first chapter, the Shogun was striped of all power, both economic and political. It might be said, therefore, that from Keiki's point of view the *Kogi Seitai Ron* had disastrous consequences. Yet more significant, in the long run, was the fact that the concept of government by deliberation survived the demise of the Shogunate.

[33] Quoted in Asai, *op. cit.*, p. 204.

Chapter IV

ASSEMBLIES AND CONSTITUTIONS

I.

THE idea of building the new government around a deliberative assembly continued to exert its influence even after the Restoration. Its most active proponents were a few Tosa samurai, who feared that unless the dominance of the Satsuma and Choshu clans could be checked a neo-Shogunate might arise on the ruins of the old.[1] At the same time other pressures were pushing the somewhat reluctant Meiji government in this direction. Lacking financial resources and wide-spread support, it found it expedient to be conciliatory if it hoped to gain friends and allies. Since at this time the war against the Tokugawa forces was still being fought, the government was particularly anxious to enlist the support of the various feudal lords. Furthermore, the government had been obliged to issue unbacked paper currency amounting to some twenty-four million *yen* or roughly seventy-two percent of the budget to help pay for the cost of the civil war.[2] It was necessary that the government enjoy the confidence of the people in order to get complete acceptance of this currency. Finally, there was the matter of foreign relations. It was necessary to indicate to the Western Powers that the new regime was not anti-foreign.

These considerations formed the background of the historic document known as the *Gokajo no Goseimon* or Charter Oath of Five Articles. This Oath was a broad statement of policy issued at a critical period for the purpose of placating potential opposition. The document was originally drafted by the Minister of Finance, Yuri Kimimasa. Yuri had come under the influence of Yokoi Shonan, who had been attracted to the republican form of government. Accordingly, his draft began with the statement, " It is to

[1] See the memorial submitted by Goto Shojiro and Fukuoka Kotei, Fujii and Moriya, *SNST*, pp. 210-212.
[2] Honjo, " The Importance of ' Goyokin ' or Forced Loans," *op. cit.*, p. 25.

be desired that the common people shall achieve their aims and that thereby the people's minds shall not grow weary." Yuri's draft was later revised by Fukuoka Kotei, of Tosa, who wished to emphasize the need for calling an assembly. Therefore he began with the statement, "An assembly of feudal nobles shall be convoked and all matters shall be decided by open discussion." Kido Takayoshi, of Choshu, and later one of the leading statesmen of the Meiji government, made the third and final revision. With an eye towards the possible reaction of the Western Powers, he added the clause, "All absurd customs of former days shall be abandoned, and all actions shall be based on international usage." [3] In its final form the Oath read as follows:

1. Assemblies shall be widely convoked and all measures shall be decided by open discussion.
2. The government and the governed shall be of one mind, and the national economy and finances shall be greatly strengthened.
3. Civil and military officials as well as the common people shall achieve their aims, and thus the people's minds shall not grow weary.
4. All absurd customs of olden times shall be abandoned, and all actions shall be based on international usage.
5. Knowledge shall be sought for all over the world and thereby the foundations of Imperial rule shall be strengthened.

On April 7, 1868 the well known Court noble, Sanjo Saneyoshi, in the presence of the Emperor and other notables read aloud the above Oath. This was followed by a ceremony in which the Court nobles and the feudal lords affixed their seals to a document affirming that they would exert themselves to " set the Emperor's mind at ease." [4]

The statement of general policy having been issued, there now remained the question of its implementation. The first step in this direction was taken by Fukuoka, who again presented a memorial calling attention to the need for reforming the governmental structure.[5] In response to his memorial, Iwakura ordered Fukuoka and Fukushima, a samurai from Saga, to draw up plans for the reorganization of the government. The result was the *Seitaisho*, which can be considered Japan's first modern constitution.

---

[3] The texts of the three drafts may be found in *SNST*, pp. 213-216.
[4] *Ibid.*, p. 216.   [5] *Ibid.*, p. 219.

In drafting this document, the authors drew on the American constitutional system for guidance. Among the reference works they consulted were: (1) a history of the United States by Elijah C. Bridgman,[6] an American missionary to China, which was translated into Japanese from the Chinese by Mitsukuri Genpo; (2) Fukuzawa Yukichi's bestseller, *Seiyo Jijo* (Western Conditions); and (3) the Constitution of the United States, which Fukushima's teacher, Guido H. F. Verbeck, the Dutch-American missionary, had used as a text in teaching English in Nagasaki.[7] The *Seitaisho* was promulgated on June 17, 1868.

We need not go into a detailed discussion of the reorganization of the government based on this constitution except to mention several points of special interest to this study.[8] Under the *Seitaisho* all authority was concentrated in a Council of State known as the *Dajokan*. But the functions of the Council were in theory divided in such a way that a separation of powers would be achieved. "The legislative branch cannot possess executive functions, nor can the executive branch possess legislative functions." Another interesting point was that government officials were to be elected for four year terms. In practice, however, neither of these stipulations was carried out. The most important change produced by the reorganization was the creation of a bicameral assembly. The upper house, composed of princes of the blood, Court nobles and feudal lords and their retainers, was given considerable authority. The functions of this body included the "establishment of the constitution, the enactment of laws, the decision of questions of policy, the selection of men to fill the offices of the three higher ranks, the supreme judicial power, the conclusion of treaties, and the power of making peace and war." The lower house consisted of representatives from the fiefs apportioned on the basis of three representatives for large fiefs, two for intermediate fiefs, and one for small fiefs. Under the direction of the upper house, it was to

[6] On Elijah Bridgman, see Susan Reed Stifler, "Elijah Coleman Bridgman, The First American Sinologist," *Notes on Far Eastern Studies in America*, No. 10 (January, 1942); Arthur W. Hummel, "Some American Pioneers in Chinese Studies," *ibid.*, No. 9 (June, 1941); *Eminent Chinese of the Ch'ing Period*, I, 505.

[7] Fujii and Moriya, *SNST*, p. 221. On Verbeck see *Dictionary of American Biography*, edited by Dumas Malone (New York, 1936), XIX, 248.

[8] The text of the *Seitaisho* is printed in "Japanese Government Documents," edited by W. W. McLaren, *TASJ*, XLII (May, 1914), 8-15. (Hereafter the "Japanese Government Documents" will be cited as *JGD*).

deliberate on matters pertaining to revenues, laws, communications, coinage, erection of fortifications, military establishments, disputes between different clans, etc.

The lower house met a number of times and deliberated on bills dealing with taxation, communications, dress, etc. It is said that there was a great deal of useless discussion and it appears that this experiment in parliamentary government was not very successful.[9] At any rate, the institution was abolished in the fall of the same year, and a committee was appointed to look into the whole matter. Among the members of this committee were two young officials from the foreign office, Sameshima Naonobu and Mori Arinori, both of whom later distinguished themselves in the diplomatic service. Having been among the students sent abroad by the Satsuma authorities, they had studied in London and travelled through the United States. On their advice another deliberative assembly known as the *Kogisho* was summoned in the spring of 1869.[10]

The chief function of this new body, it was declared, was that of enacting laws. The members, still representing the various clans, were to be at least twenty-five years of age, and were to be chosen for four-year terms. All bills required at least a three-fifths majority to pass. The assembly was given the power to summon administrative officials for questioning. Following Western legislative practice, the work was divided among a number of committees, including those on taxation, agriculture, foreign relations, mining, and domestic industry.[11]

The *Kogisho* appears to have been a strange amalgam of the old and the new. According to the biography of Motooka Keiji, a representative to the *Kogisho*, there were some members who came dressed in Western-style clothes. "When Motooka Keiji made his appearance clad in a new samurai outfit with his hair still tied in a top knot, the assembly room was filled with chairs and tables. Seeing this, he immediately went to the rostrum and argued that Japanese customs should not be abandoned in favor of European customs. . . . There were some who objected, but in the end he won out and the chairs and tables were removed."[12]

[9] Fujii and Moriya, *SNST*, pp. 223-224.
[10] *Ibid.*, p. 224.
[11] *Ibid.*, p. 226.
[12] Quoted in Osatake, *NKST*, I, 212.

Somewhat similar contrasts were revealed in the bills introduced in the *Kogisho*. There was, for instance, a measure to abolish the feudal practice of forced loans. Another bill was aimed to do away with limitations on interest charges. Both of these measures, it might be said, represented the modern aspect of Meiji Japan. On the other hand, a bill to allow those other than officials and soldiers to abandon the old custom of wearing two swords, the badge of samurai privilege, aroused much anger. Indeed so strong was the opposition that Mori Arinori, the originator of the bill, was almost assassinated and later forced to resign.[13]

The *Kogisho,* whose effectiveness was hampered no doubt by the existence of old prejudices, was soon replaced by another assembly known as the *Shugi-in.* Compared to its predecessor the *Shugi-in* had less power. Since all measures were now to be proposed by the *Dajokan,* the nature of the bills discussed underwent some change. Included on the agenda were proposals for the expansion of the armed forces, revision of the educational system and reform of the clan system.[14] No further meetings of the *Shugin-in* were held after October, 1870, and in 1873 it was abolished and its functions transferred to another body known as the *Sa-in.*

The failure of the *Shugi-in* to take root in the soil of Jap .nese politics may be explained on several grounds. Osatake believes that there are four reasons. First, the strong class system made family name a more important consideration than ability. Next, second-rate men were sent to the assembly, the outstanding men having become members of the bureaucracy. Third, many of the representatives were without experience in politics and often failed to represent the views of their clans. Fourth, they were more local than national in outlook.[15] To these may be added a fifth consideration, namely that the central government, then engaged in building up its power, was not interested in strengthening representative institutions.

II.

The very fact that institutions of the central government like the *Kogisho,* patterned more or less after Western models, were established so early in the Meiji era testifies as to the strong impression

[13] Fujii and Moriya, *SNST*, p. 227.
[14] *Ibid.,* pp. 228-229.
[15] Osatake, *op. cit.,* p. 214.

certain Western concepts and techniques of government had made on the Japanese mind. An even more eloquent testimony, however, is provided by the astonishing spread of similar institutions organized on a local basis. It is known that during the Restoration period, assemblies paralleling the *Kogisho* were established in many clans.[16] They were short-lived, however, because with the centralization of authority, following the abolition of feudalism in 1871, these assemblies were dissolved. They, nevertheless, served as precedents for other local assemblies to follow.

During the succeeding years, both local officials and local political leaders took the initiative in setting up assemblies in various communities.[17] There were also instances in which the people submitted memorials calling for their establishment. In 1875, for example, representatives from thirteen prefectures met and submitted a memorandum to the *Chihokan Kaigi* or Assembly of Prefectural Governors, asking that body to consider the creation of local assemblies. They argued that the people wanted these assemblies because such institutions would participate in the making of the constitution and because they would strengthen popular rights.[18] Between 1871 and 1879 local assemblies were set up in at least forty-eight prefectures.[19] According to a news item published in the *Aichi Shimbun* (Aichi Newspaper) in August, 1872, an assembly was established in Aichi prefecture because " if the rights of the four classes are to be protected and their interests promoted, the people should be permitted to petition and discuss matters without distinction of rank as is the practice under the Western system of legislative assemblies." All people with " worthy ideas " including local officials, wealthy individuals, samurai, Shinto priests, Buddhist priests, peasants, and merchants were urged to appear at the assembly.[20]

[16] See Osatake Takeki, " Chiho Minkai " [Local Popular Assemblies], *Meiji Seiji Shi Kenkyu* [Studies in Meiji Political History,], No. 2 (May, 1936).

[17] *Ibid.*, p. 14.

[18] Osatake, *NKST*, I, 262.

[19] See the list in *ibid.*, p. 267.

[20] Osatake Takeki, " Han Gi-in to Chiho Minkai " [Clan Assemblies and Local Popular Assemblies], *Meiji Bunka Kenkyu* [Studies in Meiji Culture] (Hereafter cited as *MBK*), No. 4 (December, 1934), p. 11.

III.

After the abolition of feudalism in 1871, the Meiji government underwent another of its numerous reorganizations. This time the *Dajokan* was divided into three boards. In the *Sei-in* or Central board was concentrated most of the power. It served as a policy-making and executive body. The *U-in* or Right board was composed of the heads of administrative departments, but there was some overlap between it and the *Sei-in* in terms of personnel, for some of its members also were in the *Sei-in*. The *Sa-in* or Left board, which is of most interest to us, represented what little there was left of the legislative branch. Although encroachment on the authority of the assembly had stripped it of practically all of its power, it still enjoyed enough support to make its outright abolition unwise. As W. W. McLaren has said, it was difficult to get rid of the *Kogisho* and the *Shugi-in* in view of the charter oath which had proclaimed that all measures should be decided by open discussion. "The Government," continues McLaren, "not feeling secure enough in its power to openly repudiate the terms of the oath and announce its determination to rule the country without consulting the people, the *Sa-in* was therefore created with advisory powers, and its members were appointed by the Emperor for the purpose of representing public opinion, but lest it should by any chance attempt an independent course, its functions were strictly limited to giving advice on projects of law proposed by the *Sei-in*." [21]

In view of its ancestry, the *Sa-in* was quite naturally concerned with various problems of representative government, especially those related to the drafting of a written constitution for the central government. In taking up the study of constitutions, the *Sa-in* was by no means breaking new ground. As early as 1843, Mizuno Tadakuni, a leading minister of the Tokugawa *Bakufu*, had ordered the translation of the Dutch constitution.[22] In the years that followed, many other foreign constitutions were translated and studied. The American constitution, as we have already seen, formed the background of the *Seitaisho*.

---

[21] Walter Wallace McLaren, *A Political History of Japan During the Meiji Era 1867-1912* (London, 1916), p. 113. (This work will be cited hereafter as *Political History*).

[22] Osatake, *NKST*, I, 277.

It would be a mistake, however, to interpret the interest shown in constitutions to mean that the central government was seeking a way whereby the popular will could be brought to bear on the operation of government. On the contrary, as Osatake has correctly stated, " it was mostly based on the idea of creating a constitution for the purpose of building a centralized state, and of calling a deliberative assembly to appease the popular mind." [23] As early as 1868, the crafty Iwakura had urged the Imperial court to create an assembly to open the way, as he put it, for the employment of men of talent. It is suspected, however, that his real purpose was to use the assembly as an instrument for exercising control over the opinions of the various political leaders.[24] In other words, just as the Shogun had planned to employ the assembly as a device to retain power, so Iwakura apparently hoped to strengthen the central government by the use of the same device.

Nor was Iwakura the only one who entertained such views. There was, for instance, Miyajima Seiichiro, an employee of the *Sa-in.* Being much disturbed by the trend of events, he submitted a report entitled, *Rikkoku Kengi* (Proposals on the Constitution and the Creation of Nations), to his superior, Goto Shojiro. " The traditional system of government in our country," wrote Miyajima, " has been that of an absolute monarchy. All political affairs are controlled from above, and the people, of course, know not what their rights are, nor what their duties are." He went on to complain that " At the present time when intercourse with foreign nations is increasing daily, the ignorant people are studying foreign systems of government, and under the guise of independence and freedom are exaggerating their rights and neglecting their duties. *In extreme cases, some are urging a republican form of government.*" [25] The solution he proposed was the creation of a constitution establishing a strong monarchy.

Although the *Sa-in* contained men like Miyajima, on the whole it appears to have been staffed by fairly progressive officials who wished to see established eventually a constitutional government patterned after European models. After a study of various foreign

[23] *Ibid.*, p. 279.
[24] Suzuki Yasuzo, " Kempo Seitei Ron no Hassei " [The Genesis of the Argument for the Establishment of the Constitution], *CK*, LVI (March, 1941), 304.
[25] *Ibid.*, p. 307. (Italics mine, N. I.)

constitutions, the *Sa-in* presented to the *Sei-in* a plan including the following points: An assembly, consisting of the *Sa-in*, forming the upper house, and the *U-in* plus prefectural officials, forming the lower house, would be set up in Tokyo. It would hold annual meetings lasting for three months. Eventually the assembly, at first consisting of appointed officials, would become a popularly-elected body. Perhaps in anticipation of such a day, the *Sa-in* even drafted detailed election laws.[26]

The *Sei-in*, however, refused to accept the proposal. It was evident that the small group of men who had seized power in 1868 and controlled the Meiji government were not yet in a mood to share power with a deliberative assembly.

[26] *Ibid.*, p. 306.

Part Two:

THE BIRTH OF THE DEMOCRATIC MOVEMENT

CHAPTER V

THE CRISIS OF 1873

I.

THE first major schism to rend the inner core of the ruling group which had been in control since the Restoration occurred in 1873. The issue which produced the split was a proposal to send an expeditionary force to Korea. For several years previous to 1873 there had been a growing demand to make war on Japan's neighbor on the continent of Asia. In the vanguard of those advocating war were the samurai who had suffered severely with the advent of the new regime. Under the Shogunate their status had been growing precarious, as we have already seen, but the Restoration virtually spelled their ruin as a separate and privileged class. The new government, unable to support the vast army of unproductive samurai, had granted them pensions in lieu of their hereditary stipends. But the government found that even this was too great a burden. So in 1873 an offer to commute the samurai pensions was made. It was hoped that by giving the samurai a lump sum of money they could be encouraged to set themselves up in business, buy land for agricultural purposes, or become small-scale producers of commodities.[1] Great efforts were also made to absorb as many samurai as possible into the governmental machinery, particularly in the police and armed forces. Yet despite all the efforts to provide them with some means of livelihood, many were unable to make the necessary adjustments. It was not unusual for those who had gone into business to fail through lack of experience. Some, refusing to adapt themselves to the new social order, simply lived in idleness and quickly exhausted the money they had received from the government.

Added to the economic distress was the loss of social prestige. At least under the Shogunate they were a part of the ruling class and enjoyed certain social privileges. With the Restoration, these

[1] McLaren, *Political History*, pp. 80-82, 86-90; Norman, *Emergence*, pp. 95-96.

47

too disappeared, for equality before the law was decreed. When conscription was adopted in 1872 even the peasant could become a soldier. This swept away a cherished prerogative of the samurai class.

Tremendous pressure, therefore, was brought to bear by the samurai to make war on Korea. They longed to return to the old order in which their martial skills would be appreciated, and in which they could once again enjoy the social prestige commensurate with their status as members of the governing class. The leading spokesman for this group was Saigo Takamori, a large, burly, powerfully muscled samurai from Satsuma. A natural leader, his " name could kindle the most ardent sentiments among the former samurai throughout the nation; his exploits even in his lifetime were translated into legend, sure omen of immortality." [2] Sensing the restlessness of the samurai, Saigo wrote to his fellow-clansman, Okubo Toshimichi, then in London, that he felt it was beyond his power to control his men. He added that " I feel as if I am sleeping on a heap of explosives." [3] To Saigo war must have appeared as the most desirable solution, for the samurai would necessarily form the great bulk of the army. And following a victorious campaign, Saigo hoped to return home " with such prestige and material support, that he would be enabled to dictate his own terms to the Tokyo government. . . ." [4]

Nor were the samurai alone in advocating a war program. They enjoyed the support of those who favored an imperialistic policy on the continent. There was a long tradition of aggressive action in Korea going back to the semi-historical Empress Jingo and continuing through Toyotomi Hideyoshi, who tried but failed to conquer and hold the peninsula as a base for the conquest of eastern Asia in the sixteenth century. This tradition, moreover, had been given articulate form in more recent times by such men as Yoshida Shoin, whose influence on some of the Meiji leaders was profound.[5] Thus, in 1871, Eto Shimpei, who later led a revolt

---

[2] E. Herbert Norman, *Feudal Background of Japanese Politics*, Secretariat Paper, No. 9 for the Ninth Conference of the Institute of Pacific Relations (in mimeograph) (New York: Institute of Pacific Relations, 1945), p. 73. (This work will be cited hereafter as *Feudal Background*).

[3] Smimasa Idditti, *The Life of Marquis Shigenobu Okuma* (Tokyo, 1940), p. 154.

[4] Augustus H. Mounsey, *The Satsuma Rebellion* (London, 1879), p. 62.

[5] Robert T. Pollard, " The Dynamics of Japanese Imperialism," *Pacific Historical Review*, VIII (March, 1939), 5-35; Yoshi S. Kuno, *Japanese Expansion on the*

against the government, wrote in a memorandum to Iwakura that " China is the battleground of Asia. Those who do not take possession of her are endangered; if, however, you take possession of her, you control the situation in Asia." [6] Other supporters included officials drawn from the lesser clans like Tosa and Hizen. Since they were a distinct minority in the Meiji government, they were prone to oppose policies proposed by men from Satsuma and Choshu mostly out of partisan considerations.

As an excuse for their proposed aggression in Korea, the war party pointed to the anti-foreign policy of the Korean government. Soon after the Restoration, a mission had been sent to Korea through Lord So, of Tsushima, the traditional emissary, to announce the change of government in Japan. But the Korean government, then under the control of the anti-foreign Regent Tai-Wen Kun, refused to receive it.[7] No envoy had been sent from Korea to Japan since 1811 and the conservative faction at the Korean court was not prepared to resume relations or recognize the new regime in Japan. In the following year, two other missions were sent, but the Koreans again refused to receive the commissioners; and when the mission proceeded to the capital without an invitation, they were reproached for having "intruded into forbidden precincts." Still undaunted Japan once again, in 1871, sent the chief secretary of foreign affairs, Hanabusa Yoshichika, accompanied by two warships, but this, too, failed to bring about the desired results.

By 1873 there was a good deal of sentiment in favor of a punitive expedition to Korea. As a Japanese writer put it, " the psychological moment was attained when the ex-samurai politicians, tired of the long quiet after so many years of excitement and danger, and dissatisfied with the apparent gradual weakening of manly national spirit under the influence of Western intercourse, eagerly longed for some stirring events in which their belligerent patriotism could again be brought into display." [8]

Asiatic Continent (Berkeley: University of California Press, 1937, 1940), II, pp. 351-355.

[6] Quoted in Suzuki Yasuzo, " Tairiku Shinshutsu no Hitsuzen-sei to Joyaku Kaisei " [The Inevitability of the Continental Advance and Treaty Revision], *CK*, LVI (April, 1941), 352.

[7] Tyler Dennett, *Americans in Eastern Asia* (New York: 1941), pp. 434-435.

[8] Nagao Ariga, " Diplomacy," in *Japan by the Japanese*, edited by Alfred Stead, (London, 1904), p. 148.

50 POLITICAL DEMOCRACY IN JAPAN

In the summer of 1873 preparations were made for the projected attack on Korea. First, the foreign office sounded out the Chinese government on its attitude towards Korea. Since Korea was generally regarded as a dependency of China, it was necessary to determine whether China would come to the aid of the Koreans in case of war. It seems that as a result of several talks with Chinese officials, the Japanese became pretty well convinced that China would remain neutral.[9] Then on the basis of information from Mori Shigeru, who was then in Korea, the foreign office outlined a plan to the *Sei-in*. The gist of the proposal was to "send the army and navy to Korea and protect the Japanese residents; moreover, send an ambassador directly into Seoul and talk with the Korean government."[10] Sanjo Saneyoshi, who held a position equivalent to that of prime minister, agreed to this proposal.

Itagaki Taisuke, of Tosa, was also in agreement. He wished, moreover, to send a large force to Fusan, and added that this should naturally result in peace talks. Saigo, however, was opposed. Apparently he feared that the Koreans would yield and therefore there would be no war.[11] Hence he made a counter-proposal to the effect that Japan should send just an envoy first, and that if he were treated with insolence or assassinated, then it would be time to send warships. Itagaki immediately approved, and withdrew his plan. Eto Shimpei and Goto Shojiro also assented.[12] Then Saigo, who hoped that he would be murdered by a Korean mob and "furnish a fair *casus belli* for his country," asked to be named envoy.[13] This was done by the *Dajokan* on August 17. So elated was Saigo by his victory that in a note to Itagaki thanking him for his support, he said, "This is the happiest moment in my life."[14] The decision of the *Dajokan* was made official when Sanjo saw the Emperor and received his approval.[15]

[9] Nobutaka Ike, "Triumph of the Peace Party in Japan in 1873," *The Far Eastern Quarterly*, II (May, 1943), pp. 291-292.

[10] Tokutomi Iichiro, *Koshaku Yamagata Aritomo Den* [The Biography of Prince Yamagata Aritomo] (Tokyo, 1933), II, 301. Idditti's account differs slightly. See, *op. cit.*, pp. 151-152.

[11] Idditti, *op. cit.*, p. 155.

[12] Tokutomi, p. 304.

[13] Idditti, p. 155.

[14] For the text of this and other letters from Saigo to Itagaki, see Itagaki Taisuke, *Jiyuto Shi* [History of the Liberal Party] (Tokyo, 1910), I, 53-63. (Hereafter the *Jiyuto Shi* will be cited as *JS*).

[15] Tokutomi, p. 305. Idditti (p. 155) however says that Sanjo reserved the right

But there still remained a serious obstacle. Not all members of the inner group were convinced of the wisdom of going to war at this time. The most conspicuous of these were the members of the Iwakura Mission. In 1871 a part of the *Dajokan* was sent abroad under the leadership of Iwakura to investigate the West at first hand and to negotiate the revision of the unequal treaties. This group did not differ from Saigo's war party in principle, but only in the matter of priority.[16] They felt that internal reforms should take precedence over foreign aggrandizement. Nor did all of the militarists urge war, as the case of Yamagata Aritomo, one of the creators of the modern army, shows. He, like the others, felt that the time was not ripe, for he told Saigo that " Our army is in the midst of reorganization at the present time; but in a year or so, the foundations of the military system will be established, and there probably will not be any obstacles to prevent the sending of an army to the continent." [17]

Now in the absence of Iwakura and his mission, Saigo had dominated the government, and under his influence plans had been perfected for the invasion of Korea. But Saigo could not carry out his plans because of a written agreement that no major changes would be made without Iwakura's approval.[18] The final decision, therefore, had to wait until the entire *Dajokan* could meet.

to submit the cabinet's opinion to the Emperor pending the return of Iwakura. Essentially the same view is presented in George Etsujiro Uyehara, *The Political Development of Japan* (London, 1910), p. 74. Genji Hamada in his *Prince Ito* (Tokyo, 1936), p. 68 says the Saigo bloc had secured a tentative approval to dispatch an expedition to Korea.

[16] Evidence for this may be found, for instance, in Kido Takayoshi, who belonged to the peace bloc. In a letter he once wrote to Omura Masajiro, who might be called the founder of the modern Japanese army, Kido said: " The Imperial court, using its power—chiefly military power—should open up the port of Fusan in Korea. We will not benefit in terms of commodities and precious metals; rather we may incur losses. Yet in order to establish the great objectives of our Empire, to bring about a change in the eyes of all the people with regard to domestic and foreign affairs, to give the army and navy incentive to practice their techniques, to make our Empire great in the future and maintain itself for all time, there is no other policy." Quoted in Suzuki, *op. cit.*, p. 352.

[17] Tokutomi, p. 308.

[18] Article 2 required that the Iwakura mission and the stay-at-home members mutually report important incidents; article 5 provided that internal changes be avoided until after the return of the mission, and that if by any chance reforms were necesasry, they must first ask Iwakura by mail. The complete text of this agreement is given in Tokutomi, pp. 274-275.

As soon as the Iwakura mission returned on September 12, Saigo pressed for a meeting; but Sanjo refused to be hurried, probably owing to pressure from Iwakura. The latter wanted Okubo, who was opposed to the Korean invasion, appointed a *Sangi* or Councillor. This was done on October 12. But the support which the peace party gained was soon nullified when on the 13th Soejima Taneomi, of the foreign office, whose views were diametrically opposed to those of Okubo, was also placed in the inner group.

The first meeting was held on October 14.[19] Iwakura outlined what were in his opinion the three problems confronting the government: Russian pressure in Sakhalin, the actions of the natives in Formosa, and the Korean issue. He said that the Russian problem was the most urgent. Itagaki, Goto, and Eto disagreed. The boundary question in Sakhalin, they said, could be settled by negotiation with Russia, while in the case of Formosa one was dealing with aborigines with no government or state. But Korea concerned the prestige and power of Japan and should be settled immediately. The only reply Iwakura's bloc could give was that internal reforms were necessary in order to become powerful enough to carry out foreign conquests. The meeting disbanded about five o'clock in the afternoon without having reached a decision.

At the next session on the 15th, Saigo gained the upper hand. It was decided that he would be sent as an envoy. The fortunes of the peace party reached low ebb on October 16, and as a result four members of the *Dajokan*, Kido, Okubo, Okuma, and Oki, submitted their resignations on the 17th. Iwakura also sent a letter signifying his intention to resign. He also refused to attend the meetings, giving illness as his excuse. Meanwhile, Saigo put pressure on Sanjo to report the results of the meetings to the Throne in order that Imperial approval could be secured. That evening Sanjo called on Iwakura to tell him about Saigo's demands. A heated discussion followed. Returning late at night, Sanjo summoned Saigo and told him that Iwakura was still opposed to the Korean war. Saigo refused to yield, and the discussion was ended at dawn.

At this point, the timid Sanjo, caught between two contending forces, suffered a nervous breakdown. Consequently he, too, submitted his resignation. Immediately Iwakura was named acting

[19] The following account of the negotiations is based on Itagaki, *JS*, I, 63-72.

head of the *Dajokan*. The scales were now tipped in favor of the peace party. Accordingly, on October 22, Saigo, Itagaki, Goto, Soyejima, and Eto proceeded to Iwakura's residence. They argued that it was only fair that he should faithfully carry out what had already been decided by the *Dajokan*. Iwakura replied that he would use the authority of his post to annul what had been decided. Then Eto came forward with a remark that the Emperor had already given his approval. To this Iwakura answered, " No matter what His Majesty says, I, Iwakura, will not permit him to do it."

On the 23rd Iwakura reported to the palace. The Emperor now reversed his earlier decision and acceded to the wishes of the peace party. Angered by the turn of events, the war party, including Saigo, Itagaki, Soyejima, Goto and Eto resigned.

II.

The crisis of 1873 marked a great divide in the political history of the Meiji era. The unity of the coalition originally formed to overthrow the Tokugawa was broken. Now that the common enemy was gone, and the confusion attending the first days of reconstruction ended, the Restoration began to appear in a different light to different people. To some the partial political revolution, which had been the Restoration, had gone too far, while to others it had not gone far enough. The conflicting cross currents of interest, submerged in the early days of the Restoration, at last appeared on the surface. And out of the break that followed, there emerged at least three groups where previously there had been but one.

Of these groups the most powerful was the one remaining in control of the government. The roster of this group included virtually all of the names of the leading Meiji political figures— Okubo, Kido, Ito, Okuma, Yamagata, Iwakura, to mention a few. In matters of basic social and political philosophy these men were in basic agreement. They believed in a program of modernization; but they also attached certain important qualifications. Modernization was to be directed towards the centralization of power, the strengthening of the military arm of the state, and eventual overseas expansion. Opposed to popular control of the government, they aimed to erect an absolute state, using what one writer has called the " mystic quality " of the Emperor to bind the various pieces together.[20] Given the agreement on fundamentals the group naturally possessed a high degree of internal cohesion, and formed a tightly-knit oligarchy. This internal cohesion, moreover, was reinforced by the fact that almost all of the men were samurai from the two clans of Satsuma and Choshu. In a time when local sentiment and local loyalties were still very strong, this was a very important consideration. The government became something of a private preserve for men from these two areas.[21] Little wonder the critics denounced the government for being a *Hanbatsu Seifu* or " Clan Government."

The second group, led by Saigo Takamori, consisted of the disaffected samurai. Saigo came from Satsuma, but in his case his dislike of the policy of modernization was strong enough to overcome his sense of loyalty to his fellow-clansmen in the central government. After retirement from public office, Saigo returned to his home in Kagoshima, where he organized *Shigakko* or " Private schools." In these " schools " which, as an authority puts it, were " really Saigo's own military academy " the samurai were organized, trained, and indoctrinated.[22] Since Satsuma had always formed an *imperium in imperio* and effective control of the central government had never been extended into the province, Saigo was able to carry on his work without much interference. From among the large samurai population consisting of about one fourth of the total, he recruited many followers. Finally in 1877 Saigo raised the banner of revolt and took the field at the head of some 30,000 men.[23] The Satsuma Rebellion, as this uprising is called, was essentially an attempt to put the clock back and restore the old feudal order. As such it was almost a foregone conclusion that it could not succeed, for Saigo was leading his movement into a historical blind alley. The government immediately dispatched its modern conscript army to do battle with the samurai. The plebeians,

[20] Tsuchiya Takao, " Nihon Zaibatsu Shiron, Josetsu " [Historical Essays on the Japanese Zaibatsu, An Introduction], *CK*, July, 1946, p. 28.

[21] It was claimed in one memorial that of 67 officials of *chokunin* rank, 18 were from Satsuma, 12 from Choshu, 7 from Tosa, and 7 from Saga; while of 2126 officials of *sonin* rank, 345 were from Choshu, 247 from Satsuma, 112 from Tosa, and 96 from Saga. *MBZ*, IV 378-379. See also the list of the 43 men who held key positions between 1869 and 1889 in Robert Karl Reischauer, *Japan, Government and Politics* (New York: Thomas Nelson and Sons, 1939), pp. 64n-65n.

[22] Norman, *Feudal Background*, p. 75.

[23] *Ibid.*

armed with rifles, proved more than a match for the samurai elite. After six months of savage fighting, the rebellion was put down. In defeat Saigo, seriously injured, asked one of his officers to put him to death. The Satsuma Rebellion proved to be the last of a series of samurai uprisings. Its failure demonstrated conclusively that the Meiji government was too powerful to be overthrown by force. "It was amply proved," as McLaren has said, "that any criticism of the Government must follow a peaceful course, under the guidance of educated public opinion, not the desperate counsel of military fanaticism." [24]

The third group, led by Itagaki Taisuke, is of the greatest interest to us. The story of its formation in 1874, the spread of its influence all over the nation, and its eventual decline is the subject of the present study.

In the debate over the Korean question Itagaki had consistently sided with Saigo and had resigned with him when the peace party triumphed. But after leaving the government, Itagaki pursued an independent course. While both were opposed to the government, they revealed their opposition in different ways. This can be explained, in part, by the fact that unlike Saigo, Itagaki's disaffection was mostly that of the "outs" against the "ins." It was a case of a member of a minority clan showing his resentment against the dominance of the Satsuma and Choshu, or Sat-Cho faction. For that reason Itagaki's opposition took the form of political action rather than armed uprising.

Itagaki fired his first shot against the Meiji oligarchy a few months after his resignation. His attack took the form of a memorial calling for the establishment of an elective assembly. Since he had been a member of the *Dajokan*, he must have known about the discussions and research going on within the *Sa-in* regarding the calling of an assembly and the drafting of a national constitution. It would seem reasonable to assume, therefore, that he decided to steal a march on the government and compel it to agree to the creation of representative institutions. In any case, he discussed the matter with his fellow-clansman, Goto Shojiro, who introduced him to Komuro Nobuo and Furuzawa Shigeru, both of whom had just returned from Great Britain. Since Komuro and Furuzawa were anxious to introduce the parliamentary system of

[24] McLaren, *Political History*, p. 105.

government into Japan, they agreed to lend assistance.[25] At Itagaki's request, Furuzawa drafted the memorial. According to some sources, it was originally written in the English language.[26]

On January 17, 1874 the memorial, signed by nine men, including Itagaki and Goto, was presented to the *Sa-in*. At the same time it was published in the newspapers. This being the first time that a political document of this kind appeared in the press, it aroused considerable interest.[27]

The memorial was a skillfully drawn document.[28] Persuasively written, it effectively exposed some of the weak spots in the government's position. " When we humbly reflect upon the quarter in which the governing power lies," it began, " we find that it lies not with the Crown (the Imperial House) on the one hand, nor with the people on the other, but with the officials alone." The memorial went on to charge that the " administration is conducted in an arbitrary manner, rewards and punishments are prompted by partiality, the channel by which the people should communicate with the government is blocked up and they cannot state their grievances." Since the memorial was being presented by a group of men who had been a minority while in office, this attack on the Meiji bureaucracy was understandable. The memorialists warned that " if a reform is not effected the state will be ruined." In order to avert such a calamity they urged the " establishment of a council-chamber chosen by the people. Then a limit will be placed to the power of the officials, and both governors and governed will obtain peace and prosperity."

Next the principle of " no representation, no taxation " was stated. " The people whose duty it is to pay taxes to the government possess the right of sharing in their government's affairs and of approving or condemning. This being a principle universally acknowledged it is not necessary to waste words in discussing it."

Then the memorial attempted to meet some of the objections which the critics were likely to raise to the demand for an elective assembly. To the contention of the government that the people were wanting in " culture and intelligence " and hence it was too early

[25] Itagaki, *JS*, I, pp. 82-83.
[26] Osatake, *NKST*, II, 374.
[27] *Ibid.*, p. 380.
[28] A translation of the memorial is included in McLaren, *JGD*, pp. 426-433. All quotations have been taken from this translation.

for representative institutions, the memorialists replied that " to give our people culture and intelligence and to cause them to advance into the region of enlightment, they must in the first place be induced to protect their rights, to respect and value themselves, and be inspired by a spirit of sympathy with the griefs and joys of the empire, which can only be done by giving them a voice in its concerns."

The argument in favor of giving the people a voice in the government was carried a step further. Almost from the very beginning the Meiji government had emphasized everything that would make the nation strong from the military point of view. This attitude was reflected in the well-known slogan, *Fukoku Kyohei* or " Rich Country, Strong Defense." So now the memorialists asked, " How is the government to be made strong? " " It is by the people of the empire becoming of one mind," they replied. " The establishment of a council-chamber chosen by the people will create a community of feeling between the government and the people, and they will mutually unite into one body. Then and only then will the country become strong."

Lastly, the objections to the Japanese suddenly copying foreign institutions were met. Some had argued that parliaments were not formed in the West in one day, but had been developed gradually over a period of many years. The implication, of course, was that the Japanese likewise should gradually evolve a parliamentary system. In reply, the memorial asserted that " The reason why foreigners have perfected this only after the lapse of centuries, is that no examples existed previously and these had to be discovered by actual experience." On the other hand, " If we can select examples from them and adopt their contrivances, why should we not be successful in working them out? If we are to delay the using of steam machinery until we have discovered the principles of steam for ourselves, or to wait till we have discovered the principles of electricity before we construct an electric telegraph, our government will be unable to set to work."

To Itagaki's memorial, the *Sa-in* gave a rather cordial reply. Since it was working on the problem of constitutions and assemblies it may have felt that outside pressure would facilitate its work.[29]

[29] This seems to be a more reasonable explanation than the one given by McLaren who in his *Political History* (p. 108) says, " The answer given by the Sa-in . . .

It said that the " principle is an excellent one, and this college having received sanction to a similar proposal made by itself, has drafted a set of regulations. The suggestion, therefore, will be adopted." [30]

But there were others in the government who were not in favor of it. Their spokesman, Kato Hiroyuki, then engaged in giving a series of lectures to the Emperor, presented a refutation. To many people this came as a surprise, since during the preceding year, Kato had published a volume with strong liberal overtones called *Shinsei Tai-i* (Principles of True Government).[31] Kato's main contention was that the time had not yet come for the establishment of representative institutions in Japan.[32] " Now in establishing a constitution and laws," he said, " it is necessary to observe minutely the state of the country and of public feeling, and to choose such a constitution and laws as are suited to them." In his opinion, the British parliament was " competent to initiate laws and constitutional measures well suited to the wants of the country," but other parliaments were not. Neither Russia nor Prussia, he observed, had been able to establish deliberative assemblies because the people were not advanced enough to share in the government. Kato felt that there was great danger in giving power to a people whose intelligence was insufficiently developed for " they do not know how to exercise them duly, and hence they fall into license. . . ."

In reply to the passage in the original memorial to the effect that the people would become more enlightened if they had a voice in the government, Kato maintained that it could be better achieved through education. Pointing again to Prussia, he said, " The self-reliant and active character of the Prussian nation at the present day which has at last raised it to the position of the most powerful nation in Europe, has not been due to the establishment of a deliberative assembly, but to the fact that since the time of

---

was an interesting example either of the confusion within the Government or of its disingenuousness."

[30] McLaren, *JGD*, pp. 433-434.

[31] Reprinted in *Meiji Kaikaki Bungaku Shu* [A collection of Literary Works on the Period of Meiji Enlightenment], volume I in the series *Gendai Nihon Bungaku Zenshu* [Collected Works on Modern Japanese Literature] (Tokyo, 1931), pp. 507-528.

[32] A translation of Kato's reply is printed in McLaren, *JGD*, pp. 433-439.

Frederick II, the Prussian Government has devoted itself to the cultivation of the people's minds."

A running debate was now begun. The newspapers took sides, some supporting Itagaki, some opposing him. Kato's attack on the memorial evoked several replies, including one by Itagaki, Soyejima, and Goto. It is not necessary to give a detailed account of these replies, except to note one important point made by Itagaki and his friends. In the course of their argument they revealed the kind of assembly they contemplated. " Now if this council-chamber be established," they said, " we do not propose that the franchise should at once be made universal. We would only give it in the first instance to the samurai and the richer farmers and merchants, for it is they who produced the leaders of the revolution of 1868." [33]

The true character of the movement initiated by Itagaki now stood revealed. Clearly Itagaki did not intend that the great bulk of the population should enjoy the fruits of self-rule. Only the samurai and the wealthy peasants and merchants were to be represented in the assembly which he proposed. Little wonder that the militarist, General Torio Koyata, called this *Joryu no Minken Setsu* or " Upper Class Democracy."

---

[33] McLaren, *JGD*, p. 445.

Chapter VI

EARLY POLITICAL SOCIETIES

THE long-run significance of Itagaki's defection was that it provided leadership for political opposition on a wide scale. In Itagaki the various individuals, groups, and interests at odds with the Meiji oligarchy found a leader of national stature. He had not only participated in the Restoration movement, but later had sat in the high council of state. He had been a member of the inner group that governed the country. Hence when he stepped down from the government and placed himself at the head of an opposition movement, he gave to it a kind of prestige and standing which no mere local political figure could have supplied.

Itagaki's assets as a leader, on the other hand, would have been worth little without a political organization which could lend him support. Lacking such support, he would probably have remained another politician without office. It is certainly to his credit that Itagaki was perceiving enough to see that if he were to challenge the government successfully he must organize a political following. It may be that the nature of the response to his memorial helped him arrive at such conclusions. His memorial had elicited a hopeful reply from the *Sa-in* and stirred up a lively debate in the press. But aside from this, it had not generated wide-spread political action on the part of the people. His memorial had not threatened the hold of the Meiji oligarchy in the least.

A few months after he submitted his memorial, Itagaki quit the capital and proceeded homeward to Tosa (modern Kochi prefecture). Years later in an essay giving his account of the origins of constitutional government in Japan, Itagaki wrote that in 1874 he had felt the need of forming a political party. It had been his opinion, moreover, that a "true" political party should be based on local units rather than on some central organization located in a big city.[1]

[1] Itagaki Taisuke, "Waga Kensei no Yurai" [The Origins of our Constitutional Government] in *Meiji Kensei Keizai Shiron* [Historical Essays on Meiji Constitu-

60

Accordingly, shortly after his return to Tosa, Itagaki founded the *Risshisha* (Society for Fixing One's Aim in Life), the first important political society. In setting up the *Risshisha*, he utilized several small political groups which had come into existence earlier. One was the *Kainan Gisha*, a kind of patriotic society formed by Tosa men, including both civilians and soldiers, who had resigned from the government after the split over the Korean affair. The other was the *Aikoku Koto* (Patriotic Party) formed by Itagaki in Tokyo. Many members from both of these organizations had drifted back to Tosa, where they were incorporated into the *Risshisha*.[2]

The headquarters of the *Risshisha* were set up in Kochi, the largest city in Tosa. Its membership, consisting mostly of samurai, was limited to natives of the province. The members were organized into neighborhood groups. Each group elected one delegate to an assembly, and the assembly chose a kind of executive committee. The president and vice-president of the *Risshisha*, elected for one-year terms, were eligible for re-election.[3]

According to a statement issued at the time of its formation, the society stood for self-government, local autonomy, natural rights, the establishment of a legislative assembly, and equality of all classes. " We, the thirty millions of people in Japan," it said, " are all equally endowed with certain definite rights, among which are those of enjoying and defending life and liberty, acquiring and possessing property, and obtaining a livelihood and pursuing happiness. These rights are by Nature bestowed upon all men, and, therefore, cannot be taken away by the power of any man." [4] Thus Locke s philosophy was proclaimed in Japan almost a century after the American Declaration of Independence.

There was, however, another aspect of the *Risshisha* about which virtually nothing was known until the publication of some documents in 1939.[5] These documents revealed that the *Risshisha* was

tional Government and National Economy], edited by Kokka Gakkai (Tokyo, 1919), p. 19.

[2] Suzuki Yasuzo (editor), *Jiyu Minken Undo Shi* [History of the Democratic Movement] (Tokyo, 1947), pp. 23-24.

[3] Itagaki, *JS*, I, 159-160.

[4] Uyehara, *op. cit.*, p. 73.

[5] See Suzuki Yasuzo, " Risshisha no ' Nihon Kempo Mikomi An ' " [Risshisha's Draft of a Japanese Constitution], *Kokka Gakkai Zasshi* [Journal of the Political Science Association], LIII (1939), 1519 ff.

a mutual-aid society for the economic rehabilitation of the *shizoku*, as the samurai were called after the Restoration. This helps to explain its name, which, it is believed, was taken from *Risshi-hen*, the title of the Japanese translation of Samuel Smiles' *Self-Help*, published in 1871 and read very widely.[6]

The announcement circulated by the *Risshisha* is of considerable interest. "The Westerners," it began, "say that self-reliance is based on knowledge and that government rests on self-reliance." It noted that since the Restoration the peasants, artisans, and merchants "had not had time to push ahead by themselves and become an independent people. Moreover, the *shizoku* have not been able to maintain their former positions, and with the three classes are falling into servility and bigotry." Now only the *shizoku*, it was asserted, "possess some knowledge and have self-reliance." The document proposed, therefore, that the "four classes should freely associate as friends, help one another, and make up for each other's deficiencies." [7] In other words, the *shizoku* would furnish knowledge and the spirit of self-reliance, while the plebeians would provide the capital and business experience.

The *Risshisha* took positive steps to assist the *shizoku* who in Tosa, as elsewhere, had fallen into dire circumstances following the Restoration. It established schools and opened a bureau for the study of law in order to aid members in law suits. It also set up tea curing establishments in various localities. A loan coöperative was also formed so that members could borrow on their pension bonds, and thus avoid the need of recourse to usurers. The *Risshisha* purchased from the government some sixteen forests. It was hoped that proceeds from the sale of timber and cleared land could be used for the development of various industries.[8]

It is interesting to note how the Tosa samurai reacted to economic distress in a different way from the samurai of Satsuma. Instead of rising in revolt, as did the latter, they endeavored to integrate themselves into the local economy. A partial explanation of this phenomenon may be found in the social and economic history of the Tosa clan.

A glance at the map will reveal that Tosa was situated on the

[6] Cf., Osatake, *NKST*, II, 450.
[7] Suzuki, *Jiyu Minken Undo Shi*, p. 26-27.
[8] Suzuki, " Risshisha no ' Nihon Kempo Mikomi An '," *op. cit.*, p. 1521.

side of the island of Shikoku facing the Pacific Ocean. Because of its mountainous terrain, it never developed into a rice surplus area. On the other hand, the semi-tropical climate encouraged the development of diversified agriculture.[9] It also became a leading center for the production of paper manufactured from a variety of upland grass which was grown locally. Although paper-making was to some extent a subsidiary industry for the peasantry, it is said that there were more than fifteen thousand families whose chief occupation was the manufacture of paper.[10]

Close commercial relations were maintained with Osaka, the great commercial center of the nation. A variety of products, including camphor, lumber, whale meat, dried bonito, sugar, tea, rice, silk thread, cotton, and oil were loaded in coastal ships and sent to Osaka.[11] As commerce developed, the penetration of money economy became more marked. Paralleling this was the emergence of the "acquisitive spirit" and a breakdown of isolation and provincialism. It was not uncommon for women and children to go off to Osaka on sight-seeing trips.[12]

The class barriers setting off the privileged samurai from the plebeians were also much less rigid in Tosa. There were found in Tosa a group known as the *goshi* or "rustic" samurai who formed a link between the peasants and the full-fledged samurai. Although the regular samurai looked with contempt on the *goshi*, the latter enjoyed privileges which went with samurai status. They were allowed to wear swords, assume surnames, and were accorded certain legal immunities. Since in Tosa it was possible for wealthy peasants and tradesmen to become *goshi* by reclaiming waste land, those with means were able to buy their way into the ranks of the privileged.[13]

[9] Irimajiri Koshu, "Tosa Han Higashi Chiho ni Kansuru Sho-Shiryo" [Various Historical Materials on the Eastern Areas of the Tosa Clan], *SKS*, VII (1937-1938), 1041.

[10] On the paper industry see, Matsuyoshi, "Tosa Han no Gokurashi Kaiage ni Tsuite," *op. cit.*

[11] Egashira Tsunehara, "Kochi Han ni Okeru Bakumatsu no Shin Seisaku" [The new Economic Policy in the Kochi Clan at the End of the Tokugawa Era], in *Bakumatsu Keizaishi Kenkyu* [Studies on the Economic History of the Late Tokugawa Era], edited by Nihon Keizaishi Kenkyujo (Tokyo, 1935), p. 118.

[12] Tanaka Sogoro, *Iwasaki Yataro* (Tokyo, 1940), p. 23.

[13] Matsuyoshi Sadao, "Tosa Han no Chonin Goshi ni Tsuite" [On the Merchant Goshi of the Tosa Clan], *KSK*, I (1929-1930), 1-17.

Politically, these factors like the development of commerce and social mobility tended to weaken the hold of conservatism and make Tosa receptive to change and reform. It was no accident that Tosa produced, in the closing days of the Tokugawa era, a leading statesman, a *goshi* by the name of Sakamoto Ryuma. Seeing that the old feudal order was dying, he wrote a brilliant essay on clan reform which, one authority says " can without exaggeration be regarded as the most penetrating criticism of feudal decay and despotic government to be found in contemporary Japanese political literature." [14] It was this same Sakamoto who organized the Tosa *Kaientai*, a kind of coast guard which attempted to combine defense with commercial shipping. That is, in order to raise money to meet expenses, the *Kaientai* also carried commodities between Tosa and Osaka.[15]

Tosa also took the lead in several other respects. Even before the Restoration, the Tosa authorities organized a *Mimpei* or " People's Militia " whose rank and file consisted largely of peasants, sailors, hunters, and merchants.[16] This anticipated by a number of years the Conscription Act of 1872 which put an end to the monopoly of the samurai class to bear arms.

Tosa was also a step ahead in abolishing the samurai class. The system of hereditary rice stipends was abandoned in 1870 and the ex-samurai were granted pension bonds instead.[17] A short while later the central government followed suit.

It can be said, therefore, that Tosa was one of the more progressive areas with a strong tradition of commercial development and political reform. But despite this rather favorable heritage, the economic program of the *Risshisha* proved to be ineffectual. It was no easy task to fit the samurai into the economic life of the community. In fact it was such a large undertaking that even the central government found no easy solution. After several years the *Risshisha* was obliged to ask the government to take back the forest land which it had originally purchased for the purpose of raising funds.

Lack of success in the economic field, however, was balanced by the effectiveness of its political program. For purposes of political

[14] Norman, *Feudal Background*, p. 65.
[15] See Egashira, *op. cit.*, pp. 122 ff.
[16] Norman, *Soldier and Peasant*, pp. 23-24.
[17] Hattori, *Meiji Ishin Shi Kenkyu*, p. 48n.

education, the *Risshisha* invited teachers to come and lecture on
the French Revolution, the Napoleonic Code, and on the political
thought of Jeremy Bentham and John Stuart Mill.[18] Local societies
affiliated with the *Risshisha* sprang up in almost every city and
county. In the various towns and villages of Tosa meetings were
held on the fifth of each month. The general public was invited
to bring political and economic problems for discussion. " The
intoxicating ideas of a liberal democracy propagated by the members of the *Risshisha* created a ferment among the lower classes in
Tosa." [19]

Although a few other political societies more or less patterned
after the *Risshisha* were founded elsewhere, Itagaki's movement
was still largely confined to Tosa. So in February, 1875 the
leaders of the *Risshisha*, hoping to broaden the scope of operations,
formed another society in Osaka called the *Aikokusha* (Society of
Patriots).[20] This society was intended to be the central headquarters for the democratic movement, but it collapsed very
shortly. This was partly due to the lack of funds to maintain the
organization; but an even more important cause was the opportunistic maneuvers of Itagaki, its moving spirit.

About three weeks after he had formed the *Aikokusha* Itagaki
unexpectedly rejoined the government, leaving his followers dumb-
founded. In a master stroke, Okubo Toshimichi, one of the
important leaders of the time, worried about the recent defections
of Meiji statesmen, lured Itagaki back into the ranks of the
bureaucracy. Since the *Aikokusha* had been founded primarily to
oppose the government, it had no alternative but to disband, now
that its leader had joined the enemy camp.

Years later Itagaki was to pursue somewhat similar tactics,
abandoning his followers at a crucial moment. His zigzag career
suggests that the blood of a political opportunist ran through his
veins. At times he seemed to be truly moved by the liberal ideas
he espoused. No doubt, too, he enjoyed the applause and adulation
that came to him as the leader of an opposition movement. Yet at
other times, he longed for the security and prestige of political
office. There is available an interesting account which throws

[18] Suzuki, " Risshisha no ' Nihon Kempo Mikomi An '," *op. cit.*, p. 1524.
[19] Norman, *Feudal Background*, pp. 67-68.
[20] Itagaki, *JS*, I, 18.

light on his earlier career. It is said that in the days before he championed the democratic cause, he was a firm believer in sharp class distinctions. He even went so far as to divide the samurai into nine grades, each indicated by different colored cards which were to be worn on the coat. "At that time," says Tani Kanjo, a fellow clansman, "he had no idea of freedom and equality," but later "he changed completely and advocated the social contract of Rousseau." [21] Probably the best characterization has been made by Mr. Norman who has said that "Itagaki had the instinctive sensitivity of a chameleon to the colouring of his political environment." [22]

Itagaki, however, did not stay in the government long. The following year, he resigned, presumably because of disagreement over policy. In 1877 the Satsuma Rebellion broke out, and echoes of the Rebellion were heard in Tosa. Although the main body of the *Risshisha* favored political action, one faction in the society advocated joining hands with the rebels. But before they could take effective action, they were seized by the police, leaving the moderates in control of the *Risshisha*.[23]

With the end of the Rebellion, the political atmosphere cleared. Armed rebellion, it had been demonstrated, was no longer feasible. Now the opposition was likely to gravitate to Itagaki and his democratic movement. At this juncture, the *Risshisha* came forth with another memorial. It reiterated the demand for representative institutions. Drafted by Ueki Emori, Yoshida Masaharu, and Takeuchi Ko, all active members of the *Risshisha*, and signed by its president, Kataoka Kenkichi, the memorial was printed and circulated all over the nation.[24]

The main point in the memorial was that although much progress had been made, the country was torn by internal strife and incapable of exercising due influence in foreign affairs. This was because the despotic government had no regard for the "opinion of the nation." According to its interpretation of Restoration history, the Shogunate had been overthrown "Because the will of the people will have its own way, as surely as water runs down hill." The memorialists urged that the duty of the government was to preserve peace, "not to interfere with the happiness of the

[21] Quoted in Osatake, *Nihon Kensei Shi*, p. 153.   [23] Itagaki, *JS*, I, 255.
[22] Norman, *Feudal Background*, p. 65.   [24] *Ibid.*, pp. 253-254.

people, and hinder them from enjoying their primary rights and privileges."

Since the government, continued the memorial, pays no attention to the will of the people, various evils have arisen. First, the cabinet imposes its own oppressive measures without respecting the will of the Emperor. Second, " the management of the government is conducted in a random and confused manner." Third, " the power of the country has been too largely concentrated in the central government." Fourth, a despotic government must not impose general conscription. Fifth, the finances of the nation are mismanaged. Sixth, the present system of land tax " constitutes an oppression too great to be borne by the people." Seventh, the government has tried to equalize the rights of the samurai and the common people. Eighth, foreign affairs have been mismanaged because a country without constitutional government cannot secure just rights from other nations. In order to remedy these evils, the memorialists proposed their panacea. The sovereign should consent to the establishment of a representative assembly.[25]

In 1878 the leaders of the *Risshisha* revived the *Aikokusha* and began a concerted drive to organize local affiliates. Often they worked through influential local leaders. Speakers and organizers were also sent out by the *Aikokusha* to lend aid. As a technique of political agitation, it was discovered that public speeches were much more effective than the press, for by this method it was possible to reach even the illiterate peasant. Sometimes only one political speech was needed to form a small group consisting of several tens of members. Perhaps it was because of their effectiveness that the police were much concerned about such political speeches. The late Yoshino Sakuzo has told about an incident that occurred in Koriyama in Nara prefecture where the local police went to incredible lengths to prevent local leaders from holding a political rally.[26] Day after day the police raised numerous and petty objections. But the sponsors, being equal to the challenge, met these objections with dogged persistence. The meetings, originally planned for October 6 to October 8, 1879, were finally scheduled to begin on the 12th. On the appointed day a crowd of

[25] The memorial is translated in McLaren, *JGD*, pp. 457-480. All quotations have been taken from this translation.

[26] Yoshino Sakuzo, " Minken Undo Danatsu Sokumen Shi " [A Sidelight on the Suppression of the Democratic Movement], *CK*, XLIV (October, 1929), 170 ff.

more than 2,000 persons assembled at 10 o'clock in the morning.
The police arrived and in a series of delaying tactics held up the
rally until 3 o'clock in the afternoon. Then the police announced
that the rally would not be allowed and ordered the crowd to
disperse. Having waited for hours, the spectators were in no mood
to obey. " We were born in isolated communities," they said, " and
have neither books nor the ability to read them. We left our work
and took the trouble to come, hoping to enrich our knowledge by
coming into contact with scholars, and to obtain benefits equal to
more than ten years of reading." [27] The angry crowd then reas-
sembled in front of the police station where they argued with the
police officers. Finally when darkness fell they gave vent to their
resentment by hurling stones and breaking the windows of the
police station.

The efforts of Itagaki and his followers to expand the democratic movement produced astonishing results. The movement,
hitherto largely confined to Tosa, now spread like a contagion.
There was a remarkable proliferation of political societies. Exactly
how many societies were formed in this period and how big a
membership they boasted is not known. It is certain, however, that
numerous groups were organized, particularly at the village level.
It has been reported that in Tokyo-*fu* alone, there were twenty-two
societies with a membership of more than 16,000 persons.[28]

Some of the organizations in the larger towns and cities grew to
be quite large. A well known organization, the *Aikoku Koshinsha*
(Patriotic Society) had more than 11,000 members. Located in
Nagoya, an industrial city known for its ceramics, silk reeling, and
textile manufacturing, the *Aikoku Koshinsha* drew the great bulk
of its members from the working class. A secret police report
claims that many joined when they were given the false impression
that by joining they would not only be exempt from taxes and
military service, but would also be granted hereditary stipends.[29]

It is noteworthy that several important societies were founded in

[27] *Ibid.*, p. 183.
[28] Nakayama Yasumasa (editor), *Shimbun Shusei Meiji Hennen Shi* [A Chronological Meiji History Compiled from Newspapers], IV (Tokyo, 1935), 164. (Hereafter this work will be cited as *SSMHS*).
[29] Sekiguchi Tai, " Meiji Jurokunen no Chiho Junshikan " [A Local Administrative Inspector in 1883], *Toshi Mondai* [Municipal Problems], XXIX (1939), 967-
970.

areas north and northwest of Tokyo where the domestic system of industrial production was widespread. The *Shokyosha* (Reform Society) was located in Nagano prefecture in the heart of the raw silk area.[30] The *Chusetsusha* (Loyalty Society) had members in Gumma and Tochigi prefectures where the textile industries thrived.[31] Many of the members of the *Yushinsha* (Society of Believers) came from Takazaki, Kiryu, Maebashi, and Chichibu, all important raw silk and textile manufacturing centers.[32]

Without the extensive use of archival material and local histories, one cannot make a statistical analysis of the membership of these societies. By piecing together scattered data, however, it is possible to arrive at some rather tentative conclusions. First of all, these societies, like the Jacobin Clubs in revolutionary France and the Democratic-Republican societies in early America, included people from nearly all social strata, excluding only those at the very top of the social pyramid. Almost everyone was represented, for among the members one could find *shizoku*, wealthy landowners, rural industrialists, journalists, school teachers, peasants, tenant farmers, and laborers.

The leadership, however, was at first confined almost exclusively to the *shizoku* class. This was because the first spark that set off the democratic movement was samurai discontent. It has been noted that the memorial of 1874 had been a gesture of protest on the part of the " outs " against the " ins." Having initiated the movement, the samurai were able to maintain themselves in positions of leadership for several years. But after about 1878 they were obliged to give way more and more to the non-samurai. Several factors account for this shift. During these years economic attrition had taken a heavy toll among the *shizoku*. Reduced to penury, they could no longer afford to devote a large part of their time to politics. On the other hand, as the movement gained many adherents, the plebeians came to outnumber the *shizoku*. Since, moreover, they provided much of the funds, the non-samurai were bound to demand some say in the management of affairs.

So noticeable was this change in the character of the leadership that it drew comments from contemporary observers. In an item published on July 9, 1880 the newspaper *Choya* concluded that to believe that the movement demanding the establishment of a national assembly is led by discontended *shizoku* is to be behind the times.[33] For a concrete example of the shift in the leadership we may turn to the political convention held in Okayama in 1879. There an attempt was made to have *shizoku* appointed to the executive committee, but the opposition of the rank and file, consisting about eighty percent of plebeians, was so strong that it failed. Then the convention drew up a strong petition to the government saying that " When we seek the reason for the extension of popular rights in the history of the West, we see that the rulers did not grant popular rights, but rather that the people themselves took the initiative and seized them." [34]

With the *shizoku* receding to the background, the mantle fell on the shoulders of the rural aristocracy. True in some instances the *shizoku* remained in control, especially in the *Aikokusha* and its successors, and they still provided virtually all of the theorists and publicists. But in the majority of the local affiliates, which gave the democratic movement its momentum, the rural gentry were in command. The best evidence of this is to be found in the fact that many of the local leaders were reported to be members of the *Fu-Ken Kai* or Prefectural Assemblies. These assemblies were established in 1877 for the purpose of giving advice to the prefectural governors. By providing these advisory bodies, the government hoped to siphon off some of the growing pressure for democratic rights. But the electorate was limited to those who paid at least five *yen* annually in land tax. Moreover, only those who paid more than ten *yen* were eligible for election to these assemblies. We can be certain therefore that anyone who was a member of the *Fu-Ken Kai* was a fairly large landowner and a local political figure.

By 1880 the rural aristocracy had captured the movement. In other words, the democratic movement was now being led by the same class that had joined the pro-Emperor cause against the Tokugawa a generation earlier. In fact there is at least one example where a big landowner in Fukui prefecture by the name of Sugita Senjuro was active in the anti-Tokugawa movement, and

[33] *SSMHS*, IV, 232.

[34] Toyama Shigeki, " Jiyu Minken Undo ni okeru Shizoku-teki Yoso " [The *Shizoku* Elements in the Democratic Movement], *Rekishi Hyoron* [Historical Review], II (May, 1947), 21.

his son, Sadakazu, participated in the democratic movement.[35] No doubt a careful search of local histories would reveal other instances of this kind, for it is generally known that political attitudes have a way of being transmitted from generation to generation. Some areas tend to be politically unstable, while in other areas the opposite is true. Probably it was no mere accident that areas like Nagano and Gumma, which were receptive to the pro-Emperor cause in the late Tokugawa era, actively supported the democratic movement some twenty years later.

[35] Ono, " Hyakusho Ikki ya, Kinno Gun Ya," *op. cit.*, p. 7.

Chapter VII

ECONOMIC GRIEVANCES

I.

JAPAN entered the family of nations in the middle of the nineteenth century under great disabilities. The long years of Tokugawa isolation had severely retarded Japan's economic growth. Between Japan and the Western powers there was indeed a wide gap. Unlike Great Britain, France, the Netherlands and other countries of western Europe, Japan had not shared in the wealth from the New World, nor had she participated in the exploitation of overseas colonies. More important still, she had not undergone an industrial revolution. In terms of technology, business organization, and capital accumulation, therefore, she was no match for her Western competitors. In commenting on the disparity in economic development, John E. Orchard has expressed the opinion that Japan of the Tokugawa era should be compared with sixteenth century Tudor England rather than with England on the eve of the industrial revolution.[1]

After the resumption of foreign trade in 1859, the backwardness of Japan's economy became painfully patent to the Japanese. The economic consequences of the opening of the century have already been touched upon in another connection, but the subject deserves further treatment here. In general the Western powers were interested in securing raw materials and in selling finished goods. The result was a steady increase in the price of export commodities like raw silk, raw cotton, and tea. On the other hand the Western nations, with their superior technology and industrial organization, were able to offer machine-made goods at relatively low prices. Cotton fabrics and yarn provide a good example. In 1874 imported yarn was selling at 29.65 *yen* per 100 *kin* (1 *kin*— 1.32 pounds) as against 42.70 *yen* for an equivalent amount of

---

[1] John E. Orchard, *Japan's Economic Position* (New York: Whittlesey House, 1930), p. 71.

72

native yarn.[2] Another import item which became quite popular was the kerosene lamp. Being far brighter than Japanese lamps, it made it possible for one to read or work at night. Accordingly, it was widely used in peasant households.[3] In some quarters, however, considerable resentment was aroused against imported goods. A measure of the intensity of the feeling is provided by the response to Sada Kaiseki, a Buddhist priest who toured the countryside lecturing against the use of foreign articles. He organized societies against foreign goods in Nagano, Aichi, Osaka, Kyoto and Tokyo and attracted thousands.[4]

Such activities, however, could not stop the import of foreign goods. In fact until the year 1881 the balance of foreign trade was unfavorable.[5] Since the Meiji government was saddled with unequal treaties, it could not resort to the manipulation of tariff rates to reduce imports.

Hence in order to lessen the need for imports, achieve self-sufficiency, and expand exports, the Meiji government encouraged the development of capitalism.[6] Soon after the Restoration it removed the various restrictions impeding the full development of a capitalistic economy. The equality of all classes before the law was decreed; local barriers and restrictions on internal trade were eliminated; the professions and trades were thrown open to all; freedom of cropping was permitted; and property rights in land were recognized.

The liquidation of the samurai class was also a part of this program. But the government, lacking the courage to abolish the hereditary stipends outright, granted the former samurai and feudal nobles pension bonds. In this way it purchased the support of the

---

[2] Horie Yasuzo, "The Development of the Domestic Market," *KUER*, XV (January, 1940), 51.

[3] Ono Takeo, *Noson Shi* [History of Japanese Agriculture], Vol. 9 in the series, *Gendai Nihon Bummei Shi* [History of Contemporary Japanese Civilization] (Tokyo, 1941), p. 138.

[4] Asano Kenshin, "Sada Kaiseki no Hakurai Hin Haiseki ni Tsuite" [On Sada Kaiseki's Boycott Movement Against Imported Goods], *SKS*, VIII (February, 1939), 1213-1232.

[5] See table in *The Recent Economic Development of Japan*, compiled by the Bank of Japan (Tokyo, 1915), p. 179.

[6] Kazahaya Yasoji, *Zaisei Shi* [History of Public Finance] in *Nihon Shihonshugi Hattatsu Shi Koza* [Lectures on the Development of Japanese Capitalism], pp. 11-12. (Hereafter the *Nihon Shihonshugi Hattatsu Shi Koza* will be cited as *NSHSK*).

feudal aristocracy, but at no little cost. In 1870, a little over 135,000 samurai received more than thirty-five million *yen* or an average of 264 *yen* per person. Six years later the Court nobles and the feudal lords were granted a total of more than 174 million *yen*.[7] All told the pension bonds cost the government more than two hundred and ten million *yen*. Incidentally as is evident from the above figures, the feudal nobility did much better than the ordinary samurai. Thanks to the generosity of the government, the feudal aristocracy were transformed into financial magnates, who later made large investments in banks, stocks, industries and landed estates.[8]

The government also took positive steps to aid industrialization. In so doing it was continuing a policy begun in the late Tokugawa era. At that time some of the clans, especially those in which the lower samurai had seized power, had turned to monopoly trade and industry in order to increase the flow of revenue into the depleted clan coffers. But in leading their clans towards industrialization, these samurai paid particular attention to military industries. Because of their military background, they were strongly impressed by the overwhelming superiority of Western arms. They purchased warships, merchant ships, and arms of all kinds. In some of the clans the manufacture of new equipment was begun. As early as the 1850's reverberatory furnaces for casting canon were set up in several parts of the country.[9] Thus " the first stage of industrialization in Japan was inextricably interwoven with the military problem, and it fixed the pattern for its later evolution." [10]

When the Meiji government came into power it took over mines, arsenals, shipyards, and foundries begun by the Shogunate and the various clans.[11] In this connection it should be pointed out that the government also assumed the debts incurred by the clans in building up these industries.[12] Because of their relation to national

[7] Yamada Seitaro, *Nihon Shihonshugi Bunseki* [An Analysis of Japanese Capitalism] (Tokyo, 1934), p. 185.

[8] Norman, *Japan's Emergence as a Modern State*, p. 94.

[9] Thomas C. Smith, " The Introduction of Western Industry During the Last Years of the Tokugawa Period," *Harvard Journal of Asiatic Studies*, XI (June, 1948), pp. 130-152; Norman, *op. cit.*, pp. 119-120.

[10] Norman, *op. cit.*, p. 118.

[11] Horie Yasuzo, " Government Industries in the Early Years of the Meiji Era," *KUER*, XIV (January, 1939), 67-87.

[12] Kanno Wataro, " Shoko to Gaikoku Boeki " [The Various Lords and Foreign Trade] in *Bakumatsu Keizai Shi Kenkyu*, pp. 412-413.

defense, the government also turned its attention to the construction of railroads and telegraph systems.

Nor were the consumers' goods industries neglected. The government hired foreign experts, purchased new machinery, and set up "model factories" to set the pace in industrialization. In 1870, for example, a filature based on Italian models was set up in Maebashi and two years later a French-model mill was established in Tomioka. Where the government did not participate directly, it gave subsidies or made loans to private individuals desiring to establish new industries.

In carrying out this program, the government worked closely with a small group of favored merchants and samurai. Some like the Mitsui and Sumitomo families became allied with the government from the very beginning.[13] In return for rendering assistance to the government in time of need, they were given numerous opportunities for profit. Some like Iwasaki Yataro, the founder of the Mitsubishi Company, got their start through the clan industries. Iwasaki was connected with the trading company set up by the Tosa clan. After the Restoration, he maintained his connections with some members of the Meiji bureaucracy, particularly Okuma Shigenobu, and through them was able to render services to the state for which he was paid handsomely. Still others were members of the nobility who enjoyed special privileges and protection in organizing companies like the Tokyo Marine Insurance Company (1879) and the Japan Railway Company (1881).

After 1881 most of the government enterprises not contributing directly to the military needs of the state were sold to favored individuals and companies at low prices. The result was, as Professor Horie has said, that "Some of the more enterprising members of the privileged class subsequently emerged into the business world as capitalistic financiers to whom the Administration offered direct and indirect aid in various forms."[14]

II.

From the very beginning the Meiji government was confronted with grave financial difficulties. Starting without reserves, it im-

---

[13] See *The House of Mitsui, A Record of Three Centuries: Past History and Present Enterprise* (Tokyo, 1937), p. 15.

[14] Horie, *op. cit.*, p. 83.

mediately incurred deficits in crushing the Tokugawa forces. To
make matters worse, in the succeeding years it took on new burdens
in the form of clan debts, samurai pensions, and state aid for a
program of industrialization. To help meet its financial obligations
the government floated two foreign loans, one in 1870 and another
in 1873. But the Meiji leaders were very wary of foreign loans
which they feared might lead to foreign political control. Under
these circumstances, they decided to levy a heavy tax on land.
The agricultural population was made to bear a large part of the
cost of modernization.[15]

The government gave early attention to the problem of taxation
since the old system of seignorial dues based on the yield and
payable in kind was expensive to administer and subject to fluctuations making difficult a modern budgetary system of public
finance. But before a land tax could be enacted, it was necessary
to recognize the right of private ownership of land and free the
peasants from the soil. This was done by a series of decrees beginning with the decree of December, 1868 which stated that " With
the exception of Imperial land and temple and shrine land, all
village land shall belong to the peasants." [16] The result was the
creation of a large number of small peasant proprietors.

The ownership of land, however, entailed the obligation to pay
a heavy land tax. Under the Land Tax Act of 1873, the land tax
was fixed at three percent of the " legal value " of the land. This
" legal value " was arrived at by the application of the following
formula: First, the money value of the average yield (over a
five year period) from one *tanbu* (0.245 acres of land was calculated on the basis of the price of rice prevailing in that district.
Then the " net profit " was obtained by deducting the cost of
fertilizer and seed rice (legally fixed at 15 percent), and land tax,
and the local tax which was usually one third of the land tax.
Finally, this " net profit " was capitalized at a rate varying from
six to seven percent.[17]

In general the land tax operated to the disadvantage of the

---

[15] Between 1868 and 1875, 82 percent of the ordinary revenues of the government came from the land tax. Ono, *Noson Shi*, p. 50.

[16] *Ibid.*, p. 45.

[17] Ono Michio, *Kinsei Noson Keizai Shiron* [History of Japanese Agricultural
Economics in Modern Times], Vol. 59 in *Keizaigaku Zenshu* [Collected Works on
Economics] (Tokyo, 1933), p. 302; Saburo Shiomi, " On the Revision of the Land
Tax," *KUER*, IV (1929), 79.

small peasant landowners during the early years. Since this is not the place for a detailed discussion of the effects of the tax, a brief summary must suffice.[18] To begin with, in computing the "legal value" of the land no allowance was made for the cost of labor nor for a reasonable profit.[19] Hence when the local tax of one percent was added, it was found that from thirty to forty percent of the yield went for taxes. The requirement, moreover, that the tax be paid in money worked a real hardship on many a cultivator. Since the average peasant worked a small holding[20] and possessed little or no working capital, he was often forced to dispose of his crop soon after harvest when as a rule prices of agricultural produce were the lowest.[21]

In addition to the problems of marketing, the cultivator had to contend with the vicissitudes of nature. Under the old system, which was more paternal, it was possible to have the seignorial dues reduced in times of poor harvests. Now, however, the tax was fixed and payable on a certain date.[22] The small peasant, therefore, was almost always forced into the grip of the village usurer in case of a crop failure.[23] And once in debt the peasant could easily lose his land since the interest was high and the debt was unsecured against sudden demand for repayment.

The land tax which was already high even when legitimately administered was made almost intolerable when abuses crept in. The interests of the government and the landowner were likely to conflict over the assessed value of the land. There are several known cases where overzealous officials placed an unduly high value on land for taxation purposes.[24] Quite naturally the land-

[18] For aditional details see Nobutaka Ike, "Landownership and Taxation in the Westernization of Japan," *The Journal of Economic History*, VII (November, 1947), pp. 160-182.

[19] Hirano Yoshitaro, *Nihon Shihonshugi Shakai no Kiko* [The Mechanism of Japanese Capitalistic Society] (Tokyo, 1934), p. 22.

[20] A survey of land holdings made in 1874 revealed that the average area cultivated by a family including paddy and dry fields was 2.353 acres. Norman, *op. cit.*, p. 153.

[21] Quotations on the Tokyo market in 1875 revealed that prices were lowest in March and April. Nakazawa Benjiro, *Nihon Beika Hendo Shi* [History of Price Fluctuations of Rice in Japan] (Tokyo, 1933), p. 322.

[22] A decree in 1872 said that those who were late in paying the land tax must pay interest of one-half percent per month and if they did not pay by July they must be declared bankrupt and the tax and interest collected. Ono, *op. cit.*, p. 73.

[23] See Max Fesca's remarks quoted in *ibid.*, p. 72.

[24] See Ono Michio, *op. cit.*, pp. 340-341; Hirano, *op. cit.*, pp. 22-23.

owners were opposed to such practices, and in one instance a group of peasants held a conference and issued the following manifesto:

According to what we hear, such high agricultural taxes as ours can rarely be found in other countries. Now Heaven created mankind; how can there be differences [among the peoples of the various countries] in the eyes of Heaven? The Japanese people alone have borne such heavy burdens, and have been held down in such servile and slavish conditions for more than 2,000 years. This is, indeed, a lamentable condition. It is for no other reason than that we have no independent spirit.[25]

The Land Tax Act affected landownership in several other ways. During the Tokugawa period large areas of forest and meadow land were owned in common by the inhabitants of one or more villages. After 1873 many peasants, not wishing to be held responsible for taxes on such land, relinquished their claims to it and permitted the state to take possession.[26] But in so doing, they lost access to fertilizer (in the form of leaves), fodder, fuel, and timber which previously they had obtained free of charge. This accelerated the decline of the more or less self-sufficient farm economy.

Since the owner of the land was made responsible for the payment of the land tax, the government issued land certificates (*chiken*) to show ownership. But in issuing the certificates favoritism was shown to certain groups. For instance, during the Tokugawa era land had been mortgaged desipte the ban on the permanent alienation of land. In such instances the debtor often retained the right to permanent tenancy. After 1873, however, the government refused to recognize such rights and granted the land certificate to the mortgage holder, making him the outright owner. Much the same thing happened with regard to reclaimed land. Wealthy merchants working in partnership with landless

---

[25] Quoted in Ono Michio, *op. cit.*, p. 383.

[26] "It is said that the fact that so much of our forest and meadow land belongs to the government finds its origin in the disposition of the village common land at that time." Ono Takeo, *op. cit.*, p. 366.

The following table will give some idea of the extent of government-owned land: (The figures are for *cho*).

	1882	1886	1887	1888	1889	1890
Gov't-owned forest land	5,391,240	5,713,403	7,139,368	7,584,680	8,040,170	3,750,140
Imperial land	1,110	31,574	32,257	41,271	1,129,048	3,654,533

This table comes from Hirano Yoshitaro, *Meiji Ishin ni okeru Seiji-teki Shihai Keitai* [The Form of Political Control in the Meiji Restoration] in *NSHSK.*, p. 54.

peasants had brought wasteland under cultivation. Since the peasants had supplied the labor they possessed certain definite rights to the reclaimed land. But the government issued the land certificates to those who had supplied the capital with the proviso that one of the two parties should buy the other's rights. Yet the very fact that the government gave the certificate to the merchant strengthened his position so that he was usually unwilling to negotiate. This gave rise to numerous disputes; and in one case the governor of Kochi prefecture suggested that the land be divided equally between the two parties, but the merchants refused.[27]

That the land tax was unpopular among the agricultural population goes without saying. Between the years 1873 and 1881 at least twelve peasants uprisings connected with the land tax broke out.[28] In view of the resentment and resistance to the tax the government made a number of concessions in 1876 and 1877, including permission to pay a part of the tax in kind, and a reduction of one-half percent in the tax rate.[29]

III.

The land tax was not the only factor affecting the economic position of the farming population. Farm incomes greatly depended on the price of rice, the principal crop. With the rise in the price of rice after 1878, the money income of the landowning population was appreciably increased. Although the government tried to regulate the price of rice through purchases and sales, and through the control of imports and exports, there was a general tendency for the price of rice to rise over the years. One reason was the increase in population. In the fifteen-year period between 1872 and 1887, the population increased a little more than 11 percent.[30]

But the sharp rise in the price of rice after 1878 came mostly from the serious currency inflation. Ever since the Restoration currency inflation had been taking place, but its effects were not immediately felt because the demand for money had increased.[31]

[27] Hirano Yoshitaro, *Gikai Oyobi Hosei Shi* [History of the Diet and Legislation] in *NSHSK*, p. 45.

[28] Ono Takeo, *op. cit.*, p. 197.

[29] For changes in the land tax see Ono Michio, *op. cit.*, pp. 368-370, 335.

[30] Watanabe Shinichi, *Nihon Noson Jinko Ron* [On the Japanese Agricultural Population] (Tokyo, 1934), p. 18.

[31] Allèn, *op. cit.*, pp. 35-36.

In 1877, however, the government was forced to print 27 million
yen in inconvertible notes in order to help defray the cost of suppressing the Satsuma Rebellion. At the height of the inflation in
1881 the notes issued by the government came to more than 142
million *yen*.[32] About the same time the amount of bank notes in
circulation was greatly expanded. A revision of the banking law in
1876 permitted national banks to issue currency against the deposit
of government bonds up to eighty percent of their capital. Many
of the ex-samurai and nobles holding pension bonds which had
depreciated in value founded banks. By 1880, one hundred forty-
eight new banks had been established and the note issue had
reached the limit of 34 million *yen* as set by law.[33] The tremendous
increase in the volume of paper money reduced its value to a point
where one *yen* in silver was worth 1.73 *yen* in paper.[34]

The inflation was accompanied by the usual upsurge in prices.
In 1881 the commodity price index stood at 151.9 as compared with
100 in 1876. The upward movement of the price of rice was even
more conspicuous for the price doubled between 1877 and 1880.[35]
Since the land tax remained fixed, all those who owned land were in
a position to profit from the price inflation. According to one
source, the change in prices affected the division of income from
land between the state and landowner as follows: [36]

Year	State	Landowner	Net Profit for Landowner
1873	50%	50%	¥1.632
On the basis of average price of rice, 1874-1877	18.7	81.3	7.398
After reduction of tax in 1877 and based on 1877 price of rice....	18	82	7.515
On the basis of average price of rice, 1878-1887	16.9	83.1	8.06

There was unmistakable prosperity in the countryside. Peasants
who had been " sleeping on straw mats and eating wheat suddenly

[32] Ono Takeo, *op. cit.*, p. 152.
[33] Allen, *op. cit.*, p. 39.
[34] Ono Takeo, *op. cit.*, p. 152.
[35] See page 141 for a graph showing price trends.
[36] Hirano, *Nihon Shihonshugi Shakai no Kiko*, p. 29.

built new dwellings and ate rice; and in extreme cases squandered their money on luxuries and drink." [37] Among the landlords and wealthier peasants, old style clothing gradually gave way to more expensive garments. The use of imported goods became more prevalent, so that foreign goods were seen even in isolated hamlets. There was a lively demand for landed property. Land values rose, sometimes as much as one hundred percent.[38] There was much speculation in land, and some borrowed money to purchase land at inflated prices.

Increased purchasing power among the farming population led to the expansion of the domestic market. Textile producers supplying domestic needs were kept busy filling new orders. Production was undoubtedly expanded by the further spread of the domestic system of production. This period also witnessed the mushroom growth of small-scale enterprises. Some of them were begun by landlords who invested their surplus funds in indigenous industries like *sake* brewing and *miso* (bean paste) manufacture. Others were started by unemployed samurai, using their pension bonds as capital. In the three urban prefectures of Tokyo, Osaka, and Kyoto alone the number of retail establishments increased from a little more than 87,000 in 1879 to 152,000 in 1881.[39]

But not everyone stood to profit from the inflation. Tenant farmers were not in a position to take full advantage of price increases. Although tenancy practices varied from locality to locality, in general the tenant assumed most of the risks of production, but paid rent in kind amounting to 50 or 60 percent of the yield. Hence as prices rose, the landlord was able to secure increasing amounts (in terms of money) for his share of the crop since the land tax which he paid did not rise. It has been calculated that, on the basis of the average price of rice for the period, 1878-1887, the division of proceeds from the land was as follows: 11.5 percent for the state (in the form of tax), 56.5 percent for the landlord, and 32 percent for the tenant.[40] Under these circumstances, it is understandable that tenants sometimes tried to pay their rent in money. In 1880 some tenant farmers in Bitchu-no-

[37] Ono Takeo, *op. cit.*, p. 79.

[38] Examples may be found in *ibid.*, pp. 117-118.

[39] Yagizawa Zenji, " Seinan Senekigo no Infureshion " [The Inflation After the Satsuma Rebellion], *KSK*, VII (July, 1932), 52-53.

[40] Norman, *op. cit.*, p. 150n.

kuni offered to pay their rent in money at the rate of eight percent of the value of the land. The landlords refused, and offered instead to make some reduction in the rent crop.[41]

There were other conditions which made the economic position of the tenant farmer precarious. Tenure was very insecure. In the majority of cases rent contracts ran from three years to five years. Although it was customary for the landlord to reduce the rent in times of poor harvest, such provisions were seldom written into the contract. Hence in this matter the tenant had to rely on the good-will of his landlord. Since the tenants were never compensated for any improvements they made, no attempt was made to improve the soil. Consequently, the yield on rented land was lower than that on land cultivated by the owner.[42]

In case of controversy or trouble between the landlord and tenant, the officials were more than likely to side with the former. There is at least one known case where the governor of a prefecture ordered the tenants to pay their rent, saying that since the rent " is the base which creates the tax, tenants are to pay with the idea that they are paying the land tax." [43] And if tenants ever fell in arrears in their rent, they could be evicted with the landlord taking all of the standing crops as a matter of course.

Wage workers were another group which could not benefit from the inflation. As is usually the case, wage boosts lagged far behind price increases. Average wages for carpenters, masons, and the like rose, in Tokyo, from 40 *sen* per day in 1877 to 51 *sen* in 1881 or an increase of 28 percent.[44] The average daily wages of workers in the production of raw silk in Gumma prefecture advanced from 12.5 *sen* in 1877 to 17.8 *sen* in 1881, representing an increase of 42 percent.[45] In any case there was a definite drop in real income. In March, 1881 an article in the *Tokyo Keizai Zasshi* (Tokyo Economic Magazine) noted:

[41] Hirano, *op. cit.*, p. 36.

[42] Paul Mayet, *Agricultural Insurance in Organic Connection with Savings-Banks, Land-Credit, and the Commutation of Debts,* translated by Arthur Lloyd (London, 1893), pp. 148-150.

[43] Hirano *op. cit.*, p. 26.

[44] Ono Takeo, *op. cit.*, pp. 155-156.

[45] Tsuchiya Takao and Ouchi Hyoei (editors), *Meiji Zenki Zaisei Keizai Shiryo Shusei* [Collection of Historical Material on Finance and Economy in the Early Meiji Period], XII (Tokyo, 1931), p. 289.

Now our workers have indeed fallen into a lamentable condition. Paper money is steadily falling in value while the price of everything is increasing and is up more than 70 percent. The price of rice has doubled; yet wages have risen only 30 to 40 percent. Expenses are high and income small. Living is getting more difficult daily. The wives are complaining loudly about starvation and the children are crying out in the cold.[46]

IV.

We may now bring together the various parts of this discussion in order to see how they help to explain the rise of the democratic movement. As was stated earlier, the movement was initiated by a group of disaffected samurai who used democratic slogans to oppose the government in power. By the latter part of the 1870's, however, a number of political figures threw in their support. Rallying together landowners and tenant farmers, they organized political societies in the rural villages and towns. Almost always these local leaders were relatively wealthy landlords. In addition they were, in many instances, rural industrialists operating local breweries and small-scale industries producing goods on the domestic system.

As landowners and industrialists they opposed the fiscal policies of the central government. They resented the fact that so much of the revenue was derived from the land tax. Moreover, they looked with misgivings on the steady flow of taxes into the central treasury, for this tended to drain the countryside of capital which otherwise could have gone into industrial development. Thus the *Risshisha* memorial, previously cited in another connection, said: "The taxes of the *fu* [urban prefectures] and *ken* [prefectures] are collected and sent directly to the Okurasho [the Ministry of Finance]. This causes great scarcity of money in the country and cripples its power of production. . . . On coming into the capital from the country one is struck with the vast difference there is between the wealth of the former and the wretched poverty of the latter. It seems as though all money had collected in the capital and ceased to circulate in the country." The memorial also complained that the government was giving this money to a few favored individuals and companies. "Hundreds of thousands of *yen* are spent in assisting certain companies, or in forming new

[46] Quoted in Hirano, *op. cit.*, p. 149.

ones, but such benevolent acts of the government are confined to certain persons or associations, and in no way exercise any benefit for the public good." [47] To make matters worse, some of these companies were attempting to bring the rural entrepreneurs under their control. We get a glimpse of this conflict in an incident concerning the export of raw silk.

In the period immediately following the opening of the country, raw silk was generally shipped to the treaty ports from the countryside by local people of some means, who held the upper hand in their dealings with the wholesale merchants in the port cities. But as the volume of trade grew, the urban merchants became increasingly powerful, until by 1880 they were advancing funds to the rural producers.[48]

In 1881 some silk dealers (including Mitsui) and silk commission houses formed the *Rengo Kiito Ni-azukari Sho* (Silk Warehousing Association). Its objectives were to create one general establishment to advance funds on silk brought in from the countryside, and to force all foreign purchasers to come to its premises. In short, it hoped to secure something of a monopoly on the silk trade. The association enjoyed the support of the government in the form of a non-interest bearing loan of one million *yen*.

The association, in appealing to the rural producers, argued that it was necessary that a central organization secure control of the trade in order to eliminate certain " bad customs " of the foreign buyers. The rural producers replied that they were in sympathy with the desire to secure better terms from foreign merchants. But they were also quick to point out that there were some discrepancies between what the association professed and what it practiced. They claimed that the association had borrowed more than a million *yen* from the banks at six percent interest, and yet was charging fifteen percent to eighteen percent on money advanced to the silk producers. " We are forced to say," they argued, " that it looks very much as if the Silk Warehousing Company had been established for the mere purpose of lust after profit, and that is, therefore, one of the reasons for our dissatisfaction with it." [49]

[47] McLaren, *JGD*, p. 471.

[48] *Sanshi Yokan* [The Essentials of Silk], edited by the Dai Nihon Sanshi Kai (Tokyo, 1926), p. 111.

[49] *Commercial Reports of Her Majesty's Consuls in Japan, 1881* (London, 1882), p. 60.

In the end the association backed down because of objections raised by the foreign merchants and the rural producers.

Between 1878 and 1881 the democratic movement gained numerous adherents from the lower classes. Small landowners, tenant farmers, and wage workers swelled the ranks. Each group had reasons for enlisting in the new cause. The poorer peasants, like their wealthy neighbors, hoped for tax reductions. Seeing that the taxes they paid were not being used for their benefit but rather for the maintenance of the army, the police, the bureaucracy, for industrialization, and for debt charges on bonds held by the samurai, money lenders, and the nobility, they demanded " cheap government." The tenant farmer, weighted down by high rents, harassed by Nature, and perennially in debt, longed for some land that he could call his own. Caught in the squeeze between high prices and low wages, the wage worker wanted some kind of relief from his misery. All of them agreed that the system of compulsory military service was undesirable. Those on the farms found conscription particularly burdensome since it took away much needed labor. The incidence of service, moreover, was inequitable. By paying a sum of 270 *yen*, an amount, incidentally, which only the wealthy could afford to pay, one could escape being called.[50] So strong was the opposition to conscription that it led to a number of peasant revolts. General Yamagata, the creator of the modern army, once complained that the people hated military service. " There are not a few," he said, " who injure themselves or run away, or by other fraudulent practices try to avoid being called." [51]

The task of knitting together these diverse elements into a coherent movement was performed by some professional politicians like Itagaki and his friend, Goto Shojiro. Although these men had their liberal moments, they were not above using the movement to further their personal careers. Gathered about them, however, were a number of writers and intellectuals. Genuinely moved by the heady doctrines of European and American democracy and sincerely desirous of seeing democracy planted in Japan, they rendered yeoman service. They advised the leaders and wrote many of their speeches for them. They peppered the government with stinging

[50] Norman, *Soldier and Peasant in Japan, The Origins of Conscription*, p. 50.
[51] Quoted in Hani Goro and Izu Kimio, *Meiji Ishin ni okeru Seidojo no Henkaku* [Institutional Changes in the Meiji Restoration], *NSHSK*, p. 47.

memorials, published long articles in newspapers extolling democratic rights, and even went on speaking tours in order to arouse their fellow citizens. In their speeches and writings they denounced the Meiji government for being a tight oligarchy of Sat-Cho politicians. In order to break the hold of this oligarchy and thus bring an end to the abuses, they said that a national assembly must be established. And so persuasively was this message conveyed and so ready were the people to receive it that by 1880 the cry for a national assembly swelled into a national chorus.

CHAPTER VIII

POLITICAL AGITATION

I.

A VILLAGE official by the name of Hamamura faced some five hundred villagers assembled in a temple in a village in Shizuoka prefecture in the year 1880. He was there to persuade his neighbors to affix their signatures to a petition asking the government to establish a national assembly. In approaching the gathering, Hamamura used a homely touch. Heretofore we had been led to believe, he told them, that we were still young. But the truth of the matter is we are now grown up and understand what is going on around us. We now wish to take a wife called "Kokkai" (National Assembly). But no one will give us his daughter in marriage if we are reticent about asking for her hand. Those who wish to get married, therefore, should step forward. Of those present about four hundred responded. As a result two "matchmakers" were chosen and sent to Tokyo bearing the petitions.[1]

In Tokyo these two men no doubt met many others who had come to the capital on a similar mission. For about this time, political associations all over the country were busily engaged in drawing up petitions. To some extent this campaign was directed and coordinated by the *Aikokusha*. In March, 1879 the *Aikokusha* called a convention in Osaka. About eighty delegates representing twenty-one local political groups in eighteen prefectures attended.[2] Another convention followed in November of the same year. It was resolved at this meeting that a petition seeking the creation of a representative assembly should be presented to the Emperor.[3]

Actually this drive had been launched about a month earlier by a political society in Okayama,[4] and when the *Aikokusha*, with its local affiliates joined in, the movement rapidly grew in scope. It

[1] Yokose Yau (editor), *Meiji Shonen no Seso* [Aspects of Life in the Early Meiji Era] (Tokyo, 1927), p. 284.
[2] Itagaki, *JS*, I, 321.   [3] *Ibid.*, pp. 322-325.   [4] Osatake, *NKST*, II, 524 ff.

only required a few months for the idea to spread. By the time the
next convention met in March, 1880, great enthusiasm had been
aroused. Several thousand persons came to this convention, and
in order to avoid confusion, the right to debate and vote was
limited to those representing societies with more than twenty
members. It is reported that there were ninety-six such organizations with a total membership of more than ninety-eight
thousand.[5] A petition bearing more than seventy-seven thousand
signatures from twenty-two prefectures plus Tokyo and Osaka was
presented to the convention.[6]

The magnitude of the movement was enough to frighten the
government. Immediately it struck back with a law restricting
public meetings and a decree ordering the convention to disband.
Having been forewarned of the government's action, the leaders,
in the meantime, changed the name of the organization to the
" League for the Establishment of a National Assembly " (*Kokkai
Kisei Domei Kai*) and a resolution to continue the organization
until its aims had been achieved was passed.[7] For the purposes of
political agitation the country was divided into twelve districts,
and a committee was set up in Tokyo for the purpose of maintaining liaison with local political groups. It was envisaged that if
the petition was granted, the League would submit a memorial to
the government regarding the method of choosing delegates to a
constitutional convention. It also was to make known its views as
to the kind of constitution it preferred.[8] Two leaders of the
Aikokusha, Kataoka Kenkichi and Kono Hironaka, were given
the task of formally presenting the petition to the government.

Kataoka and Kono were joined by a host of others who con-
verged on Tokyo bringing petitions to lay before the government.
The *Tokyo Nichi-Nichi*, pro-government newspaper, derisively
characterized the whole affair as a " fad." But it added that
" Although there are differences of opinion, some wishing joint

[5] Ukita Kazutami and Counts Itagaki and Okuma, " The History of Political
Parties in Japan," in Okuma Shigenobu (editor), *Fifty Years of New Japan*,
English edition edited by Marcus B. Huish (London, 1910), I, 150.

[6] Itagaki (*JS*, I, 356-376) has given figures on the number of signatures by
prefectures. From these the overwhelming predominance of Kochi and Hiroshima
prefectures with 47,957 and 20,152 signatures respectively is evident.

[7] Ukita, Itagaki and Okuma, *op. cit.*, p. 150.

[8] Itagaki, *JS*, I, 334-335.

petitions and others separate petitions, there is unanimity when it comes to the desire for the establishment of an assembly and a constitution. Each time a petition is presented, it is noisily praised in the press and in lecture meetings so that those in areas not participating in the movement seem to feel abashed. . . ." [9]

In 1880 at least fifty-five petitions, most of them favoring the creation of a representative assembly, are known to have been drawn up.[10] As an answer to these pressure group tactics, the government, on one pretext or another, refused to accept the petitions. When Kataoka presented the petition to the *Dajokan,* he was told to go to the *Genro-in* (Senate). But the latter body refused to accept it on the ground that it was improperly drawn up.[11] About the same time, two men representing the *Shokyosha* in Nagano prefecture arrived with a petition bearing more than twenty thousand signatures. They spent fifty days trying to get the government to accept it, but in vain.[12] The stubborn attitude of the government sometimes led to bizarre episodes. A corporal in the Imperial Guard became so enraged that he tried to commit suicide in front of the Imperial Palace with a petition in his pocket.[13] Embarrassed by it all, the authorities finally announced that hereafter all petitions were to be presented to the local prefectural government which, in turn, would transmit them to the *Genro-in.* "Hereupon," says one account, "the popular leaders immediately changed the course of their movement directed against the central government. Wishing to establish bases from which to operate, they formed groups in various localities. . . . Political societies sprang up everywhere, including the cities. Even the laws and strict watch maintained by the government could not prevent the leaders from communicating with each other secretly."[14]

II.

The government did not remain idle while the democratic movement was gaining adherents. In coping with the movement, it

[9] Quoted in Osatake, *NKST,* I, 532.
[10] See Osatake Takeki, *Nihon Kensei Shi* [Japanese Constitutional History], pp. 260-264.
[11] Itagaki, *JS,* I, 377.
[12] *Ibid.,* p. 386.
[13] *Ibid.,* p. 367.
[14] Suzuki, *Jiyu Minken Undo Shi,* p. 53.

followed a dual policy. First, whenever popular pressure became too great it agreed to concessions, granting the people more power in form but not in substance. Secondly, it resorted to outright suppression through the use of repressive laws and police power.

In the former category may be included the creation of certain institutions connected with local government. The assembly of prefectural governors (*Chihokan Kaigi*) was convoked in 1875. These governors met to discuss and give advice on matters of local interest. In 1878 the prefectural assemblies (*Fu-Ken Kai*) were formed. Since these assemblies were composed of legislators elected from each county (*gun*), they were *bona fide* elective assemblies. Property qualifications, however, limited the electorate and gave the wealthier landowners excessive representation. The chief weakness of these assemblies was that they could only advise.[15] It can be said that the creation of these institutions was not a genuine attempt to broaden the basis of government. Rather it was an attempt to placate hostile public opinion and to win the support of those groups whose opposition could be dangerous.

When it came to suppressing the democratic movement, the government had many weapons in its armory. Recognizing the importance of public opinion, the government enacted press and libel laws in 1875 and 1877.[16] When the editor of the liberal newspaper, the *Choya*, attacked these laws, he was promptly imprisoned and fined twenty *yen*. The number of arrests for violations of the press laws gives some idea of the scope of the action taken against the press. In 1875 and 1876 more than sixty arrests were made.[15] Between 1878 and 1880 the number of fines and jail sentences meted out increased until it reached three hundred and five in 1880. Most of the cases arose from alleged slander and libel. The editor of the Tokyo newspaper, the *Azuma*, for instance, was sentenced to two years imprisonment and fined one hundred *yen* for printing an editorial in which he said, " The Emperor, the Prime Minister, and Ministers are employed, after all, for the protection of the people. That is to say, we recognize that they are public servants of the state." [18]

[15] A detailed account of these institutions is given in McLaren, *Political History*, Chapter 6.

[16] For the text of these laws, see McLaren, *JGD*, pp. 539 ff.

[17] Fujii and Moriya, *SNST*, p. 544.

[18] Nishida Nagahisa, " Meiji no Shimbun " [Meiji Newspapers], *Kokumin no Rekishi* [National History], I (November-December, 1947), 57-62.

The law regulating public meetings has already been mentioned. Under this law anyone wishing to hold a political meeting or discussion was required to obtain a permit at least three days in advance. Article five of the law stated that " The police authorities shall send officials in uniform to the place of meeting. Such officers shall examine the warrant of official sanction and exercise control over the meeting." Another provision was that " No political association, intending to lecture or deliberate upon politics, may advertise its lectures or debates, persuade people to enter its ranks by despatching commissioners or issuing circulars, or combine and communicate with other similar societies." Finally the law prohibited men in the armed forces, teachers and policemen to attend political meetings or become members of political organizations.[19]

The last-mentioned provision suggests certain things about the police and the army, the main props of the Meiji bureaucracy. One of the institutions which the Meiji government inherited from the Tokugawa regime was the police. In the Tokugawa era wide use had been made of the secret police, political spies, and *agents provocateurs*.[20] In an interesting article on the Meiji police the well-known historian, Miura Hiroyuki, has shown how the Meiji government followed in the footsteps of the Shogunate in this respect. At one time, every high official in the government was provided with as many as three secret agents who could be sent out to make private investigations.[21] Later the government, following European precedents, centralized the police system under the Home Minister.[22]

In view of the historical background of the Japanese police, it is not surprising that they were used extensively to thwart political opposition. The political nature of the police was frankly expressed in the instructions sent out by the *Dajokan* on July 15, 1879. " We hear," it said, " that recently in rural areas certain societies which have the objective of discussing national affairs and the form of government have been formed and that they hold meetings and attract great crowds. In such cases, the police officers are to visit

---

[19] McLaren, *JGD*, pp. 495-499.

[20] Norman, *Feudal Background*, p. 8.

[21] " Meiji Shi no Ankoku Men " [The Dark Side of Meiji History] in his *Nihon Shi no Kenkyu* [Studies in Japanese History] (Tokyo, 1930), II, 294.

[22] Yada Soun, " Keikan Monogatari " [Tale of Police Officers], *CK*, XLIV (1929), 232-233.

such meetings, and if by any chance it is felt that they are of a nature as to stir up the people and threaten the national safety, orders to disband the meetings are to be issued, in Tokyo-*fu* the Metropolitan Police Bureau, and in the rural areas by the governors." [23]

But the police, by the very nature of their work, came into contact with the people and therefore was exposed to democratic ideas. According to one account by a man who made a speaking tour organizing political societies, the police officer assigned to trail him became very friendly and urged him to be more outspoken in his discussion of current events. He also reported that one policeman even resigned and joined the democratic movement.[24] It is quite possible that such tendencies led to the reorganization of the Metropolitan Police Bureau in 1881.[25]

Since the army could be isolated in barracks and trained and indoctrinated, it was less likely to be affected by the political currents of the times. Nevertheless, there is some evidence that even the troops were not completely immune. It is suspected that the "Takahashi Disturbance," a mutiny in a battalion of artillery troops in the Imperial Guard was influenced by the democratic movement.[26] A few months after this mutiny, General Yamagata issued his famous "Admonitions to Soldiers." "Such behavior," he said, "as questioning Imperial policies or expressing private opinions on the constitution, or criticising the published regulations of the government, runs counter to the duty of a soldier." [27] Two years later, that is about the same time that the Metropolitan Police Bureau was reorganized, the gendarmerie was created and given the "prime task of ferreting out dissident opinion within the army." [28]

With even the police and the army being infected with democratic ideas, it is little wonder that the top leaders of the Meiji government were thoroughly alarmed. The best evidence of their

[23] Quoted in Itagaki, *JS*, I, 320.
[24] Nomura Motonosuke, "Tanaka Shozo Kun to Watakushi" [Mr. Tanaka Shozo and I], *MBK* (December, 1934), p. 141.
[25] Cf., Shiota Yasumi, "Meiji Shonen ni okeru Keisatsu to Rikugun no Bunka" [The Differentiation of the Police and the Army in the Early Years of the Meiji Era], *RGK*, IV (September, 1935), 475n.
[26] Norman, *Feudal Background*, p. 83.
[27] *Ibid.*, p. 83.
[28] *Ibid.*

fear of the democratic movement is to be found in the letters exchanged between the leading statesmen of the time. In a letter dated July 4, 1879 General Yamagata wrote to his friend, Ito Hirobumi, that he had come to the conclusion that those in the democratic movement hoped to overthrow the government at the opportune moment. "Therefore," he continued, "every day we wait, the evil poison will spread more and more over the provinces, penetrate into the minds of the young, and inevitably produce unfathomable evils." [29] But Yamagata, as well as the other conservatives, were realistic enough to see that some concession in the form of a written constitution and a national assembly was inevitable. "Intelligent people," wrote Yamagata in another letter, "know that sooner or later there must be a national assembly. I feel with respect to that that unless the objective of future policy is defined, it is inevitable that the ship of state will lose its course." [30]

Even while Yamagata was writing this letter, steps were being taken to pave the way for the creation of an assembly. In an earlier chapter we saw that the *Sa-in* had been engaged in drafting a constitution. This work was continued by a committee within the *Genro-in* which had been set up in 1876. An Imperial order addressed to Prince Arisugawa Taruhiko, president of the *Genro-in* said: "We hereby desire that a constitution which is based on the system established at the time of the founding of the nation and which gives due consideration to the laws of the various foreign nations be drafted." [31] A little later another decree was issued, urging Arisugawa to speed up the work. With the decree the Emperor sent along a copy of A. Todd's *Parliamentary Government in England*.[32] Owing to the Satsuma Rebellion, the work on the draft was interrupted, and it was not completed until July, 1880.[33] Perhaps the committee took its cue from the fact that the Emperor had sent Todd's book. There were indications that the committee had borrowed heavily from British parliamentary

---

[29] Quoted in Osatake, *NKST*, II, 522.

[20] Quoted in Tokutomi, *Koshaku Yamagata Aritomo Den*, II, p. 839.

[31] Osatake Takeki, "Ito An Izen no Kempo Soan" [Draft Constitutions Before Ito's Draft], *MBK*, No. 1 (February, 1934), p. 5.

[32] *Ibid.*, p. 6.

[33] Kenneth Colegrove, "The Japanese Constitution," *American Political Science Review*, XXXI (1937), 1038.

practice.[34] When Ito heard of this he felt rather apprehensive and proposed that the *Genro-in* abandon its work. Iwakura complained that there were " points which were not in keeping with the national polity (*kokutai*) ." [35] The leading figures in the government were then asked to submit their opinions on the advisability of granting a written constitution and establishing a national assembly. All except one took a conservative stand and urged that the summoning of a parliament be delayed until a more distant date. The lone exception, Okuma Shigenobu, presented no opinion even though he was pressed a number of times to do so. When finally he made known his views in 1881, they precipitated a political crisis marking a turning point in Meiji political history.

III.

When Okuma was asked to give his views, he requested that he be allowed to talk with the Emperor in person. He said that this was because he could not express himself in writing and also because he did not wish his opinions to become known to others.[36] His request was denied. Accordingly in March, 1881 he submitted a written report, prepared by his disciples, Ono Azuma and Yano Fumio. Ono had lived in England for three years, and Yano, according to his own statement, relied on Todd's *Parliamentary Government in England* in preparing this report.[37] The main points in this report were that the first parliament should be elected toward the end of 1882, that the first sessions ought to begin early in 1883, that the leader of the party with the largest number of seats should be given the task of conducting foreign affairs, and that parliamentary secretaries and permanent civil servants should be different individuals.[38]

This report came back from the Throne late in June. When it was shown to the other members of the cabinet, Okuma was severely denounced. Ito, who had previously worked closely with Okuma on constitutional questions, was indignant. He claimed

[34] *Ibid.*
[35] Tokutomi, *op. cit.*, p. 840.
[36] Takahashi Shingo, " Meiji Juyonen no Seihen ni Tsuite " [On the Political Crisis of 1881], *Waseda Seiji Keizai Gaku Zasshi* [Waseda Journal of Politics and Economics], No. 61 (October, 1938), p. 15.
[37] Idditti, *op. cit.*, p. 211.
[38] *Ibid.*

that Okuma had given the Emperor advice which was at variance
with views which he had expressed earlier to Ito. In fact Ito felt
so resentful that he threatened to resign and refused to attend
cabinet meetings. But early in July, peace was arranged between
the two. The sulking Ito consented to come to the cabinet sessions
again.[39]

Meanwhile, another question became intertwined with this controversy within the inner group within the government. In 1871,
the government had begun a ten-year project to develop the
northern island of Hokkaido. Over the years a total sum of more
than ten million *yen* had been appropriated. The program expired
in 1881 at a time when the government was pursuing a policy of
transferring government-owned enterprises to private interests.
Consequently, some officials who had been connected with the
project, including Kuroda Kiyotaka, the head of the commission
on Hokkaido, formed a company headed by a wealthy Osaka
merchant by the name of Godai Tomoatsu. The company proposed
to buy these government properties in Hokkaido for a small sum
of 300,000 *yen* to be paid over a period of thirty years without
interest.[40] In commenting on this proposition, McLaren has said:
"The only conclusion to be arrived at in the circumstances was
either that the money had been squandered by the members of the
Commission or that they were now attempting to get possession
of a valuable property on terms so ludicrously inadequate as to
amount to theft."[41] Some men in the government, including
Okuma, opposed the proposed transaction, but the majority approved of it.[42] In this connection it is worth noting that both
Kuroda and Godai were Satsuma men and hence closely afflliated
with the Sat-Cho faction in the government.

Somehow or other the news of the pending sale leaked out to the
press. Immediately the public expressed strong opposition. On
July 26, the *Tokyo-Yokohama Mainichi* published an editorial
attacking the proposed sale. This was echoed in all the other
papers, including even those which had persistently supported the
government. Mass meetings were called in the big cities. Everywhere strong protests were registered and denunciations of the
"clan oligarchy" were heard. The incident provided wonderful

[39] Takahashi, pp. 19-21.
[40] Fujii and Moriya, *SNST*, p. 840.
[41] McLaren, *Political History*, p. 158.
[42] Fujii and Moriya, *SNST*, p. 840.

ammunition for the leaders of the democratic movement. They emphasized the point that a representative assembly would make such schemes impossible.[43]

In the midst of this the Emperor left for a tour through northern Japan, accompanied, among others, by Okuma. Kuroda, who was naturally anxious to get the final approval on the transaction, then called on Sanjo, the head of the *Dajokan*. Kuroda told Sanjo that if the latter did not agree to the sale, he had other plans; and to emphasize his point, he struck Sanjo with a candle stick.[44] Sanjo, who was easily intimidated, went off to see the Emperor and obtained Imperial assent. On August 1, 1881 the sale was officially approved.

Meanwhile rumors were circulated among the top-ranking officials that Okuma was pulling wires from behind the scenes to turn the public against the government. Whatever the truth behind these rumors, it was a fact that his popularity had shot up rapidly. It was generally known that he had opposed the Kuroda deal. But as he grew more popular, his colleagues, especially Ito, began to fear him. Okuma did not belong to the Sat-Cho clique, having come from Hizen, one of the minor clans. But he was an important figure with many disciples and friends ensconced in important government positions.[45] Ito's analysis of the situation may be seen in an entry in the diary of Sasaki Takayuki, vice-president of the *Genro-in*. "According to a confidential talk I had with Ito," says the entry, "Okuma personally favors the democratic movement. He believes that there is no hope for the present government and has allied himself very secretly with some people outside the government. . . . He is working with the Mitsubishi company and Fukuzawa Yukichi. It is indeed an evil thing." [46]

[43] Fujii and Moriya, *ibid*. McLaren (*op. cit.*, pp. 158-159) says: "Okuma, as Finance Minister, was the natural channel through which such a scandal should have been brought to the notice of the public. He called a meeting of the citizens of Tokyo and divulged the nature of the plot, not only raising thereby a storm of protest against the Government, but making himself the idol of the people. While carried along the crest of this wave of popularity he addressed a memorial to the Emperor praying for the establishment in 1883 of a National Parliament." While the above hypothesis that Okuma divulged the news is plausible, the statement that he presented the memorial at this time is in error. Actually it was presented several months before the scandal.

[44] Watanabe Kuriyama, "Meiji Juyonen Seihen ni Tsuite" [On the Political Crisis of 1881], *MBK*, No. 2 (May, 1934), p. 6.

[45] See McLaren, *op. cit.*, pp. 156-157 for his characterization of Okuma.

[46] Quoted in Osatake, *NKST*, II, 576.

The reference to Mitsubishi and Fukuzawa was concerned with another rumor which was also making the rounds. It was said that Okuma was being backed by Fukuzawa Yukichi and Iwasaki Yataro, head of the Mitsubishi interests. Fukuzawa was supposed to be directing the strategy, and Iwasaki was said to have contributed 300,000 *yen* for campaign expenses.[47] Still another rumor said that Okuma would become the next Premier and Fukuzawa would be appointed Minister of Foreign Affairs.[48]

From the available documents it is evident that some of the high officials took these rumors seriously.[49] And they had good reasons for so doing. It was more or less common knowledge that Okuma, Fukuzawa, and Iwasaki were closely linked together. Fukuzawa was a leading writer and educator of his time. He had probably done more towards the spread of Western civilization in Japan than any other individual. Shortly before the Restoration he established in Tokyo a school called Keio Gijuku. Having been strongly influenced by Utilitarian doctrines, he emphasized practical subjects like English and economics rather than the traditional classical learning. Consequently his students were well qualified for pursuing business careers, and many of them were hired by the Mitsubishi company.

Even more important was the web of economic ties that held them together. In the late 1870's, Fukuzawa and several others presented a memorial to Okuma, then Minister of Finance, urging him to establish a bank. In 1879 the Yokohama Specie Bank was founded, with one-third of the capital being supplied by the government. Iwasaki also put up some capital, thereby giving him some interest in the bank. Another link was the Foreign Trade company (*Boeki Shokai*). This company was set up by Asabuki Eiichi, an employee of Iwasaki and a graduate of Keio Gijuku. Of the total capital of 200,000 *yen*, Iwasaki provided 80,000 *yen*. The rest came from Fukuzawa and some other Keio men, and from the Yokohama Specie Bank which obtained Okuma's permission to invest in this company. Then there was the Meiji Life Insurance company organized by the Mitsubishi interests with the assistance of some Keio graduates. Fukuzawa had also taken a leading part in the negotiations leading to the sale of the Takashima Coal Mine owned by Goto Shojiro to Iwasaki for more than 900,000 *yen*.

[47] *Ibid.*, p. 575.   [48] *Ibid.*, p. 581.   [49] See *ibid.*, pp. 577 ff.

Lastly, it might be mentioned that Iwasaki had certain navigation rights to Hokkaido which he feared might be nullified if the government properties were sold.[50] This might help explain why Okuma was opposed to the sale.

In view of the enmity between Ito and Okuma provoked by the disagreement over the constitution, the suspicion that Okuma was stirring up public opinion against the government, and the close connection between Okuma and Mitsubishi (which ran counter of the ties between Choshu and Mitsui interests), one can see why Okuma became *persona non grata* to the Sat-Cho clique. If the close alliance between Satsuma and Choshu was to be maintained, it was necessary to get Okuma out of the government. Thus while Okuma was away on a tour with the Emperor, behind-the-scenes maneuvering was taking place. On September 6, Sanjo dispatched a letter to Iwakura, who was at that time in Kyoto, asking him to return to Tokyo at once. Iwakura, however, was not anxious to return. It may be that he did not wish to see the Sat-Cho faction strengthened. In any case he was not anxious to see Okuma forced out of the cabinet. On September 18, Yamada Kengi, a cabinet member, secretly went to Kyoto to urge Iwakura to return. Finally on October 6, Iwakura arrived in the capital. Sanjo called on him at once. The two came to an agreement on two things: the date of the calling of the first parliament should be announced, and the sale of the Hokkaido properties should be cancelled. On the question of the future status of Okuma no agreement was reached. But on the following day, Ito saw Iwakura and somehow or other managed to persuade him that Okuma should go. On October 11, the Emperor returned from his tour and that very evening, a cabinet session was held to which Okuma was not invited.[51] About midnight Ito and Saigo Yorimichi called on Okuma and asked him to resign. The following day an Imperial Rescript was issued, announcing that a parliament would be established in 1890.

---

[50] Tanaka, *op. cit.*, pp. 236-247.
[51] Watanabe, pp. 15-16.

Part Three:

THE POLITICS OF
THE DEMOCRATIC MOVEMENT

CHAPTER IX

THE FORMATION OF POLITICAL PARTIES

I.

THE Imperial Rescript of 1881 represented a partial victory for those who had been clamoring for a representative assembly. But if the government thought that the political agitation could be dispelled by this concession, it was to be disappointed. Within a matter of a few weeks, the *Jiyuto* (Liberal Party), organized on an even wider basis than the League for the Establishment of a National Assembly, made its appearance.

Although the *Jiyuto* was built on the foundation laid by the League, its program was much broader in scope than that of the League. The beginnings of the *Jiyuto* went back to the end of 1880. At that time there appeared a minority within the League who wished to broaden the basis of the movement and form a political party dedicated to the liberal cause.[1] At a meeting of the League in November, 1880, Ueki Emori argued that since the government had rejected the petitions, the only alternative was to form a political party and bring more people into the movement. In fact he even presented a draft of the platform and the by-laws of a party which he called the *Jiyuto*. Later under the leadership of Kono Hironaka, a number of meetings were held, and an embryonic party called the *Jiyuto* was formed.[2]

About this time, Itagaki was also working towards similar objectives. In 1881 he undertook a lecture tour in which he urged the formation of a political party. Everywhere he went he attracted large crowds. There was enthusiastic response, for example,

[1] The existence of this minority is brought out in the transcript of a secret meeting of the League held in November, 1880. Thanks to the thoroughness of the Japanese police, we have a record of the proceedings. See *Kokkai Kaisetsu Ronja Higi Tanbun Sho* [A Record of the Secret Deliberations of the Advocates of the Establishment of a National Assembly], reprinted in *MBZ*, XXII, 161-188.

[2] Itagaki, *JS*, I, 456; Otsu Junichiro, *Dai Nihon Kensei Shi* [Comprehensive Constitutional History of Japan] (Tokyo, 1929), II, 488.

when it was announced that he would be present at a political rally to be held in Osaka-*fu*. Five thousand admission tickets were printed for the occasion, but the supply was quickly exhausted. On the morning of April 10, the day of the rally, about ten thousand persons crowded around the gates. " Owing to this," says one account, " traffic was stopped. When the doors were opened all the people eagerly rushed in, knocking down the sturdily-built gates. It was a terrible sight, for they were just like a pack of wolves. In a twinkling both the main floor and the balcony became a mountain of humanity. Some were standing on the runway (*hanamichi*) and some climbed up the posts and on to the rafters. They crowded around the speaker's rostrum built on the stage, and there was no room left at all." [3]

The drive for the formation of a political party bore fruit after the Hokkaido affair of 1881. The scandal served as a catalyst to bring together the various anti-government groups which hitherto had been unable to combine. At the same time, when the government announced that a parliament would be summoned in 1890, the League lost its *raison d'etre*. Consequently, it was merged with the group led by Kono and transformed into a more powerful *Jiyuto*. After some jockeying for power among the leaders, an election of officers was held on October 30. Itagaki was named president and Nakajima Nobuyuki, vice-president. The *Jiyuto's* program was, first, to broaden liberty, protect the people's rights, promote their happiness, and reform society; second, to work for the creation of a sound constitutional system; and, third, to cooperate with others in the country who were working for similar objectives.

According to its by-laws, in addition to the president and vice-president, there were to be elected a permanent committee, five secretaries, and a standing committee of ten members. Of these officials, only the secretaries and the members of the standing committee were to receive compensation. Every local party affiliated with the *Jiyuto* was to assign one person to maintain contact with the Tokyo office. Otherwise the local groups were free to organize themselves in any way they saw fit. Every October the local affiliates were to send delegates to a national convention to be held in Tokyo.[4] From this it is apparent that the *Jiyuto* was a

[3] Suzuki, *Jiyu Minken Undo Shi*, p. 59.   [4] Otsu, p. 494-495.

loosely-knit network of rural parties with the central organization having some influence but no real control over the component parts.

In order to know something about the political coloring of the *Jiyuto*, it is well to probe into the matter of the economic and social status of its membership. In this connection, we may digress somewhat and describe briefly the so-called Brewers' Conference which was called about the time of the formation of the *Jiyuto*.

Initially this conference was summoned when the government levied new taxes on the brewing industry. In order to secure funds for a proposed program of naval expansion, the government, in 1880, doubled the tax on *zoseki*, a kind of yeast stone used in brewing. Displeased by the new tax, about three hundred brewers from Tosa met in May, 1881, and petitioned the government to reduce the amount. The request was rejected. Then just about the time the *Jiyuto* was organized, one of the brewers met with Ueki Emori and Kojima Minoru. Ueki was of the opinion that this was a matter calling for united action of all of the brewers in the nation. Later he and Kojima went to Tokyo as representatives of these brewers and there conferred with several brewers from Shinano, Ibaraki, and Fukui prefectures who had come to the *Jiyuto* meeting. Then Ueki drew up an announcement addressed to all brewers. The main theme of the announcement, which, incidentally, was published in all the metropolitan newspapers, was the freedom of enterprise. It was argued that the Japanese people had a right to be in the brewing business and that heavy taxation would destroy the industry. If the industry were destroyed, the announcement continued, the brewers would have no way of making a living. Liquor, moreover, brings joy to the people, and is not a luxury as some claim. But even if it were a luxury, there is no reason why it should be taxed more than other commodities. All taxes should be equal. If the government is having financial difficulties, why does it not tax other industries? Besides the function of government is to maintain order and protect the liberty and rights of the people. The government should not meddle in private affairs.

The Brewers' Conference attracted wide attention and enjoyed good response. In December, 1881 the government, wary of opposition of any kind, ordered the arrest of Kojima, Ueki and several others who had signed the announcement. Ueki, however, was released when a Tosa court found him not guilty. In April, 1882 Ueki inserted an advertisement in the newspapers inviting the brewers to a conference to be held in Osaka in May. As a result of this advertisement Ueki was questioned by the police. Later the governor of the prefecture banned the conference, but Ueki, ignoring the governor's orders, met secretly with some brewers on a boat on a river in Osaka. After this secret meeting, another petition was presented to the government. However, nothing came of it and the conference was later dissolved.[5]

The significance of this episode is to be found in the fact that brewers in Japan were often large landowners who rented their holdings to tenant farmers. We may say, therefore, that to some extent they were Janus faced. That is, as traders and industrialists they could espouse " freedom of enterprise " worthy as Mr. Norman has said, " of the purest Manchester Liberal in 19th Century England," but as landlords they were quite conservative.[6] Owing to the interest aroused by the Brewers' Conference, numerous merchants and rural industrialists who, like the brewers, were often landowners, were attracted to the *Jiyuto*. Thus one might say that the *Jiyuto* was a " liberal " party in which landowners occupied a prominent position. As we shall see later, this helped to make the party vulnerable to pressure from the landless peasants.

The *Jiyuto* soon found a rival in the form of the *Rikken Kaishinto* (Constitutional Progressive Party), organized in the spring of 1882. Led by Okuma Shigenobu, the party had for its nucleus a group of former bureaucrats like Kono Binken, Maejima Mitsu, Kitabatake Harufusa, and Yano Fumio. These men had resigned from the government when Okuma was driven from office. The *Kaishinto* also included intellectuals of the Keio school, and some lesser known people from two minor organizations, the *Otokai* and *Toyo Giseikai*. Wealthy merchants and industrialists, especially the Mitsubishi interests, backed the party financially.

In view of its makeup, it was to be expected that the *Kaishinto* would be more conservative than the *Jiyuto*. In a speech delivered at the first meeting of the party on April 16, Kono Binken stated that " Since the *Jiyuto* champions the cause of justice, and resolutely advocates equality, it naturally cannot help but become the ally of the poor. . . . Accordingly, it is to be expected that

[5] Itagaki, *JS*, I, 616-630.   [6] See Norman, *Emergence*, p. 170.

some of the rich and the learned would not be pleased. The *Kaishinto* will rally the latter elements. . . ." [7] At the same meeting there was distributed a pamphlet signed by Okuma and setting forth the watchword of the party, *Onken Chakujitsu* or " Moderate and Sound, Slow but Steady." In this pamphlet Okuma said that he did not wish to follow in the footsteps of Rousseau's followers or the Jacobins because they would bring about a " radical revolution." [8]

According to its by-laws, the president of the party was to be elected, but the other party officials were to be appointed. Those desiring to join the party were required to get recommendations from more than three party members. Those who violated party principles or brought dishonor to the party could be expelled by a resolution of the party meeting. Members living in Tokyo were to be assessed one *yen* a year, while those living in the rural areas were required to pay fifty *sen* a year. A monthly meeting was to be held in Tokyo. To help defray expenses, those attending were required to pay fifty *sen*.[9]

About the same time, a third party, the *Rikken Teiseito* (Constitutional Imperial Party) was founded. This group, however, never attracted many adherents since it was a government party created to offset the influence of the other two parties.

With the formation of these parties, the democratic movement reached its height. Many of the societies which had participated in the movement to petition the Emperor fell under the mantle of either the *Jiyuto* or *Kaishinto*. New affiliates were created, for the parties, especially the *Jiyuto*, carried on vigorous recruiting campaigns. The newspaper, *Choya*, claimed that there were 183 parties in October, 1882, of which 59 were connected with the *Jiyuto* and 42 with the *Kaishinto*.[10]

Both the *Jiyuto* and the *Kaishinto* continued the practice begun by the old *Aikokusha* of dispatching speakers to the local affiliates to stir up interest in political questions. Itagaki himself made many speeches. In October, 1881, for example, he appeared at a meeting

[7] Quoted in Baba Tsunego, " Nihon Seito Shi " [History of Japanese Political Parties] in *Dai Shiso Ensaikuropijiya*, XVII, 148.

[8] Quoted in Osatake, *NKST*, II, 630-631.

[9] *Ibid.*, p. 628.

[10] Tanaka Sogoro, " Shakaito Ko " [On the Rickshamen's party], *Rodo Hyoron* [Labor Review], II (April, 1947), 53.

of the *Yushinsha* in Takazaki and spoke before an audience of 1,000 local residents.[11] A secret police report on conditions in Tochigi prefecture throws light on the politics of the period. "Since this prefecture," says this report, "is only about a day's journey from Tokyo, men from both the *Kaishinto* and *Jiyuto* come frequently and get the people to join their organizations. All political groups. therefore, have been incorporated into these two parties and there are no independent political parties."[12] The same report goes on to say that the *Kaishinto* speakers emphasized slow but steady progress, eschewed violence and tried to win the support of the wealthy. In contrast, one *Jiyuto* speaker was arrested because his speech violated the law and he was forbidden to make any more speeches for a period of one year.[13]

The culminative effect of continued agitation carried on from the speaker's platform and in the press was an ever increasing diffusion of political ideas, most of which were derived from Western sources. It is, of course, difficult to measure the precise extent to which new political ideas permeated to the lower orders of society, but that it made an impression is evident. Some of the best illustrations are anecdotal in character. One Hirano Yataro, of Okayama, for example, was fined five *yen* when he said that "Even the Emperor, from the point of view of Heaven, is a human being like the rest of us," and that "national affairs ought not to be left solely to the Emperor." "The Japanese people," he said, "should arouse themselves, enhance national prestige, and imitate the Russian Nihilists."[14] Another illustration is the following poem called *Song of Liberty* (*Jiyu no Uta*) which became very popular in this period.[15]

> Be in Heaven a ghost of Liberty,
> On earth a man of Liberty.
> Liberty, Liberty, Oh Liberty!

> Follow the path of the English Revolution.
> Yesterday a King, today a rebel.
> Cromwell's beckoning with a flag of Liberty in his hand
> Almost upset Heaven.
> By putting King Charles to death
> The basis for liberty was laid.

---

[11] Itagaki, *JS*, II, 205.   [13] *Ibid.*
[12] Sekiguchi, p. 967.   [14] Yokose, *op. cit.*, p. 301.
[15] Kimura Takeshi, "Meiji Bungaku ni Arawaretaru Jiyu" [Liberty as Revealed in Meiji Literature], *Soken* [Foundation], I, No. 5 (May, 1946), 81-82.

The more concepts like equality, liberty, and popular rights percolated down to the lower classes, the lower became the social center of gravity of the movement (as represented by the *Jiyuto*). Increasingly impoverished peasants, tenant farmers, and wage workers were drawn into the *Jiyuto*, thus broadening the base of its pyramidic structure. The following newspaper account of a *Jiyuto* meeting in Tosa is very illuminating in this connection.

Finally Itagaki spoke and as usual there was great applause and cries of approval through the building, but when this had died down, two sturdy workmen wearing blue denim (their names were Umaji and Ushitaro) jumped up on the platform and commenced to speak in favour of social equality and their words were spoken with such vehemence and passion that they put to shame the Russian Nihilists. The audience looked at them with amazement because it appeared that they were not members of the audience but two of the cooks who worked in the kitchen of the hall in which the meeting was being held.

Itagaki was moved so much by the strong feeling of the plebeian class revealed here in which they understood the changed situation in which Japan found itself that he again got up to speak and greatly stirred the emotions of the audience. The people of Kochi prefecture are most earnest in disseminating the principle of democracy and if even those who perform the task of preparing food can speak with such eloquence on the rights of social equality and display such feeling and passion it goes without saying what strength and principles our party has in this prefecture which we cannot but admire.[16]

III.

From the preceding discussion it should be clear that the *Jiyuto*, the most militant and radical of the major parties, drew its main strength from the rural areas. The *Kaishinto*, on the other hand, was more urban, but at the same time was frankly devoted to the interests of the wealthier classes. It can be said, therefore, that the urban groups which played a fairly important role in the rise of Western liberalism, were not represented in any significant degree in the Japanese democratic movement. Yet this should not be interpreted to mean that no attempt was made to enlist the support of the urban proletariat. In 1880 a number of intellectuals in Tosa spent a month or so pulling *jinrikisha*. By taking up this despised occupation they hoped to secure a following among the working classes, and to encourage the samurai to take up regular

[16] Translated in Norman, *Feudal Background*, p. 68.

occupations. They published a manifesto in which they said that there was nothing degrading about manual labor. They also wrote a series of articles in a Tosa newspaper describing their experiences. As a result of these articles, says one source, " the manual laborers at last became cognizant of their rights." [17]

A more serious attempt to organize the rickshamen was made in Tokyo in 1882. At that time some radical members of the *Jiyuto* formed the *Shakaito* (Rickshamen's Party) [18] and thereby tried to link up city workers with the *Jiyuto* movement. In the *Shakaito* then we have an interesting example of an urban movement which was in a sense an offshoot of the democratic movement stemming largely from the countryside.

The immediate reason for the formation of the *Shakaito* in the fall of 1882 was the introduction of the horse-drawn street car in the city of Tokyo. Competition from the street cars led to increasing unemployment among the rickshamen. About the same time, the police, seeking the assistance of the rickshamen in apprehending criminals, had ordered them to organize themselves into a group and select their own leader.[19] Thus unrest stemming from increasing unemployment and an embryonic organization made it possible for some members of the *Jiyuto* to step in and form a political society.

Of the *Jiyuto* members connected with the *Shakaito*, the most important was Okumiya Kenji, a brilliant young man of about 22 or 23 years of age. Born in Tosa, he had learned English and was widely read in the works of Mill, Spencer, Buckle and Guizot. For a time he was connected with the Mitsubishi Company, but later resigned and joined the *Jiyuto*. Some years later he became a socialist. Implicated in the famous High Treason case, he was executed in 1911 along with Kotoku Shusui and a number of other socialists.[20]

Okumiya and his friends worked with Miura Kamekichi, the " boss " of the rickshamen. A circular signed by Miura and urging

---

[17] Suzuki, *op. cit.*, p. 49.

[18] If the " sha " 車 in *Shakaito* 車會黨 were written with another ideograph also pronounced " sha " 社 we would get a word meaning " Socialist Party." It would not be surprising if the men who organized the party hoped to get the connotation of the word socialist into the Rickshamen's party by using this device.

[19] Tanaka, pp. 50-51.   [20] *Ibid.*

the men to organize was issued.[21] For advertising purposes, men wearing hats with slips of gold-colored paper on which the word *Jiyu* or Liberty was written were sent out.[22] Mass meetings were also called. *Jiyuto* members attired in *happi* (a short coat worn by coolies) addressed some of these meetings. On one occasion when the police interrupted a speech being delivered by Ueki Emori, the crowd became angry and fought with the police, nearly beating them to death.[23] Little wonder that the pro-government *Tokyo Nichi-Nichi* commented in an editorial that " The object of this is to stir up the people's minds. It is to impart radical views to laborers like rickshamen, provoke discontent, make them disgusted with the government, and force them to wish something would happen. It was for this purpose that organizations like the Workingmen's *Jiyuto* in Kochi, and the *Aikoku Koshinsha* in Aichi were formed." [24]

The by-laws of the *Shakaito* provided for a president and ten officers. Meetings were to be held twice a month and dues were to be three *sen* per month. In case a member became ill, died, or suffered loss from fire, the party was to make a grant of money.[25]

It is quite evident that the *Shakaito* represented a marriage of convenience between the rickshamen and the *Jiyuto*, and thus between trade unionism and a political party. The rickshamen hoped to secure the support of the *Jiyuto* in opposing technological progress. Like the European workmen who smashed machines in the early days of industrialization, the rickshamen resisted change. The *Jiyuto*, on the other hand, wished to utilize the power of the city poor to strengthen the democratic movement. This is indicated in the following account written by Ito Jintaro, one of the *Jiyuto* members who worked with Okumiya. " The object of the *Shakaito* was not merely to destroy the horse-drawn street car. We were going to organize the rickshamen in the city under the pretext of destroying the horse-drawn street car, and if things went well, utilize them to attack people like Iwasaki." [26]

---

[21] See Kada Tetsuji, *Meiji Shoki Shakai Keizai Shiso Shi* [A History of Social-Economic Thought in the Early Meiji Era] (Tokyo, 1937), p. 634.

[22] Tanaka, p. 51.

[23] Ishikawa Kyokuzan, *Nihon Shakai Shugi Shi* [A History of Japanese Socialism] reprinted in *MBZ*, XXI, 342.

[24] Tanaka, p. 51.

[25] *Ibid.*, p. 52.

[26] Ishikawa, p. 341.

This alliance between the two groups proved to be short lived. Not long after the *Shakaito* was organized, Okumiya and several others were arrested and imprisoned for fighting with the police.[27] Thus the attempt to organize and enlist the aid of urban labor ended in failure.

[27] Tanaka, p. 53.

CHAPTER X

INTELLECTUAL CURRENTS

THE impact of Western civilization on a decaying feudal system led to the release of new energies and a reorientation of the economic, political, and cultural life of the nation. With the end of the long period of national isolation under the Tokugawa, a new spirit filled the air. The two decades following the Restoration of 1868 were marked by a penchant for change and innovation. During this period, too, the incoming tide of foreign influences reached its high-water mark. " Indeed," says Professor Anesaki, " there was never a period in Japanese history when foreign assistance was so welcomed and made use of as in the eighth decade of the nineteenth century." [1] Truly this was the age of *Bummei Kaika* or " Civilization and Enlightenment."

Changing conditions called for new intellectual moorings. After the fall of the Shogunate, a freer atmosphere prevailed. The orthodox Confucian doctrines, which the Tokugawa rulers had fostered to facilitate their rule now seemed somewhat anachronistic. A redefinition of the relation of the individual to the state and to society was made necessary. And in the realm of political theory, as well as in more mundane matters like technology and military organization, the Japanese turned to their Western mentors for enlightenment and guidance.

I.

The new generation of political theorists first turned to British Utilitarianism. For this they could hardly be blamed. The very fact that Utilitarianism was the dominant political philosophy of Britain, the great Power, must have been recommendation enough. Perhaps equally important was the fact that this doctrine, with its strong bias towards individualism, accorded well with the new temper in Japan. Furthermore, the simplicity of the formula, " the

---

[1] Anesaki Masaharu, *A History of Japanese Religion with Special Reference to the Social and Moral Life of the Nation* (London, 1930), p. 350.

greatest happiness of the greatest number," which the Utilitarians used to explain social phenomena, no doubt appealed to the Japanese who by tradition were not interested in problems of profound philosophical nature.

The first important European work to be translated after the Restoration was John Stuart Mill's well known essay, *On Liberty*. It was translated in 1871 by Nakamura Masanao (or Keiu), who began his career as a Confucian scholar, but after several years of study in England became a Utilitarian and a Christian.[2] Widely read and quoted, the translation of Mill's classic essay made a strong impression on the youth and intellectuals of the time. One of those influenced by it was Kono Hironaka, who later became one of the prominent leaders of the democratic movement. The following passage from his biography, although possibly exaggerated, is illuminating.

I bought a book called *Jiyu no Ri* [Principles of Liberty] by John Stuart Mill and translated by Nakamura Masanao. . . . I read this book on horseback while homeward bound, and there was a sudden great revolution in my thinking which had been nourished by Chinese studies and *Kokugaku* [native Japanese studies] which tended to be anti-foreign. All my old ideas excepting only those on loyalty and filial piety were completely destroyed. At the same time, I learned that we should esteem man's liberty and rights. Furthermore, I realized of my accord that government must be on the basis of broad public will. It made a deep impression on my mind, and engraved deeply on my breast, a belief in freedom and people's rights; and it was, indeed, a great turning point in my whole life. . . . It was March [of 1872] that I read the Principles of Liberty which brought about a great revolution in my mind."[3]

Translations of other well-known works on political science appeared in the 1870's. A part of De Tocqueville's *Democracy in America* was translated in 1873, and the following year a partial translation of Bluntschi's *Allgemeine Staatslehre* was published. A translation of Montesquieu from the English edition appeared in 1875 as well as Mill's *Representative Government*.[4] After 1877 the popularity of the earlier Utilitarians like Bentham and Mill declined

[2] Anesaki (*ibid.*, pp. 352-353) says: "He [Nakamura] combined his Confucianism with Christian theism which he professed to advocate, although he was never baptized nor did he believe in the Trinity or in miracles."

[3] *Kono Banshu Hensan Kai, Kono Banshu Den* [The Biography of Kono Banshu] (Tokyo, 1924), I, 186-187.

[4] A list of important works, including translations, relating to the democratic movement may be found in *MBZ*, V, 511-517.

and Herbert Spencer became the idol of Japanese intellectuals. A measure of the appeal his writings had is provided by the large number of translations. Between 1878 and 1896 at least thirty-three translations of his books were issued.[5]

The chief attraction of Spencer appears to have been his emphasis on ethics and morality. Many of the intellectuals, especially those of samurai origin, who had been exposed to Confucianism in their formative years, had found the materialism of the earlier Utilitarians somewhat distasteful.[6] Another feature of Spencer's writings which no doubt attracted the theorists of the democratic movement was his intense hostility to the bureaucracy. Spencer provided many good weapons for attacks on Meiji officialdom.

An incident surrounding the publication of a translation of *Social Statics* affords an interesting commentary on Spencer's standing among Japanese scholars. Matsushima Tsuyoshi, a scholar who had studied English with some missionaries and who had become interested in the relation between Western civilization and Christianity, happened to read *Social Statics.* Deeply moved by Spencer's disquisitions on justice and benevolence, he felt that it should be made available to Japanese readers. When he had completed the translation of about one third of the book, he showed it to a friend. This friend urged him to have it published, and it finally appeared in 1882 in six volumes. It immediately enjoyed a wide sale. The *Risshisha* ordered copies by wire in lots of tens and hundreds. So great was the demand that the translator, who had originally expected to receive about twenty-five *yen* in royalties, actually was paid twenty-five hundred *yen*. Itagaki called *Social Statics* the text book of the democratic movement, and later when he went to London, he called on the author. Influenced by the chapter which argued that individuals had the right to ignore the state, one person created a sensation by taking steps to renounce his citizenship.[7] Ironically enough, Spencer himself was not sympathetic to the democratic movement. Once when Mori Arinori, the Japanese

[5] Shimoide Junkichi gives the list in " Miru to Spensa Meiji Bunka ni Oyoboshita Eikyo ni Tsuite " [On the Influence Exerted by Mill and Spencer on Meiji Culture] in *Meiji Shakai Shiso Kenkyu* [Studies in Meiji Social Thought] (Tokyo, 1932).

[6] This is the view of Suzuki in *Jiyu Minken Undo Shi*, p. 81.

[7] This is based on an account given by Matsushita to Shimoide Junkichi in 1928, and published in " Shakai Heiken Ron Kaidai " [A Bibliographical Note on Shakai Heiken Ron], *MBZ*, V, 33-37.

Minister to the United States, sought his views on the reorganization of Japanese institutions, Spencer gave "conservative
advice."[8] Later he approved the provisions in the Meiji constitution preserving the absolute sovereignty of the Emperor.[9]

For every translation there appeared several books by Japanese
authors. Most of them inclined heavily towards the liberal side.
Even Kato Hiroyuki, who later became the spokesman and staunch
defender of the Meiji bureaucracy, wrote several books which were
highly critical of the government. In his *Kokutai Shinron* (A New
Theory of National Polity), published in 1874, he said:

> Both the ruler and the people are human beings. They are certainly
> not of a different race. But how is it that when it comes to rights there
> should be such vast differences? People who are born in a country with
> such a base national polity are indeed most unfortunate.
>
> No one, even among those who are respected for their wisdom, has
> realized that such a state of affairs is bad. On the contrary, it is evident
> that they believe that the ruler is sublime and the people are base, and that
> they are fostering such vile beliefs more and more. Especially in our
> country, the views of Nationalist scholars [Kokugakusha] do violence to
> truth, and are indeed despicable. . . . They say that all the land belongs
> personally to the Emperor and that all the people are his retainers. . . .
> They argue that it is the proper thing to obey faithfully Imperial Rescripts
> and not question anything which pertains to the Emperor. This, they say,
> is national polity [kokutai] and makes our country superior to all other
> nations. Such base views and vulgar opinions are indeed ridiculous.[10]

However, a few years later Kato recanted. Success made him
more conservative and the liberalism of his earlier days embarrassed
him. Accordingly, he not only let the book go out of print, but
even went so far as to insert an advertisement in a newspaper
informing the public that he no longer subscribed to such views.[11]

---

[8] David Duncan, *Life and Letters of Herbert Spencer* (New York, 1908), I, 213.
[9] Uyehara, *op. cit.*, p. 204, who cites as his authority an article in *Taiyo* for
March, 1909.
[10] Quoted in Ishikawa, *op. cit.*, p. 333.
[11] The advertisement said: "During the last four or five hundred years,
Copernicus, Galileo, Newton, and lately Lamarck, Goethe, and Darwin have studied,
by means of experiments, the principles of various things. Physics has abolished
delusions and established true principles. Recently philosophy and political science,
too, with the help of physics have finally begun to study reality. . . . My *Shinsei
Tai-i* and *Kokutai Shinron* were written before I knew about these principles. It
had been my hope to correct these errors but I have not had time to do so. Hence
this advertisement. I have allowed the books to go out of print. As for those
still circulating, I wish that the people reading them will not take the views
expressed therein to be those which I now hold." *MBZ*, V, 15.

The shift in Kato's position was probably due in part to personal reasons,[12] but it also mirrored the rise of new trends in Meiji thought.

The first wave of Utilitarianism was quickly overtaken by successive waves of European thought. As the Japanese became more familiar with Western political thought, they became discriminating in their preferences. Increasingly different political groups began to choose the kind of political theory which best served their interest. The *Kaishinto*, for example, eventually became the repository of a somewhat modified form of the earlier Utilitarianism. The main body of the *Jiyuto* was attracted by Herbert Spencer. The radical wing of the *Jiyuto*, however, fell under the influence of French thought. Rousseau, whose *Social Contract* was first translated in 1877 became the guiding light of this group. Through their manifestoes, speeches and articles they popularized the doctrine of natural rights, and spread the idea of liberty and equality. Returned students who had come into contract with French revolutionary tradition also served as carriers of French thought. It is noteworthy that even an aristocrat like Saionji Kimmochi, who later becamé the last *Genro* (Elder Statesman), was affected by his sojourn in France. On his return he participated in the publication of the *Toyo Jiyu Shimbun* (Oriental Liberal Newspaper), causing consternation in official circles. An Imperial order forced Saionji to sever his connections with the paper.

For a number of years the government could offer little intellectual defense against the diffusion of the doctrine of natural rights. As one writer says, the officials had difficulty " defending themselves against the powerful forensics of the theorists of liberty, equality, and natural rights, since their minds, too, were to some degree swayed by the *a priori* reasoning of Liberalism." [13] In 1881 the *Genro-in* (Senate) issued a summarized translation of Edmund Burke's writings for the purpose of counteracting the influence of Rousseau's ideas. According to Kaneko Kentaro, who made the translation, copies were distributed to local officials who used the book for " instructing the people under their jurisdiction." [14]

The first really effective intellectual defense of the government's

[12] For Kato's connections with the bureaucracy through his sons and daughters, see A. M. Pooley, *Japan at the Cross Roads* (London, 1917), p. 93.
[13] Uyehara, *op cit.*, p. 115.
[14] Osatake, *NKST*, II, 621.

position was made some time later by Kato, who by now had completely gone over to the government. In a new book entitled, *Jinken Shinsetsu* (A New Theory of Human Rights), Kato attacked the natural rights doctrine. Using the Darwinian theory of natural selection, he refuted the claim that man was born with the right of liberty, equality, and self-government. He argued that there were variations among men, owing to differences in heredity and environment. Just as there is a struggle for the survival of the fittest among lower animals, so there is a like struggle going on among men. In the light of this, he said, there can be no such thing as natural rights.

Besides, he continued, rights are acquired, not natural. Rights came into being with the rise of states. In turn states owed their existence to the emergence of a strong ruler, who brought security to man and society. From this Kato came to the conclusion that legislators must be men of ability. Since Kato more or less equated ability with wealth, he urged a limitation on suffrage.

One of the arguments frequently used against the government with telling effect was that Japan must follow the example set by the civilized Western nations with respect to parliamentary government. In answer to this, Kato maintained that the growth of rights depended on the state of civilization. In this context, laws and rights found in Western nations were unsuited to Oriental nations since the latter had a lower level of civilization. In other words, Japan was not yet ready for parliamentary government.

Kato, however, was astute enough to see that the theory of the survival of the fittest was a double-edged sword. For if in the competition between the democratic movement and the government the former won out, Kato, in terms of his theory, would be forced to admit that the victory was a legitimate one. Accordingly, once he had used the notion of the survival of the fittest to attack natural rights, he then modified it, emaciating it in the process. First, he said, it was not physical prowess that counted among human beings, but rather mental fitness. Then he introduced a distinction between " real " and " false " survival. He admitted that sometimes inferior groups attained power, but claimed that this was a temporary phenomenon, and that it could not become permanent. He specifically criticised the democratic movement, saying that if the people, thinking only of promoting their own interests, fought the government and the aristocracy, they would bring harm to society. The implication was that even if the democratic movement should succeed, it would only be a case of " false " survival.

The publication of Kato's book was the beginning of a trend in Japanese political thought. Kato, who was able to read German, as well as English, made use of a number of German treatises.[16] Thereafter the Meiji bureaucracy came to rely increasingly on Prussian thought to provide justification for its position. This tendency reached a high point in the drafting of the constitution. As we shall see in a later chapter, Ito and his associates paid careful attention to Prussian political theory and turned to Prussian advisers for guidance in drawing up the document which became the constitution of 1889.[17] Here we have an example of one autocracy indirectly coming to the aid of another.

Thus it can be said that English Utilitarianism and French political thought contributed to the strength of the democratic movement by providing it with an ideological basis. By turning to the writings of Mill, Spencer, and others the anti-government forces were able to secure ready-made arguments with which to embarrass the government. But, as we have seen, not all Western thought was helpful. Prussian ideas of statecraft, by strengthening the position of the government, had the effect of weakening the democratic movement.

II.

The transformation of Japan occurred at a time when socialism had already become a factor in European politics. Just four years before the Restoration, the First International was formed under the leadership of Marx. In 1871, while the Meiji government was still in the midst of reorganization, the Paris Commune fell. The growth of the democratic movement in Japan was roughly paralleled by the rise of the Social Democratic Party in Imperial Germany, and the emergence of Nihilism as an element in the politics of Tsarist Russia. Significantly enough the Japanese were in possession of some information, although not always accurate,

---

[16] See Kato's footnotes to *Jinken Shinsetsu* in *MBZ*, V, 386-388.

[17] More than twenty German advisers and experts were employed in connection with the drafting of the constitution. See *The Japan Weekly Mail*, August 6, 1887, p. 112.

concerning these European developments, and there is reason to believe that this knowledge affected the course of the democratic movement.[18]

So far as is known, the words " socialism " and " communism " first appeared in Japanese publications in 1870 in a book by Kato Hiroyuki entitled *Shinsei Tai-i* (Principles of True Government). The author described communism and socialism in these words:

> Although there are some differences between the two, they are by and large similar. They are theories which propose to bring equality to all phases of the everyday life of the common people, including clothing, food, and shelter. The reason these schools of thought arose is this: If individuals were left to themselves, they say, there would arise distinctions between the rich and the poor, owing to differences of ability and effort. The rich would get richer, and the poor would become poorer. This would lead to the impoverishment of the entire world. They therefore propose that everything, including clothing, food and shelter, and privately-owned land, equipment, and industries be owned by the government. By this means differences between the rich and poor would be abolished. . . . [but] it is an unbearably harsh system. . . .[19]

During the 1870's information on socialism became more plentiful. In at least one university lectures on socialism were given. An American, the Reverend Dwight W. Learned, is believed to have been the first person to lecture on the subject. A graduate of Yale University, he went to Japan in 1875 and joined the faculty of the well-known Christian university, Doshisha. At first he taught various subjects, but about 1879 he began giving courses on economics, in which he discussed socialism. Being sympathetic to *laissez faire* economics, he was severely critical of socialism. He said, however, that capitalism was accompanied by some evils. His solution for these evils was not socialism, but " true humanism " and " true Christianity." [20]

---

[18] For example, the situation in Paris just before the Commune was reported by Tada Rokunosuke. This report is reprinted in *MBZ*, XXI, 399-404. The First International and other European socialist developments were described by Ozaki Hiromichi who apparently obtained his information from Theodore Woolsey's *Communism and Socialism*. See Ozaki's article, " Kinsei Shakaito no Genin o Ronzuru " [On the Origins of Modern Socialist Parties], reprinted in *MBZ*, XXI, 408-414.

[19] The *Shinsei Tai-i* is reprinted in *Meiji Kaikaki Bungaku Shu* [A Collection of Literary Works on the Meiji Enlightenment] which is volume I in the series, *Gendai Nihon Bungaku Zenshu* [Collected Works on Modern Japanese Literature] (Tokyo, 1931), pp. 507-528. This quotation comes from p. 522.

[20] Sumitani Etsuji, *Nihon Keizaigaku Shi no Issetsu* [An Act in the History of Japanese Economics] (Tokyo, 1934), pp. 65-124.

The most important source of information on socialism, however, was the press. Towards the end of the 1870's there were published a number of news dispatches describing the activities of the Social Democrats in Germany and the Nihilists in Russia. Bismarck's attempts to suppress the Socialist party, for instance, were reported. One item intimated that the Iron Chancellor was seeking absolute powers under the guise of putting down the socialists.[21] Japanese writers also speculated as to the reasons for the emergence of socialism in Europe. It was generally believed that the existence of social and economic inequality was an important factor. Some thought that despotism encouraged the rise of socialist parties. A few attributed socialism to the decline of Christianity.[22]

Owing to the nature of the source of information, the Japanese public was never presented with a systematic treatment of the socialist doctrine. As a result many people apparently received the impression that socialism called for an egalitarian social order in which private property would be abolished. Thus the result was that not only conservatives but even liberals expressed strong opposition to socialism. One writer has examined the newspapers supporting the democratic movement in order to see how they reacted to the question of socialism. He found that they criticised the doctrine because, they said, it would lead to the end of private property. Many of the articles appearing in these newspapers staunchly defended private property, for to them it was the basis of security, livelihood, happiness, wealth, and progress. Modern democratic thought, it was claimed, rested on the system of private property. If property were abolished the social order would collapse and society would revert to a barbaric state.[23] Something of the general attitude on this subject can be seen in the following extract taken from an article on " Delusions on the Equality of Wealth " which appeared in the newspaper, *Kochi*, on February 20, 1881.

It is characteristic of social nature that there be some differences in wealth among us. So even if equality of wealth were achieved by means of temporary pressure, in a little while the characteristic nature would

---

[21] Reprinted in Yokose, *op. cit.*, pp. 420-421. Yokose also reprints some press dispatches on Nihilism.

[22] Hayashi Shigeru, " Jiyu Minken Ron no Shakai-teki Genkai " [The Social Limits of Japanese Democratic Thought], *Kokka Gakkai Zasshi*, LIII (August, 1939), 1100.

[23] *Ibid.*, pp. 1093-1094.

emerge, owing to differences in effort. More important, this so called equality is an extreme form of inequality. The toil of the diligent (that is the wealthy) would always be sacrificed for the lack of effort on the part of the lazy (that is the poor). The diligent would exert themselves more and more and the lazy would avoid work more and more. Who would be willing to create wealth for others instead of planning for one's progeny? To strengthen the right of private property is to protect one's rights and to lay the basis for attaining one's happiness. Therefore, disregard of this not only works to the disadvantage of the wealthy, but also to the disadvantage of the poor. This is because commerce and industry would not be created if the wealthy did not put their capital to work. And if commerce and industry are not created, how can the poor secure their livelihood? This is, of course, a principle of social economy; so the error of wishing to regulate social nature by means of puny action needs no elucidation on our part.[24]

There was a general belief that socialist parties would be formed in Japan. " The spread of socialism," said the newspaper, *Azuma,* " will probably not stop on the continent of Europe . . . and it appears that it will spread to our empire. . . ." [25] The press noted the existence of social and economic inequality in Japan and warned that if the government continued to suppress the democratic movement, the disaffected people would be forced to turn to socialism. Some of the papers contended that the way to prevent socialism in Japan was to establish constitutional government which would protect the rights and liberties of the people.[26]

Actually, of course, there was no reason for the Japanese to be so apprehensive about socialism. Industrialization in Japan was still on a small scale, and as yet there existed no large and class-conscious proletariat. There was, on the other hand, ample grounds for the leaders of the movement to be extremely wary of any doctrine which would pave the way for the modification of existing property rights. It will be recalled that many of the leaders and wealthier members of the *Jiyuto* were landowners, renting out land to tenant farmers. Consequently, they were sensitive to pressure from landless peasants demanding cheaper rents and a more equitable distribution of land. In fact in the fall of 1882 there was formed an Oriental Socialist Party. As we shall see later, this party was in reality a peasant party and socialist in name only. But to

---

[24] Quoted in *ibid.,* pp. 1096-1097.
[25] Quoted in *ibid.,* pp. 1106n.
[26] *Ibid.,* p. 1109.

the rural propertied groups, who associated socialism with the abolition of private property, the formation of a peasant party which, from the name, appeared to adhere to socialistic principles, must have been a serious menace.

III.

To round out this discussion of intellectual currents, it is necessary to comment briefly on the development of the political novel. Traditionally associated with the culture of the lower classes, the novel was apparently considered beneath the dignity of serious political writers as a medium of expression. So unlike the ponderous treatises on political theory and government which appeared fairly early, the political novel was not used as a means of popularizing liberal ideas until the last phase of the democratic movement.

One of the first political novels to appear was a rather jejune work by Toda Kindo entitled *Jokai Haran* (Waves on the Sea of Love) (1880). The principal characters—a geisha, her lover, and a villain — represented democratic theory, the Japanese people, and the government respectively. The villain wooed the geisha, but without success. In the end, the geisha and her lover were married, and the villain, having a change of heart, became a friend of the couple. The plot obviously expressed the pious hope of the author that the democratic movement would succeed.[27]

Most of the political novels appeared after 1882. One reason for its increased popularity after this date was the growing severity of government suppression. Political opinions disguised in the form of novels were less likely to incur official wrath than when stated baldly in political tracts. Another reason, according to some writers, was the influence of Victor Hugo. When Itagaki Taisuke took a trip to Europe in 1882, one of the things he did was to call on Victor Hugo. Itagaki sought the well known novelist's advice on how to stimulate the growth of democracy in a country like Japan. Hugo's reply was that the people should be encouraged to read political novels. When Itagaki inquired what kind of novels he would recommend, Hugo is said to have replied, " Anything of mine written during the past decade would be good." Following

[27] Homma Hisao, *Meiji Bungaku Shi* [History of Meiji Literature] which is volume 10 in the series, *Nihon Bungaku Zenshu* [Collected Works on Japanese Literature] (Tokyo, 1935), pp. 265-266.

Hugo's advice, Itagaki purchased a number of political novels and brought them back to Japan. Later he had some of them translated and published serially in newspapers. Others were abridged or reworked into Japanese novels and issued in book form.[28]

Novels of various nations were included among the translations appearing after 1880. English writers, for instance, were represented by the works of Bulwer-Lytton and Disraeli. There was, however, a noticeable preference for French and Russian novels. As an example of a French novel, the partial translation of *Memoire d'un Medean* by Alexander Dumas may be cited. It was first published in 1882, but was banned by the authorities a year later.[29]

The case of Russian novels is of special interest because there are indications that some of them influenced one or two of the local revolts which broke out in 1883 and 1884. Beginning in 1881 there were published a series of books dealing with Nihilism in Russia. Two of them, *Fujo Risshi Oshu Bidan* (Stories of Inspiring European Women) translated by Tanaka Shoji, and *Rokoku Kibun Retsujo no Gigoku* (The Arrest of an Unusual Russian Heroine) translated by Somata Sakutaro told of the exploits of Vera Zassulic, who attempted to assassinate General Trepov, the Prefect of St. Petersburg. Others were *Rokoku Kyomuto Jiji* (On the Russian Nihilist Party) translated by Nishikawa Tsutetsu, and *Kyomuto Taiji Kidan* (Unusual Accounts of the Suppression of the Nihilist Party) translated by Kawashima Tadanosuke from a little known French novel. These books together with portions of Stepniak's (S. M. Kravchinski), *Underground Russia* which dealt with Kropatkin, Sophia Perovskaia, Vera Zassulic, and V. Ossingsky, formed the basis of a novel by Miyazaki Muryu. First printed in the *Jiyuto* organ, *Eiri Jiyu Shimbun* (Illustrated Liberal Paper), this novel was later published secretly under the title *Kishushu* (The Devil's Cry). It is said that the author was imprisoned several months for publishing this novel.[30]

The Japanese also published original works during this period. A particularly famous novel was *Keikoku Bidan* (A Beautiful Story

[28] Suwa Jiro, " Yugo to Itagaki Haku Sono Ta " [Hugo and Count Itagaki and Others], *Denki* [Biography], July, 1935, p. 40.
[29] Homma, p. 194.
[30] Kimura Takeshi, " Kyomuto Jitsuden Ki—Kishushu Kaidai " [Bibliographical Notes on Kyomuto Jitsuden Ki—Kishushu], *MBZ*, XIII, 25-32.

of Statecraft) written by Yano Fumio, a prominent member of the *Kaishinto*. The novel featured the struggle of Thebes to throw off Spartan domination. The central figure, Epaminondas, became a popular hero in Japan, and many young men imitated his speeches as reported in this book.[31] Another popular novel was *Kajin no Kigyu* (A Chance Meeting of a Beautiful Lady) written by Shiba Shiro. This lengthy and melodramatic work was substantially a world history of the decline of nations and their oppression by their more powerful neighbors. The plot revolved around the adventures of the hero, a young Japanese who went to Philadelphia to study, and two young women whom he met in that city. One of these was a Spanish girl whose father was involved in a movement to make Spain into a constitutional monarchy. The other was an Irish girl. Her father had died in prison following his arrest. He had been working for Irish independence. The novel was painted on a board canvas, the action taking place in America, Egypt, Spain, and Korea.[32]

A noteworthy feature of these novels was the glorification of resistance to oppression. In those novels inspired by the activities of the Nihilists, the resistance of a small group to the oppressive measures of an autocratic government was portrayed. In other novels the authors sympathized with the small and weak nations which had been crushed by their stronger neighbors. Since these novels were published at a time when, in domestic politics, the democratic movement was feeling the heavy hand of the government, and, in foreign affairs, the efforts of the Japanese to get rid of the unequal treaties were coming to nought, we can say that even the works of fiction mirrored the political situation in Meiji Japan.

---

[31] Anesaki, *op. cit.*, p. 354.
[32] *Kajin no Kiyyu* is reprinted in *Meiji Kaikaki Bungaku Shu*, pp. 139-326.

CHAPTER XI

TWO THEORISTS: NAKAE AND UEKI

THE preceding discussion of intellectual currents dealt mainly with the development of those aspects of Meiji thought which appeared to have a significant bearing on the course of the democratic movement. For this reason the primary focus of interest was on general trends. The political philosophies of individual thinkers were treated only in so far as they illustrate the character and direction of these broad trends.

Such a treatment, however, runs the risk of distortion through oversimplification. Probably every important thinker could be fitted into a general scheme and given a convenient label; but in so doing the individual variations and revealing nuances of their thought would be lost. It is therefore useful, at times, to leave the realm of the general and probe into the particular. For such an approach may have the advantage of giving the subject matter a third dimension.

In this chapter the political thought of Nakae Chomin and Ueki Emori will be discussed. They have been chosen because they belonged to the wing of the *Jiyuto* which was most liberal in its outlook. In their thought, therefore, it should be possible to trace, to some extent, the intellectual origins of the movement, and to assess the strength of its liberalism.

I.

Nakae Tokusuke (pen name Chomin) was born in Tosa, the cradle of the democratic movement, in the year 1847.[1] His early education, like that of most children of samurai families, consisted of the study of Chinese classics. When he was 17 or 18, however, he began the study of Dutch, a change which was undoubtedly

---

[1] Biographical details on Nakae Chomin have been taken from Kaji Ryuichi, " Nakae Chomin," *Tembo* [View], October, 1946, pp. 58-71; Kojiro Tanesuke, " Heimin no Mezamashi Kaidai," [Bibliographical Notes on Heimin no Mezamashi], *MBZ*, VII, 39-40.

124

influenced by the opening of the country. At the age of 19, he was sent by his clan to Nagasaki, where he took up the study of another foreign language, French. He apparently made good progress for two years later he served as an interpreter for the French Minister, Leon Roches. After the Restoration, he taught French. About this time, too, he became interested in the problem of translating philosophical terms of foreign origin into Japanese. Some of the terms which he created still exist in the language. Because of his interest in the French language, he was most anxious to study in France, but unfortunately he lacked the means. Finally on the recommendation of his fellow-clansmen, Goto Shojiro and Itagaki Taisuke, he was sent as a government student in 1871. Ironically, he traveled to France with Iwakura, probably unaware that some day he and Iwakura would be on opposite sides of the political fence.

While in France, Nakae attended primary school in order to get a good grasp of the language. He also busied himself studying philosophy, history, and literature. Shortly after his return in 1874, he took a position in the *Genro-in* as a secretary, but soon resigned over differences with Mutsu Munemitsu, who later became foreign minister. This was followed by a brief spell as principal of a foreign language school. Later he established a school of his own and trained a total of about 2,000 students.

Besides education, Nakae was interested in literary activities. Betraying his early training in Chinese classics, he wrote in a ponderous and formidable style. It is only fair to say, however, that according to the standards of his day it was considered brilliant writing. In 1881, when the democratic movement was at its height, he started, with Saionji and several others, the *Toyo Jiyu Shimbun* (Oriental Liberal Paper). He also launched about the same time a magazine called *Kyorin Sodan*. The announced purpose of this magazine was to "translate theories regarding the political ethics of the great Powers of Europe and America, and to explain in a simple manner the true principles of liberty and rights of the state and individual."[2] In his journal, he published numerous translations and essays on Western political thought. His translation of J. J. Rousseau's *Social Contract* first appeared in this magazine. Probably because of this, and because of his

---

[2] Homma, *op. cit.*, p. 247.

interest in French thought, he became known as the " Rousseau of the Orient."

Through his writings and political activities he became well known as a liberal. When the government made the notorious Peace Preservation Law in 1887 in order to rid Tokyo of important figures who had opposed its policies, Nakae was affected. Driven from the capital, he sought refuge in Osaka. There he became associated with several newspapers. After the promulgation of the constitution, he reentered politics, and was elected a member of the House of Representatives from Osaka. But he later resigned his seat in protest over an appropriation bill. He resumed writing for newspapers, and also tried his hand at business enterprises, but without success. Towards the end of his life he became a supporter of Japanese imperialism and advocated war with Russia. He died in 1901.

The great bulk of Nakae's voluminous literary output consisted of short pieces on current politics, published in newspapers and magazines. Of his books, *Ichinen Yuhan* (One Year and a Half), written shortly before his death and edited and published posthumously by his disciple, Kotoku Shusui, is probably the best known.[3] Consisting of running commentaries on politics, political personalities, social questions, and philosophical problems, it is a good guide to his general outlook and his philosophy of life. But for an understanding of his political thought, an earlier work, *San Suijin Keirin Mondo* (Dialogues of Three Intoxicated Men on Politics) is more useful.[4]

As the title indicates, the essay is cast in the form of a dialogue in which three men, mellowed by generous amounts of wine, discuss current political problems. The major portion of the work is taken up by a heated debate between two protagonists: a European scientist and a Japanese militarist. The third individual, Nankai, who acts as the moderator, serves as the vehicle for Nakae's ideas.

The *San Suijin Keirin Mondo* is a fairly long work, and in the

---

[3] *Ichinen Yuhan* is reprinted in *Shakai Bungaku Shu* [Collection of Social Literature] which is volume 39 in the series, *Gendai Nihon Bungaku Zenshu*, pp. 3-32.

[4] The following discussion is based on *San Suijin Keirin Mondo* reprinted in a collection of his writings issued under the title, *Fude Nao Ari, Shita Nao Ari* [I Still Have My Pen and My Tongue] (Tokyo, 1922), pp. 1-97. (A more accessible source is the reprint in *MBZ,* VII).

course of the discussion, numerous subsidiary matters are treated; but its main arguments may be fairly easily summarized. The scientist opens the debate, and it is immediately evident that he is something of an idealist in politics. In his attitude toward both domestic affairs and foreign relations, he is far ahead of his times. But in his approach to these questions, he is of the nineteenth century. He is both a democrat and a pacifist because he believes in evolution. Everything, including political forms, is evolving towards a higher stage. In politics, the first stage of evolution is monarchy where a strong individual becomes the king. In time this type of government gives way to constitutional government. Under constitutional government the right of suffrage, the right of freedom of religion, the right to own private property, and similar rights are recognized. The third stage is democracy. Here we find combined liberty and equality. To the scientist, equality is most important, for he believes that without it liberty would have little meaning. A significant feature of democratic government is that it permits the full development of personality which can only grow in a free system. Democracy, moreover, is necessary for the achievement of universal peace. A believer in one world, the scientist advocates the abolition of armaments. He is even willing to say that although individuals may have the right of self-defense, nations do not.

To his opponent such views appear to border on the ludicrous. He believes that man, by nature, likes to win and hates to lose. He is also of the belief that there will always be wars. In fact war contributes to progress. Look at the civilized countries of the world, he says, and you will find that they are great Powers. Contemporary Europe is on the brink of war. France and Prussia are heading for a clash, while Great Britain and Russia have conflicting ambitions in Asia. This provides an opportunity for small nations like Japan. Taking advantage of war among the Powers, Japan should seize territory and become a large nation herself. While no country is mentioned my name, it is evident that China is to be the victim. " It is necessary," he says, " that we slice off a part of the territory of a big country and thereby become wealthy ourselves. Now, thanks to the benevolence of Heaven, there is a large and sprawling country right near us. Its soil is fertile; its armies are weak. What could be more fortunate? If

this huge country becomes strong and wealthy, it will be impossible
to seize a portion of it and make ourselves wealthy even if we
should wish to do so. . . . Why does not the small nation seize it
quickly? " [5]

In this debate, Nakae was quite obviously presenting, perhaps
in an exaggerated form, ideas then entertained by certain political
groups in the country. There were, for instance, in the extreme left
wing of the *Jiyuto* men like Oi Kentaro who wished to extend the
idea of democracy to economic matters. He approached the heart
of the agrarian problem and urged the equalization of landownership and a ban on the mortgaging of land.

On the other hand, among the militarists in the government,
plans were already maturing for aggression on the Asiatic continent.
Leaders like Iwakura, for example, were urging the creation of a
bigger army and navy, using as an excuse international rivalries in
Korea.[6] In this connection it is worth noting that even the newspapers which supported the democratic movement took a nationalistic stand with reference to foreign relations. They viewed the
world as being dominated, in the main, by the principle of the
" strong devouring the weak." [7] Democratic reforms, therefore,
were often advocated, not so much because of their intrinsic worth,
but rather because they would lead to greater national unity and
hence to enhanced national power. And it can be said, in passing,
that this tie between democracy and national power represented
a weakness in Japanese democratic theory.

[5] *Ibid.*, p. 61.
[6] See Ono Michio, *op. cit.*, p. 315.
[7] For example, the following quotation from the newspaper, *Azuma*, for June 21,
1879 reveals this attitude:
"Everyone knows that in our present-day world, it is impossible to associate
with others on the basis of morality. It should be noted that morality cannot
stand alone; it can become effective only where there is something supporting it.
That the possession of power and influence lies not in morality, but in that which
is behind it can be seen in Russian actions in Poland. The Russian hawk preying
on Poland does not depend merely on intellectual and financial power. If Russia
were deprived of her might, how could she partition Poland like a wolf attacking
sheep? Coming closer to home, look at the situation in Japan during the Kaei
period [1848-1853]. If we had possessed the power to defend ourselves, we should
never have been held in contempt by the nations of Europe and America." Quoted
in Oka Yoshitake, " Meiji Shoki no Jiyu Minken Ronja no Me ni Eijitaru Toji no
Kokusai Josei " [The International Situation as Was Viewed by Those in the
Democratic Movement in the Early Years of the Meiji Era] in *Seiji Oyobi Seiji Shi
Kenkyn* [Studies in Politics and Political History] edited by Royama Masamichi
and published in honor of the late Yoshino Sakuzo (Tokyo, 1935), p. 477.

Nakae's own position was somewhere in between the extremes represented by the scientist and the militarist. He felt that the former was much too idealistic, while the latter subscribed to views which were no longer applicable. The egalitarian principle expressed by the European, Nakae found distasteful. By way of refutation, he advanced his pet theory of the two types of democracy. In England and France democracy was attained by means of pressure from below. In this type of historical process the people could determine the amount of democracy they were to have. The other type was where democracy was conferred from above. With this kind of democracy, the people cannot set the amount. Curiously Nakae was of the opinion that whether democracy was attained from below or granted from above, there was no difference in its characteristics. To him there was only a difference of degree. With respect to foreign affairs, Nakae rejected militarism. So long as there was a balance of power in Europe, he felt that there was no need to worry about national defense. Besides, he said that Asia was capable of defending itself against foreign aggression. Lastly, he was opposed to the conquest of China. The following passage in which he states his views on future policy summarizes his position.

There should be established constitutional government which would enhance the glory of the Throne above, and promote the well-being of the people. There should also be created a bicameral assembly with the upper house consisting of hereditary nobles, and the lower house chosen by election. The detailed provisions should be taken from European constitutions presently in effect. . . . With reference to diplomacy, make peace the aim, and aside from requirements for national safety, do not expand power and build up the armed forces. Freedom of speech and publication should be gradually made more liberal, and education and industry should be gradually expanded." [8]

II.

In justification for exhuming certain forgotten writers of the American south, Vernon Parrington once said that time was not a just winnowner, but was partial to success, and that lost causes had a way of " shrinking in importance in the memory of later generations." [9] Much the same thing could be said of men who

[8] *Fude Nao Ari, Shita Nao Ari*, p. 96.
[9] Vernon L. Parrington, *Main Currents in American Thought* (New York, 1927-1930), II. i.

supported the democratic movement in Japan. Deliberately belittled by official historiography, they have been by and large relegated to obscurity for having opposed the government and emerged the loser.

In this category may be placed Ueki Emori. Unlike Nakae Chomin, who has acquired a niche in Japanese thought, Ueki is unknown except among specialists in Japanese constitutional history. So far as is known he has never been the subject of a full length biography. Nor has his *zenshu* or " complete works " ever been issued. His name will elicit no sign of recognition from school boys, for he appears nowhere in the textbooks.

Yet to those who have devoted some attention to the history of Meiji political thought, he appears as a man of considerable stature. His name flits in and out of Meiji history, for he was an active participant in politics, writing polemical articles, speaking to mass meetings, and organizing political societies. A list of books on liberal thought in the Meiji era would include at least eight titles by him.[10] Nor would these account for all of his literary output. He was not only a frequent contributor to newspapers, but also drafted or wrote, it is suspected, many of Itagaki's speeches and articles. He was Itagaki's " brain trust " or as the Japanese historians put it, his " wisdom bag." [11]

Ueki was born in Tosa in 1857.[12] His father, a samurai of moderate circumstances, was a private secretary to the chief of the Tosa clan. He has related in his autobiography that he was a very independent child. At the age of eleven he began to study Chinese classics. Later he was sent to a school maintained by the Tosa clan in Tokyo, but withdrew when he learned that the policy of the school was to train soldiers. He then went to live with Itagaki, who was much impressed by his ability. He turned his attention

---

[10] *Kaimei Shinron* [New Theory of Enlightenment] (1878), *Minken Jiyu Ron* [On People's Rights and Liberty] (1879), Horitsu Ippan [On Laws] (1879), *Genron Jiyu Ron* [On Freedom of Expression] (1880), *Tempu Jinken Ben* [In Defense of Natural Rights] (1883), *Ikkyoku Gi-in Ron* [An Essay on Unicameral Assemblies] (1884), *Kokkai no Jumbi* [Preparation for a National Assembly] (1886), *Kokkai Soshiki: Kokumin Dai Kaigi* [The Organization of the National Assembly: People's Convention] (1888).

[11] Yoshino Sakuzo in *MBZ*, V, 27.

[12] For biographical data see, Hayashi, " Ueki Emori no Kempo Shian to Iwayuru Risshisha An no Kiso," *op. cit.*; Kawahara Jikichiro, " Tempu Jinken Kaidai " [Bibliographical Notes on Tempu Jinken], *MBZ*, V, 59-60.

to the study of politics, and became convinced that it was necessary to work for the creation of a representative assembly.

Later Ueki took up one of the favorite professions for intellectuals — journalism. In 1876 he ran afoul of the law when he published an article entitled, " A Government that Makes Monkeys of Men " (Hito o Saru ni Suru Seifu). The following year he started a newspaper and a magazine with Itagaki and other members of the *Risshisha*. He also went on a lecture tour, and later organized in Osaka the *Kokkai Gambo Kai* (Society Desiring a National Assembly). By this time he was drawn into the vortex of the democratic movement. As we have already seen, in 1881 he organized the national conference of sake brewers, and he was also instrumental in organizing the *Jiyuto*.

Meanwhile, he contributed to a number of newspapers and periodicals and published, in addition, a series of books. He was also at one time or another the editor of several local newspapers. When the first Diet met in 1890 he was elected to the House of Representatives from Kochi prefecture. He died from illness in 1892 at the age of thirty-five, bringing to an untimely end an active career in journalism and politics.

An analysis of Ueki's writings brings out several interesting features of Meiji political thought. Despite his familiarity with Western political principles, he still remained something of a product of his times. Having come from a samurai family, and having been closely associated with samurai, he still retained the notion that the samurai, being, in his mind, superior to the plebeians in intelligence, knowledge, and political experience, should constitute a political elite. The difficulty, however, was that the Restoration settlement had destroyed the economic basis of the samurai class. Hence economically the samurai were often worse off than the commoners. This explains, in part, why Ueki espoused the cause of the majority. He was opposed to property qualifications for voting and for eligibility to office because, he said quite frankly, it would disqualify most of the samurai.

Much of Ueki's writings was concerned with the constitution and the form of government since that was the focus of the dispute between the government and the political opposition. He began with the assumption that the people formed the basis of the state because a state cannot exist without people. For the state to be vigorous, therefore, the people must be energetic. The ancients were mistaken when they thought that if the people were obedient, the state was well ruled.[13] It is necessary, however, that the people be self-reliant and free if they are to be energetic.[14] In Ueki's mind, the people were the stuff from which states were made, and the constitution its framework, or to use his analogy, the people were the materials that go into a house, the constitution the way in which it was built. He felt that a written constitution would provide peace and security, and prevent disorder by providing for emergencies. When Lincoln was assassinated there was no disorder because of the provisions of the constitution.[15]

Ueki revealed good political insight in his insistence that the constitution be discussed and drafted in a constitutional convention.[16] We can easily guess what his reaction was to the Meiji constitution which was drafted secretly and granted by the Emperor as a " gift " to the people.

Ueki envisaged a constitutional monarchy for Japan, with the state organized on a federal basis. His preference for such a scheme probably reflected to some extent the conflict between local interests and the growth of the central government. Involved also were patronage considerations, for local autonomy always provides more officers for local inhabitants.

According to Ueki's draft of a proposed constitution, the federal government was given certain powers. It could make laws governing relations between states; it could declare war and make peace, and conclude agreements with foreign countries. It had the exclusive power to levy customs duties and internal tariffs; it could control the postal service and make laws regulating the possession of arms. It could not, on the other hand, interfere in the internal affairs of the states, change boundaries without the permission of the states, or prevent new states from joining in the union.[17]

The legislative power was to be vested in an unicameral legislature. He apparently felt very strongly on this point because he wrote a book to defend his views against advocates of bicameralism. He argued that bicameral legislatures were feudal survivals and

---

[13] *Minken Jiyu Ron* (hereafter cited as *MJR*), *MBZ*, V, 188.
[14] *Ibid.*, p. 192.
[15] *Ibid.*, pp. 190, 192.
[16] Hayashi, *op. cit.*, p. 1272.
[17] Hayashi, *op. cit.*, pp. 1270-1273.

not necessarily grounded in reason. It was his conviction that unicameral legislatures would be more responsive to the popular will.
He rejected the suggestion that the lower house be elected directly
and that the upper house be chosen by the prefectural assemblies
for the reason that the level of civilization was still low. The
meaning of constitutional government, Ueki maintained, is to
promote justice for all the people. But to obtain this, it is essential
that representatives whose interests are similar to those of the
people be obtained. An upper house representing an aristocratic
minority could not maintain justice. And as for the contention that
the level of civilization in Japan was low, Ueki's answer was that
this condition could be remedied by ensuring freedom of speech,
publication, and assembly, thus enabling the people to cultivate
characteristics suitable for constitutional government.[18]

The legislators sent to the unicameral assembly were to be elected
from electoral districts, but the voters were to be given the
privilege of voting for men outside their districts if it was felt that
they would make better legislators. Ueki defended this peculiar
system by asserting that since constitutional government implied
self-government, he was opposed to putting restrictions on voters.[19]
Since he did not give details as to voting procedure, it is impossible
to tell whether he had proportional representation in mind; but in
any case the scheme would appear to be unworkable because it
would violate the idea of a legislator representing a certain territory.

The term of office for legislators was to be two years. This was
because the Japanese electorate was still politically inexperienced.
The entire legislature, moreover, was to come up for re-election
every two years, making it more representative.[20] Ueki proposed
to pay the lawmakers the relatively large sum of three thousand
yen plus travelling expenses. He rejected the proposal that legislators should serve without pay. He claimed that those with
knowledge and ideas about national affairs were numerous among
the samurai and therefore they would probably receive many votes.
And since they were poor, they should be paid.[21] Here again we
see patronage considerations at work. The creation of an elected

---

[18] *Ikkyoku Gi-in Ron*, reprinted in *MBZ*, VII, 282-312.
[19] *Kokkai Soshiki: Kokumin Dai Kaigi*, reprinted in *MBZ*, VII, 442-445. This is
an account of an imaginary constitutional convention which met before 1880.
[20] *Ibid.*, p. 451.
[21] *Ibid.*, pp. 447-449.

legislature would have provided nearly five hundred positions, many of which undoubtedly would have gone to needy samurai.

Everyone paying taxes, except minors, convicts and priests, was to be given the right to vote. In England, said Ueki, the landed and moneyed interests created property qualifications; but this would not provide happiness for the greatest number, since the lower classes are the most numerous. Besides, said Ueki, the people are liable for military service and taxes irrespective of the property they own. The lack of property does not necessarily make people less patriotic; in fact people with property desire a static order, while the propertyless will strive to serve the state. The capstone of his argument, however, was that the property limitations would exclude samurai, who are the most qualified for participation in politics.[22]

Ueki proposed that voting be carried out by means of signed ballots. It was conceded that this might encourage coercion of the voters by moneyed interests, landlords, and money lenders. On the other hand, he held, as did John Stuart Mill, that voting was a solemn obligation. In a nation like Japan where the people had little political experience, this requirement would make the voters more prudent.[23]

According to his proposed constitution, when the ruler disagreed with the decisions of the legislature, he was empowered to order its dissolution. But he was under obligation to call for a new election within thirty days. If he failed to do so, the people could take the initiative and elect representatives and form a legislature. The ruler also had the power in times of emergency to call for troops in addition to the standing army. The ruler, however, had no power in matters affecting the rights of the people, the disbursement of funds, and changes in state territory.[24]

Another field to which Ueki devoted attention was that of civil rights. To Ueki nature, or more specifically Heaven, was the source of human liberty. Quoting with approval Rousseau's famous dictum that man is born free, he remarked that liberty is a gift of Heaven and that failure to take this gift is to commit a crime against Heaven and to bring shame upon oneself. Heaven, moreover, gave man the faculty to work, but he cannot work without

[22] *Ibid.*, pp. 437-441.
[23] *Ibid.*, pp. 445-447.
[24] Hayashi, *op. cit.*, pp. 1277, 1280, 1281, 1273.

liberty, for that is " like putting a bird in a cage." [25] Man also desires happiness and it is his natural right to secure it.[26] Without liberty there can be no happiness or peace. In fact wars have been fought for liberty, and if one cannot secure it, it would be better to die.[27] Ueki however said, like the Utilitarians, that people have the right to liberty so long as they do not violate the equal rights of others.[28]

His insistence on the limitation of the power of government may be regarded as an extension of his theory of natural rights. Since natural rights come from Heaven, they take precedence over the state and its laws. The state, therefore, cannot make and enforce laws which would destroy the liberty and rights of the people, nor can it interfere in the private affairs of the people.[29] Besides, having been created by Heaven, all men are equal, the rulers being just as human as the people.[30]

Ueki was much disturbed by the apathy of the Japanese towards political questions. Since ancient times, the Japanese have thought only of themselves and their families, he complained. Some have even maintained that ignorance is bliss; but that is not the way to achieve true peace and happiness. Unwilling to leave all matters up to Heaven, Ueki urged the people to demand and also to defend their rights. He saw that laws were influenced by the customs and temperament of the people and held that if the people desire liberty, suitable laws will be enacted. As if to bring the argument close to home, he pointed out that even if the peasants harvested a big crop, it would do them no good if there were a " brutal " government which taxed them heavily. Also if there are military disturbances, and the government issues currency, it is no different from being taxed. Under such circumstances, how can one be silent? " Silence is the source of misfortune." [31]

Ueki also appealed to nationalism. He likened the people to links in a chain which is no stronger than its weakest link. A country is strong when the people are free, have rights, and are self-reliant. The English defeated the Spanish armada because they were free. Without popular rights, national independence can-

---

[25] *MJR*, p. 186.
[26] *Tempu Jinken Ben*, reprinted in *MBZ*, V, 467. (Hereafter this work will be cited as *TJB*).
[27] *MJR*, pp. 186-187.
[28] *TJB*, p. 469.
[29] Hayashi, *op. cit.*, p. 1270.
[30] *MJR*, p. 187.
[31] *Ibid.*, pp. 184-185.

not be maintained, for the ruling group might sell out the country. Because a free people are united, the government of a free people would be in a position to negotiate successfully with foreign nations. If the foreigners saw that a country had an autocratic government, they would make excessive demands, knowing that the country did not have much power.[32] Here he was undoubtedly referring to the negotiations being conducted by the Japanese government to get rid of the unequal treaties.

A whole pamphlet was devoted to the defense of the freedom of speech and thought. Ueki sought the source of freedom of speech, as of other rights in nature. His arguments, however, were somewhat far-fetched. Men have tongues, teeth, cheeks; so, he said, they have the natural liberty to give vocal expression to their ideas.[33] It is, moreover, the will of Heaven that men live. Therefore men are justified in defending themselves against anything that impedes living, including the infringement of the right of free speech and thought.[34]

There were other reasons, for Ueki, besides natural rights for maintaining freedom of speech. What makes a state a state is that the people have a unified feeling towards that state. This is produced by the freedom of speech. By this means, the people let their desires be known. This in turn contributes to unity. In answer to Ueki's arguments, it might be noted that this "unified feeling" could conceivably be produced just as easily by suppressing free speech.

Ueki denied that government officials had any right to control speech because their intelligence is "shallow" and their knowledge "limited." On the contrary, to check the actions of officials, free speech is necessary. "The people must be informed of and also check the actions of officials regarding public affairs. Otherwise the ultimate violation of the people's freedom and rights cannot be avoided." He added that "To criticise freely the merits of legislation is necessary for the well being of the people." [35]

In a section very reminiscent of John Stuart Mill's classic defense of free speech, Ueki refuted the contention that uncontrolled speech would lead to prejudiced opinions and heretical views. It

---

[32] *Ibid.,* pp. 191-193.

[33] *Genron Jiyu Ron*, reprinted in Suzuki Yasuzo, *Nihon Kensei Seiritsu Shi* [History of the Establishment of Japanese Constitutional Government] (Tokyo, 1933), p. 359.

[34] *TJB*, p. 567.   [35] *Genron Jiyu Ron, op. cit.,* p. 360.

is through discussion that incorrect views can be corrected. Furthermore, how is one going to determine what is just? Like Mill, Ueki defended the right of one man to stand alone. Lastly, he made what would appear to be an untenable distinction between speech and action. In his view, unlawful action may be punished, but speech must be left free.[36]

Obviously Ueki's political thought is open to various criticisms. There are noticeable gaps in his blueprint for government. It is not clear, to cite an example, whether the Emperor is to " rule " or " reign." Was he to have the power to dissolve the legislature as stated in the constitution, or was that to be done only on the advice of ministers of state? Was there to be a cabinet, and if so, what was its relation to the legislature? Ueki, moreover, seems to have been completely unaware of the rôle of political parties in representative government. Also he did not make provision for the representation of states in the federal government, nor did he provide means for settling disputes that might arise between states. Furthermore, contradictory elements are evident in his thought. He was often an advocate of natural rights, but he also appealed at times to ultilitarian doctrines. In fairness to Ueki, however, it should be remembered that many Utilitarians were at times guilty of slipping natural rights into their system of thought.

These and other criticisms should not blind us to the fact that he made positive contributions to the struggle for democracy in Japan. It should be evident from the brief summary of his writings in the foregoing pages that Ueki had a precocious understanding of the political process. He saw clearly what political reforms would be necessary if Japan were to become a democracy. He revealed his dislike for the autocratic Meiji government in no uncertain terms, writing and working against it when it was not always safe to do so. He probably made as spirited a defense of democratic government as has ever been made in Japan. Taking a considerable body of Western political thought, he clothed it partly in Japanese dress and made it available to his contemporaries. In so doing, he helped to provide the democratic movement with a critique of the existing order and a blueprint of the new. Now that the ideas he espoused are no longer anathema in Japan, it is quite possible that he will be rescued from oblivion in the near future and given his rightful place in Meiji political history.

[36] *Ibid.*, pp. 359-364.

Chapter XII

DEFLATION AND DEPRESSION

THE autumn of 1881 marked a divide in the history of the democratic movement. Prior to this time, the chief objective of the movement had been to secure a popularly-elected legislative assembly. With the Imperial decree of 1881 promising the establishment of a parliament by the year 1890, this phrase came to an end.

The succeeding phase was characterized by the emergence of political parties and by greater interest in the problems relating to the organization of government. As was evident in the previous chapter, men like Ueki Emori were convinced that the promise to call a parliament did not necessarily guarantee the creation of true parliamentary government. They saw that there still remained a number of important questions, the answers to which would have a vital bearing on the character of the government that would be established under the new constitution. Indeed the period between 1881 and 1890 was an important one, for only continued popular pressure would have produced a constitutional structure providing institutional checks on the Meiji bureaucracy.

In 1881 it appeared that there existed in the *Jiyuto* a reasonably effective instrument for exerting such pressure. The *Jiyuto*, which inherited the political experience acquired by the earlier societies, was born at a propitious moment when the democratic movement had reached a high mark. In a short time it became a national party enjoying widespread support, and there seemed to be no reason why it could not grow into a powerful political party.

And it might have if its economic environment had been more favorable. It was its misfortune that the years between 1882 and 1885 were depression years. As farm incomes dropped there appeared cleavages within the *Jiyuto* which the party organization could not successfully bridge. In the end these cleavages weakened the *Jiyuto*, thus contributing to its dissolution in 1884.

I.

Since the internal dissension may be traced to the economic depression which gripped the country from 1882 to 1885, it is necessary to begin the discussion with the currency deflation of 1881 which started the economy on its downward spiral.

The currency inflation and the attendant prosperity following the Satsuma Rebellion of 1877 reached the high-water mark in the year 1881. During the intervening years there was a marked upswing in the business cycle. Many small commercial and industrial enterprises were launched. Thanks to the sustained rise in the price of rice, the income of the rural landowning classes was increased appreciably. The wage worker and tenant farmer, on the other hand, suffered a reduction in real income, owing to the prevalence of high prices. Nevertheless, the signs of prosperity were everywhere present.

But in certain quarters this state of affairs was looked upon with some misgivings. Large industrialists preferred " sound money." So did the government, which found that inflationary prices meant in effect a reduction in government revenues. This in turn hampered the policy of expanding armaments and of encouraging industrialization through the liberal use of subsidies. Land values followed the upward trend of rice and commodity prices. This encouraged speculation in real estate. With interest rates remaining high, the price of bonds, many of which were held by the members of the nobility, was further depressed.[1] Lastly, continued prosperity stimulated imports since more people were able to afford higher priced goods.[2] This resulted in an unfavorable balance of trade, and an outflow of specie.

It is against this background that the new fiscal policy set by Matsukata Masayoshi, the Minister of Finance, must be viewed.

---

[1] The following table shows the drop in the price of bonds:

Year	Pension bonds	7% *Kinroku* bonds	Industrial bonds
1878	¥ 101.58	¥ 83.50	¥ 79.70
1879	97.82	81.30	78.19
1880	92.00	71.85	73.50
1881	85.00	69.50	60.00

Yagizawa, *op. cit.*, p. 61.

[2] Godai Tomoatsu, a well known Osaka merchant, said: " In view of the gradual increase in the amount of imports, we can say that sooner or later there will come a day when foreign goods will spread widely into the rural areas." Quoted in Ono Takeo, *Noson Shi*, p. 153.

In September, 1881 he presented a memorial to the *Dajokan* in which he said:

Finance is to a state what blood circulation is to a human being. Without the circulation of blood, death follows; without finance in good order, the decline of the state must follow. How can we expect peace and happiness? Therefore, the pressing need today is to achieve the redemption of paper money by setting up a plan for currency operations and accumulating specie, and for controlling imports by increasing production.[3]

In order to achieve this end, he proposed the recall of paper money and the creation of a central bank. He realized, however, that a depression would follow, making his deflationary policy most unpopular. Accordingly, he first fortified his position by obtaining Imperial approval. Then he proceeded to deflate the currency.[4] The upswing in the business cycle which had begun in 1877 came to an end. " Just as the state," says one authority, " was a potent factor in initiating the expansion, it also proved itself to be capable of reversing this movement. With autocratic vigor and unflinching faith in the outcome, Matsukata embarked on a deflationary policy as he assumed the office of Finance Minister in October, 1881." [5]

Between the years 1881 and 1885 Matsukata froze government expenditures at existing levels, and using the surplus, he retired notes and purchased specie from abroad. The total amount involved was a little more than 40 million *yen*. The following table gives further details.

TABLE I

RETIREMENT OF PAPER NOTES

Year	Direct Retirement	Transferred to Reserve Fund	Total
1881	¥ 7,000,000	¥ 3,832,521	¥ 10,832,521
1882	3,300,000	5,227,760	8,527,760
1883	3,340,000	5,000,000	8,340,000
1884		7,006,545	7,006,545
1885		5,400,000	5,400,000

Source: Yagizawa Zenji, " Meiji Shoki no Defureshion to Nogyo Kyoko " [Deflation in the Early Meiji Era and the Agricultural Panic], *SKS*, II (June, 1932), 258-259.

---

[3] Quoted in *ibid.*, p. 157.

[4] *Ibid.*, pp. 157-158.

[5] Shigeto Tsuru, " Economic Fluctuations in Japan, 1868-1893," *The Review of Economic Statistics*, XXIII (1941), 180.

It is apparent that the circulation of bank notes and government notes decreased sharply during these years. The bank notes declined from a little more than 34 million *yen* in 1882 to 30 million *yen* in 1885. The reduction of government notes was even more marked, dropping from more than 109 million *yen* in 1882 to 67 million *yen* in 1886.[6]

As one would expect, this currency deflation was accompanied by a sharp break in the price structure. Prices quickly receded from the high levels attained in 1881. The extent to which prices dropped can be seen in the following graph.

FLUCTUATIONS IN RICE AND COMMODITY PRICES

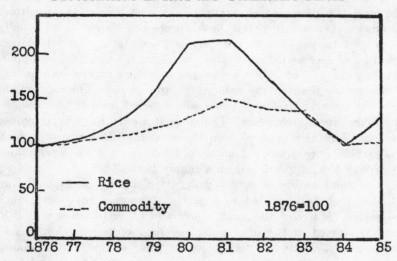

Source: Based on data in Yagizawa, " Meiji Shoki no Defureshion to Nogyo Kyoko, " SKS, II, 264-265.

While everywhere prices, and with them personal incomes, were tumbling, taxes moved in the opposite direction. Both through the imposition of new taxes and the upward revision of rates, the tax burden was increased. A stamp tax and a tax on patent medicines were created in October, 1882. In December, increased tax rates on *sake* brewing, tobacco, soy sauce, stock exchanges,

[6] Yagizawa, "Meiji Shoki no Defureshion to Nogyo Kyoko," *SKS*, II (1932), 261, 263.

brokers, and corporations were announced. Additional taxes on soy sauce, and a tax on confectionary followed in 1885. Perhaps even more important, certain expenditures were transferred from the central government to the local governments. The maintenance of local prisons became the responsibility of local governments. Subsidies for public works heretofore provided from the central treasury also were withdrawn.[7] This necessitated increases in local taxes and other charges. The amount of money collected for local purposes rose from a little less than 24 million *yen* in 1879 to more than 35 million *yen* in 1882, gradually dropping thereafter to 28 million *yen* in 1885.[8]

For the poorer families in the rural communities, the increase in local taxes became especially burdensome. Since the wealthier landowners controlled the prefectural assemblies, they usually managed to pass on to the poorer peasants a relatively larger portion of increased taxes. This was done, for example, by apportioning the cost of public works and irrigation control on a family basis rather than on the amount of land owned. Thus a contemporary observer wrote: " Those who suffered from the breakdown of dikes were landowners. Therefore it would have been proper to pay [for their upkeep] from the land tax. But since the local assemblies were composed mostly of landowners, it was finally done this way [i. e., apportioned on a family basis]." [9]

The combination of currency deflation, falling prices, and continued high taxation led to a serious economic crisis and much suffering. Many of the small stores and other business establishments started in the brief period of prosperity were forced into bankruptcy. With the decline in the price of rice, farm incomes took a sharp drop. Since the land tax remained fixed and local taxes rose, the margin between income and outlay often disappeared. Table II comparing the income from land in certain districts between 1880 and 1884 shows clearly the plight of the cultivator.

[7] Ono Takeo, *op. cit.*, pp. 159-160.

[8] *Ibid.*, p. 161.

[9] *Taguchi Ukichi Zenshu* [Collected Works of Taguchi Ukichi], VI, 451 as quoted in Toda Shintaro, *Nihon Shihonshugi to Nihon Nogyo no Hatten* [Japanese Capitalism and the Development of Japanese Agriculture] (Tokyo, 1947), p. 65.

TABLE II

FARM INCOME IN 1880 AND 1884 IN SELECTED AREAS

Area	Year	Income from .245 acres	Expenses, fertilizer	Land tax	Local tax	Profit
Aichi	1880	¥ 24.15	¥ 6.00	¥ 2.25	¥ 1.08	¥ 14.81
	1884	9.98	4.00	2.25	1.35	2.28
Gumma	1880	33.30	8.73	2.00	1.35	21.27
	1884	15.00	8.33	2.00	2.02	2.66
Chiba	1880	17.08	8.38	0.90	0.27	7.54
Ibaraki	1884	6.22	3.13	0.90	0.65	1.54
Shizuoka	1880	16.96	7.30	1.60	0.71	7.35
	1884	4.93	5.90	1.60	0.97	3.55*
Shiga	1880	18.90	11.00	1.42	0.61	5.85
	1884	7.20	5.55	1.42	0.71	0.44*
Tottori	1880	16.48	8.00	1.74	0.47	6.27
	1884	6.65	5.50	1.74	0.75	1.34*
* Loss						

Source: Adapted from table in Ono Takeo, *Noson Shi*, p. 118.

To make matters worse, the already heavily burdened peasants were harassed by a series of natural calamities which in some extreme cases destroyed the entire crop. In 1881 floods and insects did damage in several localities. The following year rain storms, hail storms, and floods affected almost the entire country. Floods struck again in 1883, and in 1884 severe rain storms raged throughout the land.[10] The effect which poor harvests had on the peasants is described in the following account.

When I stepped out of the house, the entire village presented a desolate spectacle. The faces of the peasants grew increasingly pale everyday. Poor harvests extending over several years had reduced their reserves, and they could not even have their three meals of rice cooked with potatoes. Moreover, the time to pay their land tax approached; the time to pay their rent drew near. Money lenders foreclosed mortgages on land without hesitation, and took away their horses. I still remember the time several tens of tenant formers crowded into our house to complain about their difficulties. They begged my mother to reduce the crop rent. There were some among them who had been drinking, and they used violent language.[11]

As is apparent in the above quotation, the average peasant, caught between the economic depression and poor harvests, found

[10] Ono Takeo, *op. cit.*, pp. 281-285.
[11] Miyazaki Torazo, *Sanju Sannen no Yume* [The Thirty-three Year Dream] (Tokyo, 1902), p. 27.

himself hard put to meet his financial obligations. Between January 1, 1881 and February 21, 1886 more than a quarter of a million peasants obtained loans from an emergency fund created by contributions from the government and assessments on landowners. In spite of such aid, between 1883 and 1890, about three hundred and sixty thousand peasant proprietors were dispossessed for failure to pay taxes.[12] The tragic part of this process was the incredibly small amount of money that was actually owed. If the figures presented by one authority are correct, the total amount in arrears was 114,178 *yen*, or an average of only 0.31 *yen* per person; but the total value of the land sold or confiscated by the government came to almost five million *yen*, or roughly 27 times the amount in arrears.[13] Additional statistics on the dispossession of the peasantry during the years 1883 to 1885 are given in the following table.

TABLE III

DISPOSSESSION OF THE PEASANTRY, 1883-1885

Year	No. of persons dispossessed	Amt. of tax owed	Av. per person	Area of land sold	Value of land sold	Price of public sale
1883	33,845	¥ 25,889	¥ 0.76	4,531 *cho*	¥ 905,645	¥ 267,187
1884	70,605	30,533	0.43	8,319 "	1,260,606	545,519
1885	108,055	26,423	0.24	8,933 "	2,664,879	244,192

Source. Ono Michio, *Kinsei Noson Keizai Shiron*, pp. 397-398; Watanabe Shinichi, *Nihon Noson Jinko Ron*, p. 34.

If such a large number of agricultural producers lost their holdings through inability to pay their taxes, we can be almost sure that a yet larger number were dispossessed through mortgage foreclosure. For understandable reasons, Japanese peasants are strongly attached to their land. They feel sentimental ties to their holdings which had been cultivated by their ancestors for generations. Perhaps equally important is the fact that once they lose their land, they will inevitably become tenant farmers, or agricultural workers who have neither security nor status. Or if they chose to migrate to the cities, they would have to take up degrading occupations such as pulling rickshas. The average peasant, there-

[12] Ono Michio, *op. cit.*, pp. 332-336.
[13] Mayet's figures cited by Norman, *Emergence*, p. 144.

fore, will resort to every possible means, including recourse to loans at usurious rates, to retain his land. Although no accurate statistics are available, Paul Mayet, the German agricultural adviser to the Japanese government, has estimated that in the three-year period between 1884 and 1886, land worth 203,300,000 *yen* was foreclosed, and that mortgages on land came to 165,800,000 *yen*.[14]

The reverse of this peasant dispossession was the concentration of land in the hands of the landlord class and money lenders. Undoubtedly many of the small landlords suffered losses during this period. On the other hand, those with extra capital were in a position to acquire land at bargain prices.

The case history of the well known Saito family provides a good illustration. In recent times, this family owned about 1,500 *cho* (3,675 acres) of land, making it one of the largest landowning families in northern Japan. Several centuries ago, this family owned and cultivated 10 to 18 *cho* of land. In addition to farming, it engaged in brewing, and also acted as pawn brokers and money lenders. About 1879, the ninth generation Saito gave up farming and decided to rent all of his holdings to tenant farmers. Then in 1882 he ceased being a pawn broker because the amounts involved were too small. Seven years later he gave up *sake* brewing to concentrate on money lending, taking land as security. His money lending operations extended into several counties. In 1890 he was able to add 660 *cho* of land to the 450 *cho* he already owned.[15] It was said that "once his evil hand touched middle peasants and landlords, they went bankrupt." [16]

Other statistics also reveal the trend towards the concentration of landownership. According to one source, the percentage of tenant land to the total cultivated area was 31.1 percent in 1873, but increased to 36.75 percent in 1883, and to 39.34 percent in 1887.[17] Corroborative evidence pointing to the economic decline of the smaller landholders may be found in the decrease in the number of persons qualified to vote and eligible for election to prefectural assemblies. In 1881 there were 1,809,610 persons eligible to vote because they paid taxes of five *yen* or more; but in 1887 this

[14] Ono Michio, *op. cit.*, p. 398.
[15] Ono Takeo, *op. cit.*, p. 58.
[16] Toda, *op. cit.*, p. 67.
[17] Inaoka Susumu, *Nomin no Jotai Oyobi Nomin Undo Shoshi* [A Short History of the Condition of the Peasantry and Agricultural Movements], in *NSHSK*, p. 8.

number had been reduced to 1,488,107, representing a loss of 321,503 persons (or 18 percent) in five years. Similarly, in 1881 persons paying more than 10 *yen* in taxes came to 879,347; but in 1887 this number dropped to 802,975 (or a loss of 9 percent).[18] Lastly, statistics on the number of landlords in Niigata prefecture owning land valued at ten thousand *yen* or more show an increase from 341 to 393 in one year between 1884 and 1885.[19]

II.

So far the effects of the depression have been described in terms of impersonal statistics. But when we turn to contemporary accounts, both official and newspaper, we can get a much more graphic picture of the suffering of the peasants who were caught in the depression.

In 1885 the Ministry of Home Affairs dispatched officials to various districts, especially in the northern areas, to investigate conditions then prevailing in the countryside. The report sub-mitted by these officials on the situation in Aomori prefecture reveals that the peasants were hit by the poor harvest during the preceding year as well as by the sharp drop in the price of horses, now selling for less than four *yen* a head in contrast to forty *yen* in 1881. Many of the poor were sleeping on straw since they possessed no blankets. " Generally speaking," continued the report, " seven or eight out of ten people are living almost like horses and cattle." [20] Naturally under such conditions, most of the peasants were unable to pay their taxes; but some, when threatened with dispossession, mortgaged their holdings, while others sold out at a sacrifice.

Although conditions in Akita prefecture were in general not so bad, certain mountainous areas were hard hit. " In all the areas we have inspected," says the report on Akita, " there has been an increase in robbery recently. Moreover, the fact that most of the goods stolen consist of food is one proof that there has been an increase in the number of poor who are short of food." The official goes on to report that he saw many beggars and that farm laborers were more than willing to work for nothing more than three meals a

[18] Based on Hirano's figures as cited in Norman, *op. cit.*, pp. 146-147.
[19] From the table in Ono, *op. cit.*, pp. 67-68.
[20] *Ibid.*, p. 171.

day. Nevertheless, tax collection was not reduced appreciably, indicating the probability that many of the peasants had mortgaged their holdings to secure funds for the payment of taxes.[21]

In Ishikawa prefecture beggars were found almost everywhere, and by the spring of 1885, the police were unable to cope with them. From the report on Kanagawa prefecture, we learn that when kitchens were set up to serve rice gruel to the poor, countless numbers gathered before the doors were opened at 3 p. m. and that there were many quarrels over who should be first in line.[22]

Newspaper accounts of this period run in a similar vein. In Fukuoka prefecture, for example, some of the poor were eating bark. Bark stripped from pine trees was soaked in running water and dried; it was then pounded and mixed with flour. This mixture was dropped into boiling water and made into dumplings.[23] In Naka *gun* (county) in Wakayama prefecture, more than ten thousand people out of a population of eighty thousand barely survived by eating a little rice gruel, and there were more than three thousand on the verge of starvation. Philanthropists in the various villages contributed grain and money.[24] In Kaga, eight hundred persons asked to be imprisoned rather than starve and suffer in the cold.[25]

Such human misery plus the redistribution of wealth which accompanied the economic depression was bound to have political repercussions. In fact, to anticipate the story somewhat, it can be said that the depression determined, to a considerable extent, the final outcome of the democratic movement. In the following chapters the political consequences of the depression will be discussed in some detail.

[21] *Ibid.*, p. 172.
[22] *Ibid.*, pp. 173-174.
[23] *Ibid.*, p. 181.
[24] *Ibid.*, p. 178.
[25] Mayet, *op. cit.*, p. 67.

CHAPTER XIII

PARTY STRUGGLES

I.

THE economic depression, with its whirlwind of peasant dispossession, struck the *Jiyuto* in a vulnerable spot. As we
have seen, the leaders of the rural political societies and parties
affiliated with the *Jiyuto* were drawn, for the most part, from the
rural aristocracy. It was the wealthier landowners, money lenders,
and rural industrialists who, in alliance with a group of ex-samurai,
organized the peasantry and launched a national movement against
the government. But the bond between the leaders and the rank
and file was put to a severe test by the economic depression. As
economic stagnation became more pronounced, bitterness and
antagonism sprang up between the propertied and the propertyless, between landlord and tenant, and between creditor and debtor.
Utilizing the experience gained in the long agitation against the
government, the poorer peasants pushed ahead to form local
political groups with names like "Debtors' Party," "Tenants'
Party," and "Poor Peoples' Party." Instead of campaigning for
political rights, these "parties" applied pressure for economic concessions like cheaper rents, lower interest rates, and even debt
moratorium. Such demands, of course, were not looked upon with
favor by the rural leaders, who became uneasy for fear that the
movement would get out of hand.

This reaction on the part of the leaders was very likely intensified
by the fear of socialism. We have already indicated in another
connection how the Japanese press tended to identify socialism
with the abolition of private property and were therefore opposed
to it. Learning, moreover, of the rise of Social Democracy in
Germany and of Nihilism in Russia, various newspapers felt uneasy
that such doctrines might conceivably spread to Japan. Thus the
newspaper *Azuma* said: "Although there are no such disaffected
parties in our country today . . . should these parties ever achieve

148

their aims in America and Europe, our country will be affected immediately. It will be impossible to prevent socialism from making an adverse impression on the minds of our people. . . . If the situation we fear reaches this stage, the spread of Socialism and Nihilism among our people will be quicker than sending messages by telegraph." [1]

We can easily imagine how the more conservative Japanese must have felt when they learned of the formation of the *Toyo Shakaito* or " Oriental Socialist Party " in 1882. Actually the *Toyo Shakaito* was not a socialist party, but a peasant party. The fact, however, that a peasant party was operating under the name " socialist " quite likely made it even more repugnant to the landed gentry.

The *Toyo Shakaito* was organized in Shimabara, the scene of the famous Christian rebellion of the 17th century, in May, 1882. It appears to have been the outgrowth of another party which was formed earlier in Nagasaki, but proved to be too conservative for some of its members. Its leaders were Tarui Tokichi and Akamatsu Taisuke. By his own admission, Tarui was not especially familiar with the principles of socialism, but is said to have learned a great deal from one Taketomi Tokitoshi.[2] The announced program of the party was that: (1) the speech and conduct of the party members shall be guided by moral standards; (2) equality shall be the guiding principle of the party; (3) the greatest happiness of the masses shall be its objective. The party planned to publish a magazine written in simple Japanese, and another in Chinese. It was hoped that its activities would be extended to Korea and China.[3]

The true nature of the *Toyo Shakaito*, however, was better revealed in its activities than in its declared principles. In brief, the party grew out of the perennial problem of landownership and land tenure. During the Tokugawa period, wealthy merchants had purchased land in this area which was then under the Saga clan. In order to protect the tenant farmers and landless peasants against oppression by the merchants, Nabeshima Kanso, the head of the Saga clan, issued a series of edicts declaring a long-term moratorium on interest payments, on debt, and finally on the pay-

---

[1] Reprinted in Yokose, *op. cit.*, p. 426.
[2] Kada, *op. cit.*, p. 839.
[3] Ishikawa, *op. cit.*, pp. 336-338; Norman, *Emergence*, p. 181n.

ment of rent. This was enthusiastically received by the poor. Since
the tenant farmers were released from the obligation to pay rent,
in time they came to regard the land as being their own.[4] In the
early 1880's, however, the owners of the land began taking steps to
regain possession of their land. Since this move was resisted by the
tenants, it led to violent disputes. About this time a member of
the *Toyo Shakaito* by the name of Watanabe Masataka was very
active in the area and apparently succeeded in securing a number
of recruits.

In May, 1882, a group of party members put up a large picture
of Nabeshima in front of his shrine with the following message
written at one side of the picture. "In the year Tempo Mizunoe
Tora [1842], Lord Nabeshima, with a heart of universal love, established a system of equal distribution of wealth. Our Party, bathed
in his luster, and having admiration for his virtues, present this
picture. [signed] *Toyo Shakaito*, Matsuura-*gun*, representing 3,000
persons." Since this incident was reported in the press, the people
began to take notice of the party. The press notices were unfavorable because the newspapers generally took the position that
socialist parties, being an evil, must be destroyed before they had
a chance to grow. As soon as the existence of the *Toyo Shakaito*
became known to the Home Minister, he ordered it to dissolve.[5]

The same year also witnessed the first of a series of armed
uprisings against the government. Known as the Fukushima Incident, this outbreak was precipitated by the arbitrary action of
Mishima Tsuyo, the governor of Fukushima prefecture. Mishima
proposed to inaugurate a program of public works, but was opposed
by the prefectural assembly headed by Kono Hironaka.[6] In voting
against the governor's proposals, the prefectural assembly was
probably reflecting the views of the peasantry who feared being
called for forced labor on public works. However, when Mishima,
with the permission of the Home Minister, ignored the adverse
vote of the assembly and decided to proceed with his project a
mob of about ten thousand persons attacked and destroyed the
police station at Kitakata. Mishima, who had once given vent to
his antidemocratic views by saying, "As long as I am in office, I

---

[4] Honjo Eijiro, *Kinsei Noson Mondai Shiron* [Historical Essays on Modern
Agricultural Problems], (Tokyo, 1925), pp. 244-250.

[5] Details have been taken from Kada, *op. cit.*, pp. 839-840.

[6] Baba, *op. cit.*, p. 150.

will not allow the *Jiyuto* and other assassins and bandits to raise their head," [7] took this opportunity to arrest Kono and several other *Jiyuto* members. Kono was accused of having taken an oath which said in part: " Our Party makes it its mission to over-throw the despotic enemy which is a public enemy of liberty, and establish a parliamentary system." He was sentenced to seven years imprisonment, while the others were given six-year terms.[8]

Both the formation of the *Toyo Shakaito* and the Fukushima uprising were symptomatic of the growing tendency of the demo-cratic movement to get more radical and violent. A secret police report described the political situation in Tochigi prefecture in the following words: " When we compare the strength of the two parties, the *Jiyuto* was far stronger than the *Kaishinto* until last year. But because their speeches are radical, and their actions violent, the *Jiyuto* has lost its popularity since last year. More-over, the main office in Tokyo has been pressing members in this prefecture for contributions. There is a tendency for the wealthy, to say nothing of the poor, to dislike this." [9] As a result there was a decline in the membership and income of the *Jiyuto*. In many instances, pledges for contributions were not kept, making it difficult to maintain the party headquarters and to keep up the party paper *Jiyu*. Accordingly, the leaders of the *Jiyuto* began a campaign to raise funds in the fall of 1882, but it was not very successful.[10]

At this juncture, the government made a diabolical move to split the *Jiyuto*. It involved getting Itagaki and Goto to leave the country at this critical period.

Judging from the sequence of historical events, one may assume that the government had been contemplating this move for some time. The first overt act occurred in April, 1882 when an attempt was made on Itagaki's life. He was stabbed by a youth as he came out of a hall in Gifu after having delivered one of his political speeches. The assailant, Aibara Shokei, was a young school teacher who had become convinced that Itagaki was a traitor to his country. The attempted assassination created a sensation which was highlighted by the report that Itagaki had shouted, " Itagaki may die, but liberty will not die." [11]

[7] Norman, *Feudal Background*, p. 85.
[8] Baba, *op. cit.*, p. 150.
[9] Sekiguchi, *op. cit.*, pp. 967-968.
[10] Itagaki, *JS*, II, 126-129.
[11] There is doubt as to whether Itagaki actually made this remark. See Sakai

While Itagaki was convalescing, the government dispatched an Imperial messenger bearing a gift of three hundred *yen*.[12] Since, as a rule, such gifts were reserved for those who were judged to have rendered meritorious service to the state, it must have greatly surprised Itagaki and his followers. The government, which had opposed Itagaki for years, now had the effrontery to present him with an Imperial gift.

It appears likely that this was a part of a plot to wean Itagaki away from the *Jiyuto*. The hand of Ito Hirobumi, working through Fukuoka Kotei and Inouye Kaoru, can be seen behind this move. Inouye was not only a close friend of Ito's, but was also an agent for the Mitsui interests. At first an attempt was made to persuade Iwasaki, the head of the Mitsubishi firm, to provide the necessary funds, but it failed. In the end an arrangement was made with the Mitsui interests through Inouye whereby they agreed to furnish twenty thousand dollars. In return, the contract between the Mitsui Bank and the Japanese army, allowing the former to handle army business, was extended until 1885. This somewhat dubious deal was closed after the leading figures in the inner circle, including Matsukata, Iwakura, Yamada, and Saigo, gave their approval.[13]

Unquestionably Goto knew who was providing the money, but it is possible that Itagaki was kept in the dark. Nevertheless, it seems reasonable to assume that he was aware of the purpose of this scheme and that he was an opportunist enough to agree to it. No doubt the fact that the movement was beginning to get out of hand was an important consideration in his decision to leave his followers in the lurch.

About July, 1882 Itagaki suddenly revealed to his close friends that he was contemplating a trip to Europe. The reason he gave was that he had never been abroad, and also that it was not wise to leave the study of constitutional problems entirely up to the government. But one group within the *Jiyuto* led by Oishi Masami, Baba Tatsui, and Suyehiro Tetcho strongly disapproved. They

Kunio, *Ijin Ansatsu Shi* [History of Assassinations of Great Men] (Tokyo, 1940), p. 472.

[12] Shirayanagi Shuko, *Meiji Taisho Kokumin Shi: Kensei Juritsu Hen* [Popular History of the Meiji and Taisho Periods: The Establishment of Constitutional Government] (Tokyo, 1940), p. 472.

[13] Osatake Takeki, "Seito Shi no Issetsu," [An Episode in the History of Political Parties], *MBK*, No. 2 (May, 1934), pp. 27-46.

pleaded that this was no time for the leader of the party to leave
the country. They, moreover, were suspicious of the source of his
funds. They knew that Itagaki could not afford such a trip. Other
Jiyuto members in Tokyo, and the Tosa *Risshisha* voiced opposition to the proposed trip. But Itagaki refused to listen. Angered
by Itagaki's intransigence, Oishi, Baba, and Suyehiro resigned from
the staff of the party newspaper, and eventually from the party
itself.[14] Several years later, Baba came to the United States and
published in Philadelphia a pamphlet in English. In this pamphlet
he made a scathing attack on the government. He also rebuked
Itagaki in the following words: " Thus everything was going on
favorably for this popular movement. But one serious mistake
which we made in this movement was the election of a leader who
was utterly incapable of the management of a political party." [15]

Despite the opposition to the trip, Itagaki and Goto departed for
Europe in November, 1882. They were away for seven months.
During their absence the *Jiyuto* and *Kaishinto* engaged in a bitter
controversy, which not only removed all possibilities of the two
parties uniting against the government, but also discredited political
parties in the eyes of the public. Ito's scheme turned out to be a
master stroke.

II.

As soon as the news of Itagaki's proposed trip leaked out, the
Kaishinto paper, *Tokyo-Yokohama Mainichi*, published an editorial
intimating that the government was paying for the trip. It took
the position that unless Itagaki revealed the source of his funds,
the public would be suspicious. The *Jiyuto* newspapers issued a
denial that Itagaki had been bought off.[16]

The *Jiyuto*, embittered by the defection of its leaders and the
attack by the *Kaishinto*, launched an offensive against its rival
party. The *Jiyuto* paper, now under the editorship of Furuzawa
Uro, printed in retaliation a series of articles under the general
theme, *Gito Bokumetsu* or " Destroy the False Parties," and *Umi
Bozu Taiji* or " Subdue the Sea Monster," i. e., the Mitsubishi

[14] *Ibid.*, pp. 30-35.
[15] Baba Tatsui, *The Political Condition of Japan, Showing the Despotism and
Incompetency of the Cabinet and the Aims of the Popular Parties* (Philadelphia,
1888), p. 11.
[16] Osatake, " Seito Shi no Issetsu," *op. cit.*, p. 36.

Company. Okuma was accused of being an agent of the Mitsubishi interests, and his conduct in office as Minister of Finance was attacked. To understand properly the background of this move, it is necessary to digress somewhat and discuss the rise of the Mitsubishi Company.

Iwasaki Yataro, the founder, was born of an impoverished samurai family in Tosa. In his youth he was chosen by Goto Shojiro to manage the commercial company established by the Tosa clan. When the clans were abolished in 1872, Iwasaki secured possession of the company, together with eleven ships, its chief assets. During the Japanese invasion of Formosa in 1874, he transported troops for a large fee, and thereafter the Mitsubishi Company, as his firm was called, made rapid progress. Since the government was anxious to expand the merchant marine, it provided him with an annual subsidy of two and a half million *yen*. With this subsidy plus his profits Iwasaki was able to purchase more ships, until presently he had secured a monopoly on coastal shipping.[17]

To counter the growing power and influence of the Mitsubishi, the rival Mitsui firm, together with a few other financiers, organized a competing company in 1880. But the government support which Iwasaki enjoyed through Okuma proved too much for the newcomers. The situation was changed, however, when Okuma was driven from office in 1881. The following year, Shinagawa Yajiro, an official in the Ministry of Agriculture, organized with the Mitsui interests, a semi-official shipping company known as the *Kyodo Unyu Kaisha*.[18]

In launching its campaign against the Mitsubishi Company, the *Jiyuto*, in effect, served the interests of this new company. It would seem that this was not entirely fortuitous, for the new company was owned in part by the Mitsui, and the latter, it will be called, had financed Itagaki's trip. It might also be indicated at this point that Komuro Nobuo, one of the founders of the new shipping company, was a friend of Furuzawa's, the editor

[17] G. C. Allen, " The Concentration of Economic Control," in *The Industrialization of Japan and Manchukuo*, edited by E. B. Schumpeter, (New York: Macmillan, 1940), p. 628; F. Barret, *L'Evolution du Capitalisme Japonais* (Paris, 1945), I, 132.

[18] Otsu, *op. cit.*, II, 572-573.

of the newspaper *Jiyu*. It has been suggested that this might have been a factor in the campaign against the Mitsubishi.[19]

The anti-Iwasaki movement elicited considerable response among the members of the *Jiyuto*. The Mitsubishi, with its monopoly of coastal shipping, had charged high rates, arousing the enmity of rural producers. The *Jiyu* claimed in a series of articles that Mitsubishi enjoyed an income of at least eleven million *yen* per year from freight charges alone.[20] The influence of Mitsubishi, furthermore, had stretched out into the countryside. It sometimes advanced funds to rural producers, making them agree in return that they would ship the produce on Mitsubishi vessels, insure it with the Mitsubishi Marine Insurance Company, and store it in Mitsubishi warehouses. In outlying areas like Hokkaido, Shikoku, and Kyushu, it was the custom to sell commodities first to dealers in the big cities. The latter in turn shipped them abroad or to other sections of the country. Mitsubishi, however, dealt directly with the producer. Such practices deprived the middlemen—rural wholesale merchants, commission agents, shippers, and port brokers—of much business.[21]

In the spring of 1883 a number of political rallies attacking both the *Kaishinto* and the Mitsubishi Company were sponsored by the *Jiyuto*. Since rural producers and merchants had been antagonized by the Mitsubishi, it was not difficult to whip up strong feeling against the so-called "Sea Monster." The following dispatch printed in the *Jiyu* provides some idea of the atmosphere of the times:

We have learned that the rally and execution of the Sea Monster sponsored by the Nanso [Chiba] *Jiyuto* was held in the Rensho Temple in Yamabe-*gun*, Oami-shuku. The speakers were Saito Takasuke, Ohara Kenji, and seven or eight local people. Those who went from Tokyo were Nagata Kazutsugu and Kato Heishiro. Despite the hot weather, there was a crowd of about 600, and their applause shook the building. . . . The following day, the 15th, a meeting was held in Yamato-ro in Shigehara in Nagara-*gun*. Outside several banners with the words, " Hurrah for Freedom, Kill the Sea Monster " were put up and vases filled with flowers were displayed. This was an unusual sight in this neighborhood. Not unlike the day before, the crowd applauded.

---

[19] Yanagida Sen, "Angaido Shujin Komuro Nobusuke," *MBK*, No. 2 (May, 1934), p. 155.

[20] Tanaka Sogoro, *Iwasaki Yataro*, p. 291.

[21] Shirayanagi, *op. cit.*, pp. 452, 454; Tanaka, *op. cit.*, pp. 291-292.

Moreover, the most spectacular and pleasant feature of the day was the destruction of the Sea Monster. On that day, after 6 p. m. there was dragged out, as soon as the speeches were concluded, a black monster more than 10 feet high, its head big enough to be encircled by a pair of arms, and securely tied with straw rope. This monster was tied to a tree in the court yard and several tens of men surrounded it. Several men raised their bamboo spears as if they were going to stab it. Then someone stepped forward and read in a loud voice the death sentence. When this was finished, the bravos stepped forward and jabbed their bamboo spears into the arms and legs and body of the Sea Monster, shouting all the while in unison. It was a spectacular and pleasant sight to see them rip and tear it apart. By this time there had assembled a great crowd of spectators, who looked on with astonishment. Seeing the Sea Monster beautifully demolished, it is said they instinctively sang songs of triumph.[22]

It was into an atmosphere charged with bitter accusations and recriminations that Itagaki returned. While he had been in Europe, supposedly studying constitutional problems, the differences between the two parties had widened into an unbridgeable chasm. Whatever basis might have existed for a common front against government policies was clearly destroyed.

During his absence, too, local groups, deprived of national leadership, had become increasingly more radical in their outlook and much more inclined to violent action. For instance, a *Jiyuto* member, Akai Kageaki, was arrested in November, 1882, for plotting the assassination of government leaders. He had come to the conclusion that a parliament would not be called in 1890 as promised unless those in office were removed. Accordingly, he had taken an oath with two others that " if there should come a time when there are people who are no longer of use to the state, we will punish them on behalf of Heaven without hesitation." When a copy of this oath was found by a detective, the men were arrested and imprisoned.[23]

Not only did the government plot to split and weaken the movement, but it also took positive steps to suppress it. Use was made of the supplementary regulations strengthening the law governing public meetings and associations issued in June, 1882. Under this law, the power of the police to interfere in political meetings was increased. Political associations were forbidden to " advertise a summary of the discourses, excite the public by sending out commissioners or circulars, or correspond and join together with other

[22] Quoted in Tanaka, *op. cit.*, pp. 293-294.   [23] Baba, *op. cit.*, p. 150.

similar societies." The Minister of Home Affairs was empowered to suspend permanently any meetings or association deemed " prejudicial to the public peace." " In case his order is not complied with, or the association or meeting continues secretly in existence, the offenders shall be liable severally to a fine of not more than one hundred nor less than ten *yen*, or to minor imprisonment for not more than two years nor less than two months." [24]

Despite such stringent regulations, the leaders of the *Jiyuto* were not yet ready to abandon the movement. Some party leaders suggested in August, 1883 that a drive be undertaken to create a fund of one hundred thousand *yen* to be used for the purpose of restoring order within the party and for bolstering the movement in general.[25] How much money was actually collected cannot be ascertained, since only a partial list of contributions covering Kanagawa, Tochigi, and Ibaraki prefectures is available. However, if it can be assumed that this list is more or less representative, it is apparent that the party still had the support of the wealthier people in the rural areas. As is shown in the following table, there were many contributions of twenty-five *yen* and over, an amount far beyond the means of the average peasant.

TABLE IV.

A PARTIAL LIST OF CONTRIBUTORS TO THE *JIYUTO*, 1883

Amount (*yen*)	No. of Contributors	Total Amount
500	1	500
100	27	2,700
50	28	1,400
40	2	80
30	17	510
25	34	850
20	13	260
15	5	75
10	20	200
7	2	14
6	1	6
5	18	90
4	2	8
3	5	15
2	1	2
1	1	1
	187	6,711

Source: Itagaki, *JS*, II, 135 ff.

[24] McLaren. *JGD*, pp. 499-501.   [25] Itagaki, *JS*, II, 131.

Corroborative evidence may be found in the secret police report already cited where the financial status of *Jiyuto* members in Tochigi prefecture is said to be as follows: [26]

22 persons were worth	5,000 *yen* or more			
8 " " "	2,500 *yen* to 3,000 *yen*			
48 " " "	500 *yen* to 2,500 *yen*			
79 " " "	0 *yen* to 500 *yen*			

Other steps were taken a few months later to create a more closely-knit organization and to strengthen the Tokyo headquarters in order to maintain better party discipline. More than sixty representatives met at a *Jiyuto* meeting in March, 1884 and passed a resolution which contained, among others, the following points:

(1) in a centralized state, party organization must also be centralized; (2) the leaders of the party must be given more authority; (3) closer relations should be maintained with local groups; (4) the basis of the party should be strengthened with more money; (5) contacts should be made with Western countries; (6) men with martial qualities should be trained.[27]

In order to achieve these objectives some changes were made in the party organization. Representatives of local parties were to be elected at local meetings. Party finances were to be based on direct individual contributions rather than on funds provided by local parties. This provision would have given the Tokyo headquarters more financial independence. A standing committee was to be appointed by the president of the *Jiyuto* from members of local parties. This committee was to divide its time between Tokyo and the rural areas for the purpose of achieving closer liaison between headquarters and the affiliated societies. It was also to submit reports on local conditions and to encourage rural members. Each member of the committee was to receive twenty *yen* plus travel allowances each month.[28]

It is evident from subsequent events that the attempt to tighten party discipline was unsuccessful. We can assume that the one hundred thousand *yen* fund was not raised. The standing committee was unable to function effectively, partly because of the law on public meetings and associations which forbade political parties to communicate with each other. Many party members and

---

[26] Sekiguchi, *op. cit.*, p. 967.   [27] Itagaki, *JS*, II, 156-159   [28] *Ibid.*, pp. 161-164.

sympathizers were arrested for violation of the law, and for allegedly insulting public officials.[29]

It is in this context that the dissolution of the parties must be viewed. On the one hand, increasing government suppression made it more difficult to maintain control over local parties, while the deepening depression increased the pressure from the poorer peasants and tenant farmers, on the other. Caught in this dilemma, the leaders of the *Jiyuto* decided to dissolve the party and wait for more propitious times rather than incur the stigma of being privy to outbreaks of violence.

In the announcement issued at the time of dissolution in October, 1884, it was asserted that the party could not control the masses because the law prevented the establishment of branch parties, that since the freedom of assembly was denied, the people had to resort to secret meetings, and that the lack of free speech and press prevented the people from exchanging views. Under such circumstances, it concluded that even if one were equipped with " divine power " it would be impossible to control a large number of enthusiastic persons.[30]

About this time the *Kaishinto* also underwent internal changes although the party was not dissolved like the *Jiyuto*. It is significant that one of the causes of the change was disagreement over the land tax. Numa Morikazu and several other prominent *Kaishinto* men contended that the land tax must be reduced in order to give the people a chance to achieve economic recovery. They proposed that a memorial be submitted to that effect. Okuma, however, opposed the plan, arguing that state expenditures were necessarily high and that anyone urging that the land tax be reduced was uninformed about current affairs. As a consequence of this disagreement, Okuma, Kono, and several others withdrew from the party. Numa and Ozaki Yukio carried on, but with Okuma gone, *Kaishinto* was virtually reduced to a nonentity.[31]

[29] *Ibid.*, p. 166.
[30] *Nihon Kensei Kiso Shiryo* [Basic Historical Materials on Japanese Constitutional Government], edited by Gikai Seijisha (Tokyo, 1939), pp. 462-467.
[31] Otsu, *op. cit.*, pp. 697-7.00.

CHAPTER XIV

LOCAL REVOLTS

THE cleavage between the leaders and the rank and file of the *Jiyuto*, mentioned in the previous chapter, became evident with the outbreak of local revolts in the years 1884 and 1885. After the dissolution of the *Jiyuto*, the members of the local affiliates, disappointed by the defection of their national leaders, and goaded by the continuing depression, banded together in certain areas and raised the flag of revolt. A long and detailed analysis of these uprisings would take us too far afield. Accordingly, the treatment here will be selective, with emphasis on those revolts which shed light on the dissensions within the democratic movement.

It is worth observing, first of all, that geographically these uprisings were concentrated in the mountainous regions north and northwest of Tokyo. A partial explanation of this phenomenon is to be found in the fact that this area was especially noted for the development of the raw silk industry and the textile industry, largely organized under the " putting out " system. Here numerous peasant households derived a relatively large part of their income from subsidiary industries. Hence, they were often economically dependent on local entrepreneurs who provided them with equipment and materials. In this sense, they were closer in economic status to industrial workers than to independent cultivators. Moreover, from an economic point of view, they were closely linked to the big urban centers, and, in the case of raw silk producers, even with foreign markets. They could not help but be affected by matters like price fluctuations, foreign exchange rates, and credit facilities. They, therefore, were not politically in the same category as peasants engaged in farming on a more or less subsistence level in isolated communities beyond the reach of the national market. Peasants of the latter type would tend to be absorbed in local issues, while those economically enmeshed in a larger market were likely to think more in terms of national politics.

The first revolt to be discussed here occurred in May, 1884 near the city of Takazaki in Gumma prefecture. There is no doubt that the revolt was either directly or indirectly influenced by the democratic movement. In 1879 a well known political society called the *Yushin Sha* had been organized in Takazaki. Also at the time of the Fukushima affair in 1882, several men had gone from this region to confer with Kono Hironaka. The presumption would be that the leaders of the revolt were in contact with other political societies.

The groundwork for the Gumma uprising was laid in April, 1884. The ringleaders were Kiyomizu Eisaburo, a wealthy individual from Kita Kanra-*gun*, and a member of the prefectural assembly; Hibi Son, a pseudo priest, who was wanted by the authorities for violation of the law on public meetings; and Inouye Momonosuke, a staunch proponent of liberal principles from Ibaraki prefecture. These three arranged a meeting which was attended by several *Jiyuto* representatives from the Tokyo headquarters, and several thousand local inhabitants. Later, the trio were joined by Yuasa Rihei, a village official. He was dissatisfied with mere talk about constitutional government and wished to resort to direct action. The group toured the countryside, forming so-called " athletic clubs " to provide military training in the mountainous areas.[1]

About this time a railroad running through the mountains was completed. It was rumored that the ceremonies marking the occasion would be attended by the Emperor. The group decided that they would take advantage of this opportunity to assassinate high-ranking officials who would be present for the occasion. Since the plotters did not wish to attack the Emperor, they agreed to make the attempt at Honjo while the train made a brief stop. According to the plan, 2,500 men were to attack the Takazaki garrison, while another 3,000 men, disguised as hunters and tourists, and distributed in groups of twenty and thirty, would wait for the dignitaries at Honjo. But for some reason the ceremonies were postponed indefinitely.

Meanwhile, the rank and file became extremely restless. After some hesitation, the leaders decided to go ahead with the revolt. A small delegation was sent to Chichibu in Saitama prefecture to seek assistance. On May 16, a party of about 3,000 men divided

[1] Itagaki, *JS*, II, 204-206.

into three groups set fire to a house and godown owned by a usurer who had incurred the hatred of the local inhabitants. Then the rebels proceeded to the Matsuda police station, only to find that the police had already fled. Next the Takazaki sub-station was attacked. But by this time. their provisions ran out, and some of the men dispersed. Moreover, the expected help from Chichibu failed to materialize. As a result, Hibi, who had been leading the revolt, ordered his men to disband. Everyone took to hiding, but eventually forty-two men were rounded up. The leaders of the revolt received prison terms running from twelve to thirteen years.[2]

In the fall of the same year, another revolt broke out, this time in Chichibu-*gun*. Although the revolt occurred in Chichibu, the economic unrest, which led to the uprising, extended into all of the surrounding prefectures. This general area produced a great deal of raw silk, and owing to the persistent decline in the price of this commodity, the smaller landholders and tenant farmers were severely impoverished. The economic situation is so clearly described in the following dispatch published in the *Yubin Hochi* for November 7, 1884 that it merits lengthy quotation.

Briefly, the cause of the present uprising is poverty. Now, although Chichibu-*gun* is mountainous and isolated, it is rich in products, producing large quantities of raw silk, silk cloth, and firewood. It is the wealthiest county in Saitama prefecture. However, with the development of the raw silk export industry, the methods of production have changed greatly. In the past, raw silk was made into thread, then woven into a lining material called *Chichibu-ginu* and shipped out. Women and children worked all year round, and although the returns were not large, their labor was rewarded, and they were relatively well off. With the growth of the raw silk industry, it became more profitable to spin the silk and ship it to Yokohama in the form of raw silk. Accordingly, weaving was abandoned.

When raw silk prices were high, their income from three or four months work amounted to more than what had been earned previously in a whole year. Therefore, they all became producers of raw silk. But since raw silk prices have dropped continuously, there has been much suffering. Moreover, because the raw silk industry was so prosperous, forests, which had been a source of firewood, were cleared and the trees replaced by mulberry trees.[3]

The economic crisis generated strong pressures for political

---

[2] *Ibid.*, pp. 209-232.
[3] Quoted in Hirano Yoshitaro, *Buruja Minshu Shugi Kakumei* [The Bourgeois-Democratic Revolution] (Tokyo, 1948), pp. 284-285.

action. Peasant parties known as *Komminto* (Distressed People's Party) and *Kyuminto* (Poor People's Party) sprang up. They launched a campaign for the repayment of debts in annual installments, closing of schools for three years, lowering of miscellaneous taxes, reduction of village expenses by one-half, and revision of the conscription law.[4]

Many of the debt-ridden peasants demanded of their creditors that no payment be required on loans for five years and that thereafter debts should be repaid in twenty annual installments. Feeling ran high against moneylenders. The following police report on Yoshikawa Miyajiro, a usurer whose house was burned down later by the rebels, is revealing.

The famous usurer had considerable dealings with the *Shakkinto* [Debtors' Party]. . . . For some time there had been strong protests from the chief of the debtors . . . but he [Yoshikawa] replied: I will not deal with representatives. If the man wants to make any pleas, let him come in person. He borrowed the money knowing full well the consequences. And now he says that the interest is high, that the loan should be extended, and so on. I am sick and tired of it. I am justified in presenting a writ of summons to the debtor. And so saying, he refused to have anything to do with representatives. Finally, he got a writ of summons. . . . He went to the Omiya Court House everyday with a stick in his hand, and a pistol in his belt. . . . When asked why he went around carrying such weapons, he replied that it was because the *Shakkinto* was around. . . . Hence the people called him a greedy and stubborn old man, and even those who had no dealings with him hated him.[5]

On October 8, 1884 a group called the *Enki Sha* (Society for the Postponement of Debt Repayment) was organized. Besides asking the creditors for an extension on loans, they sent manifestoes to former members of the *Jiyuto* in the neighboring prefectures of Gumma, Nagano, and Yamanashi.[6]

Meanwhile, the *Komminto* persuaded an ex-samurai by the name of Tashiro Eisuke to become its leader. Tashiro was widely known in the vicinity, and appears to have had contacts with other local leaders, because it was to him that the Gumma rebels appealed for help. Interestingly enough, it was brought out in the trial that although Tashiro owned some land, it was mortgaged and that he

---

[4] Ono Takeo, *op. cit.*, p. 193.
[5] Quoted in Sakai Toshihiko, "Chichibu Sodo" [The Chichibu Revolt], *Kaizo*, X (October, 1928), 5.
[6] Ono Takeo, *op. cit.*, p. 193.

had also signed several promissory notes.[7] Tashiro exemplified a phenomenon which must have been fairly widespread, namely the dropping down of the smaller landholders into the ranks of the landless peasants.

In order to raise some money for the revolt, a group of men broke into several homes of wealthy families and obtained money at sword's point.[8] Then on November 1, a mob assembled in the temple grounds in the village of Shimo-yoshida in Chichibu-*gun*. A description of the assembled throng reveals clearly that they were peasants: " All of them were dressed in rags. Their faces were black and the palms of their hands were like those of bears. They were all peasants, who, until yesterday, had been in their fields engaged in cultivation or in the forests cutting wood." [9] Some of the men carried swords and others had guns or bamboo spears. Although the exact number involved is not known, it is said that there were from seven to ten thousand men. They were organized into two groups with Tashiro as the leader, and two other men acting as vice-chief and chief of staff respectively. Strict regulations were laid down against looting, raping, disobeying orders and so on. Those violating these regulations were to be decapitated.

Incidentally, an item from a contemporary newspaper provides some indication that this uprising was related to the democratic movement and was not merely a revolt caused by the economic depression. An assistant civil engineer who was captured by the rebels and taken to their main camp has left this account:

In the center were placed some chairs. A man who appeared to be the leader sat in front dressed in *haori hakama* [dress for formal occasions]. He had fair complexion, piercing eyes, and a beard. The others who formed the general staff sat up straight. . . . The leader told me in a loud voice to truthfully give my address, name, social status, and age. I replied without hesitation that I was employed in this prefecture. Thereupon he asked me to state what political principle I ordinarily subscribed to, whether *Jiyuto, Kaishinto,* or *Teiseito*.[10]

The first objective of the rebels was to destroy the prison at Maebashi and rescue those imprisoned for political activity. Then they planned to attack the Takazaki barracks and obtain ammuni-

---

[7] Sakai, *op. cit.*, p. 7.
[8] *Ibid.*, pp. 9-10.
[9] Hirano, *op. cit.*, p. 287.
[10] From *Jiji Shimpo*, November 28, 1884 as quoted in *ibid.*, p. 289.

tion. After that they hoped to march on to Tokyo. The first night, the rebels burned two houses belonging to moneylenders and also destroyed the account books containing the records of loans. Next the rebels attacked and burned the police station after the police had fled. By threatening some rich families, the men obtained three thousand *yen*. The homes of those who refused to contribute funds were either wrecked or burned.[11]

Realizing the seriousness of the uprising, the government immediately dispatched a battalion of troops together with some military police. Finally on November 4 the revolt was suppressed after the rebels had overextended their lines. About three hundred men, however, escaped into Nagano prefecture. These men are reported to have said: " The object of the present undertaking is to get land taxes lowered, miscellaneous taxes reduced to one-fourth of their present levels, abolish schools in isolated areas, do away with banks and conscription, and have debts made payable in ten annual installments with no interest charged. Furthermore, the plan is to have simultaneous uprisings in four places, Shikoku, Osaka, Tokyo, and Yamanashi and overthrow the government." [12] But despite such high hopes, all of them were rounded up by November 9. Eventually, Tashiro and some of the other leaders suffered the death penalty.

Since the Chichibu uprising was on such a large scale as to resemble a miniature civil war, it attracted wide attention. It made a particularly strong impression in the neighboring prefectures to which fled some of the remnants of the rebel forces after the suppression of the rebellion. As a consequence, the vigilance of the police was redoubled. This, in turn, led indirectly to the uncovering of another plot against the government. This conspiracy, known as the Iida incident, involved an ambitious plan to foment widespread popular revolt.[13]

Like other communities in the region, the town of Iida in southern Nagano prefecture had been strongly influenced by the democratic movement. The sentiment in favor of the movement was intensified in the fall of 1883 when twenty-five men were arrested for having held a secret meeting against the exactions of landlords.

[11] Sakai, *op. cit.*, pp. 2-5; Otsu, *op. cit.*, p. 658; Ono, *op. cit.*, p. 193.
[12] Quoted in Ono, *op. cit.*, pp. 194-195.
[13] Details have been taken from Kobayashi Hirobito, *Ina Nomin Sodo Shi* [History of Peasant Revolts in Ina] (Tokyo, 1933), pp. 64-70.

Much of the political activity in this area was centered around a person by the name of Yanagizawa Takesada who had organized in Iida a political society known as the *Aikoku Seirisha* (Patriotic Truth Society). He was also a member of a club composed of *Jiyuto* members organized in the city of Nagoya under the name *Kodo Kyokai* (Justice Society). Another important member of this club was Muramatsu Aizo, a student of the Russian language. He had made a careful study of the tactics employed by the Russian revolutionaries in the assassination of Alexander II. It appears that Muramatsu was the strategist of the group. This group published a statement in the newspapers that "Any plan which proposes to meet the present situation with words is too roundabout. We should get like-minded men together and achieve our long cherished objective of changing the form of government by the use of force." [14]

In May, 1883 a small group met with Yanagizawa in Iida to map out plans for the rebellion. Three months later the conspirators met again in Tokyo. At this meeting they asked Ueki Emori to write a manifesto which was later printed in Iida.[15] Some banners were also made. The battalion banner read: "Party of Patriots—Revolution for Freedom. Hurrah for Liberty." The squad banners were more to the point for they said: "Reduction of Taxes—Revision of the Conscription Law—Revision of the Revenue Stamp Law—Help for the Poor."

Careful plans for the revolt were made. The first step, according to this plan, was to burn the town of Iida. The chief purpose of this, it appears, was to attract the troops stationed in Nagoya, thereby leaving the city unguarded. Next the conspirators planned to march on to Nagoya, burn the ammunition dump, break open the Nagoya jail and incorporate the prisoners into the rebel forces. A battle with troops dispatched from Osaka was anticipated. The next step in the plan was to seize the city of Osaka itself. The conspirators were convinced that if these two cities—Nagoya and Osaka—could be taken together with their garrisons, the revolt would succeed. In case the revolt failed for one reason or another, the men planned to flee into the mountainous areas and carry on guerrila warfare.

In the meantime, the outbreak of the Chichibu revolt had led the

[14] *Ibid.*, p. 65.   [15] *Ibid.*, p. 66.

police to take extraordinary precautions, including more stringent control of the sale of ammunition and gun powder. One day an express company handling a shipment of barrels marked " sugar " found powdered material leaking from one of the barrels. For some time the expressmen had been mystified by the fact that certain barrels of sugar were lighter than others. So the matter was reported to the police. This led to the discovery that the barrels contained gun powder consigned to Yanagizawa. The police swooped down on his home and seized a membership list containing the names of more than three hundred members of his political society. Yanagizawa, however, had taken the precaution of writing in "resigned" after all of the names. Eventually the police questioned those whose names were on the list, but they were unable to implicate a single one. The person responsible for this was probably Muramatsu. It seems that he had applied the lessons learned from the Russian revolutionaries and had organized everything so carefully that only a few key men knew about the plans for the rebellion.

In addition to those described above, there were several other local uprisings and plots against the government. None of them, however, were successful. Everywhere the government emerged victorious.

Perhaps the main reason for this was the lack of proper coordination. By the 1880's the Meiji government had been in power for more than a decade during which time it had built up a strong police force and a trained conscript army capable of dealing with local revolts. Accordingly, only a broad national movement with a grand strategy could have succeeded in winning democratic rights and liberties. It is true that some of the leaders were aware of this to some extent and tried to work with other groups with similar aims. In the Chichibu revolt, for instance, the leader, Tashiro, urged that the uprising be postponed to allow more time for preparation, but his proposal was not accepted.[16] He claimed after his arrest that if the revolt had been postponed for thirty days, simultaneous revolts would have occurred in Saitama, Nagano, Kanagawa and Gumma prefectures.

In the case of the Iida conspiracy, we saw that the plan of the revolt envisaged the seizure of two important cities. This would

---

[16] Sakai, *op. cit.*, p. 13.

indicate that by this time the leaders had come to realize that revolts confined to small mountain villages and towns could be easily isolated and suppressed.

Despite these evidences of the awareness of the problems of strategy and timing, it is clear that the revolts of this period were not characterized by brilliant leadership. Once the *Jiyuto* was dissolved, the democratic movement was left without national leadership. Power thereafter passed into the hands of local leaders. But the latter found it extremely difficult to maintain contact with other groups, especially in view of the extensive use of the secret police on the part of the government. This led some of the leaders to overestimate the strength of the local bands they led.

The task of effective leadership was rendered more difficult, too, by the impatience of the rank and file. The recurring pattern in these revolts of demands for cheaper rent, lower taxes, and debt moratorium, followed by attacks on the houses of local usurers and landlords and the police station, reveals the desperate economic condition of the small landowners and tenant farmers. It is not surprising that the rank and file, with forced tax sales and mortgage foreclosures staring them in the face, pressed for immediate action. The consequence was, as we have seen, a series of premature revolts which were quickly put down.

Although the suppression of these revolts did not signify the end of the democratic movement, it never regained the intensity which it possessed in the early 1880's. Hereafter it became more conciliatory and compromising. The government, on the other hand, having survived the critical years now had time on its side. After 1885 business conditions improved, lessening the pressure exerted by the impoverished peasants. This enabled the government to proceed with administrative reforms and the drafting of the constitution whose promulgation in 1889 marked the end of the political struggle of the early Meiji era and the triumph of the absolute state.

Part Four:

THE ABSOLUTE STATE

CHAPTER XV

ITO AND THE CONSTITUTION

IN THE Imperial Rescript of October 12, 1881, the government
solemnly promised to adopt a written constitution and convoke
a parliament by the year 1890. In adopting this policy, the government was bowing to popular pressure which had grown to such
proportions as to make continued procrastination in these matters
unwise. Somewhat reluctantly the top men in the bureaucracy
came to the conclusion that they could no longer hold the line
against the democratic movement. But in making concessions to
popular demands, they saw to it that in return they secured a
breathing spell, during which time they could build new dikes to
channel the flood.

From the point of view of the government, there was much work
to be done. It was necessary that, in the intervening years before
1890, the constitution, election laws, and other basic laws relating
to the structure of government be drafted and imposed on the
people before public sentiment became even more hostile to the
government. There was, therefore, a sense of urgency in high official
circles which is clearly revealed in the documents of the period.
For instance, in a letter written to Ito Hirobumi in July, 1881,
Inouye Kaoru pressed for the adoption of a Prussian-style constitution. But he also urged that this be done quickly, giving the following reasons:

To put into effect a Prussian-style constitution is an extremely difficult
task under existing conditions, but at the present time it is possible to
carry it out and win over the majority and thus succeed. This is because
the English-style constitution has not become firmly fixed in the minds of
the people. Among the samurai in the countryside more than one-half, no
doubt, have a lingering desire to uphold the Imperial House.
But if we lose this opportunity and vacillate, within two or three years,
the people will become confident that they can succeed, and no matter
how much oratory we may use, it will be difficult to win them back. Most
of the political parties will be on the other side rather than ours. Public

opinion will cast aside the draft of a constitution presented by the government, and the private drafts of the constitution will win out in the end.[1]

Somewhat similar sentiments were expressed by Ito in a letter to Ito Myoji on September 14, 1881. Ito Hirobumi was anxious to establish a peerage to bolster the Emperor system and to provide members for a House of Peers which he envisaged. In this letter seeking Ito Myoji's support, he said:

I believe that this [the creation of a peerage] is an absolutely indispensable instrument for fortifying the position of the Imperial House. . . . We are both worried about the recent tendency of both the government and the people to slip unknowing into the spirit of republicanism. If we do nothing about it, and it finally reaches an irredeemable situation, no matter how good a plan we have, it will be useless. Therefore, I hope to find a way to save the situation by taking advantage of the fact that as yet the after glow of the feudalistic pro-Emperor sentiment has not completely died down [and create a peerage] even though this is contrary to the spirit of the times and goes against the feelings of the people. I hope you will support me in this.[2]

By 1881 the men who formed the inner core of the Meiji government had formulated definite ideas about the character of the constitution which they thought Japan should have. In a memorandum drawn up in July, 1881, Iwakura laid down the general outline of the new constitution. Among his more important recommendations were the following: The new constitution should be granted by the Emperor. The Imperial House Law should be outside the scope of the constitution. The Emperor should take supreme command of the armed forces, and should appoint cabinet members, with the Diet having no power to intervene in the organization of the cabinet. There should be a bicameral assembly, with the upper house consisting of peers and Imperial appointees, and the lower house chosen on the basis of restricted suffrage. Only the government should have the right to initiate legislation. In case of failure to approve the annual budget, the budget for the preceding year should be followed.[3]

As is evident from the material cited above, the keystone in the

[1] The letter is reprinted in *Ito Hirobumi Den* [The Biography of Ito Hirobumi], published by the Shunbo Ko Tsuisho Kai (Tokyo, 1940), II, 249.

[2] *Ibid.*, p. 218.

[3] Suzuki, *Nihon Kensei Seiritsu Shi*, pp. 184-185. A convenient summary in English may be found in Colegrove, " The Japanese Constitution," *op. cit.*, pp. 1040-1041.

constitutional arch as Iwakura, Ito, and Inouye envisaged it was the Emperor. Throughout the early years of the Meiji era, the architects of the new regime had labored seduously to build up his political stature. And to a large degree they succeeded. But there are also indications in the documents that on occasion there was opposition. [4] Perhaps more important, the trend of the times was against them. As Ito frankly states in the passage cited above, there was a " tendency for both the government and the people to slip unknowingly into the spirit of republicanism." To offset such tendencies, Iwakura, in a memorial presented in February, 1882, suggested increasing the property held by the Imperial Household. Looking ahead to the period after 1890 he anticipated that " the anti-government views will get stronger and stronger since the extreme democrats always go beyond the proper degree." He was fearful that the provisions of the constitution would be disregarded. " Even the Emperor," he stated, " will be controlled by the Diet, and the Throne will be as good as gone. The Imperial Prerogative will be eventually nullified." He therefore urged that the Imperial Household property be increased, making it " sufficient to pay for the cost of the army and navy from its yearly income. If this is done, no matter how radical a view may arise later in the Diet, and again even if the funds for the national treasury are not appropriated, it would be possible to mitigate it." [5]

In short the problem, as it appeared to leaders like Iwakura, was to fit the Emperor into the new constitutional structure, while at the same time providing institutional safeguards to buttress his position against democratic influences.

Even though the top strata of the bureaucracy were agreed as to the general outline of the constitutional system to be erected, there still remained many problems connected with the actual drafting of the documents. How could they be worded, for instance, to make them palatable to the rural gentry which had been in opposition all these years? Should detailed provisions be incorporated into the constitution, or should the constitution merely set the general pattern? Answers to these and similar questions had to be found.

[4] For example, documents cited in pages 42 and 106 of this work.
[5] Quoted in Ono Hisato, *Meiji Ishin Zengo ni Okeru Seiji Shiso no Tenkai* [The Development of Political Thought in the Restoration Period] (Tokyo, 1944), pp. 627-628.

As they had done on previous occasions, the Japanese again turned to the West for guidance. In March, 1882, Ito Hirobumi, who was the leading figure in the government by now, was appointed head of a mission to study European constitutions. Nine assistants, chosen from the Sat-Cho clique, and the Court nobility, were also named.[6] The mission set sail on March 14 and proceeded to Europe via the Indian Ocean and the Suez Canal. After arriving in Europe, Ito dispatched Saionji, with some men familiar with the French language, to Paris to study the constitution of the Third Republic. Ito went to Germany with a larger group. Years later, Ito asserted that he took an " extended journey in different constitutional countries to make as thorough a study as possible of the actual workings of different systems of constitutional government, of their various provisions, as well as of theories and opinions actually entertained by influential persons on the actual stage itself of constitutional life." [7] The facts, however, appear to be otherwise.

From the very beginning Ito went to Germany because it had already been decided that Japan should adopt a Prussian-style constitution. In Berlin arrangements were made for the mission to hear lectures by the well known jurist, Rudolf von Gneist. The fact that Hirata Tosuke, a member of the mission, had once studied under Gneist may have influenced the choice.[8] For some reason, only Ito, Ito Myoji, and Aoki, the Japanese Minister to Germany, who acted as interpreter, were present at Gneist's talks.[9] Later Ito also heard lectures from Mosse, a disciple of Gneist.

We can surmise that Ito found Gneist's lectures most gratifying. The German jurist firmly believed that constitutions must be rooted in the history of the country. Ito agreed with him, and in fact later used this argument to reject suggestions that various provisions be borrowed from American, French and other liberal constitutions. Gneist also had other advice which Ito found easy to accept. Questions of diplomacy, military organization, and similar matters should not be subject to the decisions of the Diet.

---

[6] Osatake, *NKST*, II, 671.

[7] Ito Hirobumi, " Some Reminiscences of the Grant of the New Constitution," in *Fifty Years of New Japan*, I, 127.

[8] Osatake, *NKST*, II, 671.

[9] Yoshino Sakuzo, " Gneist, Stein, to Ito Hirobumi " [Gneist, Stein, and Ito Hirobumi], *Kaizo*, XV (February, 1933), 65-66.

The legislature should have no power over the property owned by the Imperial Household. Ministers should be given great power and the authority of the Diet should be kept down. If the Diet refuses to pass an appropriations bill, the previous year's budget should be used. Gneist also recommended that the suffrage be limited. Lastly, he was opposed to calling a constitutional convention.[10]

At the end of the course under Gneist, the members of the mission moved to Vienna, where they listened to Professor Lorenz von Stein. Like Gneist, Stein gave conservative advice. Being opposed to popular government, he did not approve of universal suffrage, nor of party cabinets. He was also convinced that only the government should have the right to initiate bills. And he thought that the Imperial Household should be kept above the constitution.[11]

In his lectures, which began on September 18 and lasted until October 31, Stein covered a wide area of the subject matter of political science. Included among the subjects he discussed were Plato and Aristotle, legislation, political parties, administration, German administrative justice, diplomacy, and statistics.[12] At the end of each lecture session, Ito asked questions and his assistants took full notes.[13] Ito was much impressed with Stein, and even tried to hire him as an adviser to the Japanese government, but Stein refused the offer.

Altogether Ito spent about seven months studying under Gneist and Stein. He no doubt learned a great deal, but it is also certain that his prejudices were confirmed. " By studying under two famous German teachers, Gneist and Stein," he wrote to Iwakura, " I have been able to get a general understanding of the structure of the state." But he added, " Later I shall discuss with you how we can achieve the great objective of establishing Imperial authority. Indeed, the tendency in our country today is to erroneously believe in the works of British, French, and American liberals and radicals as if they were Golden Rules, and thereby lead virtually to the overthrow of the state. In having found principles

---

[10] Suzuki Yasuzo, *Kempo no Rekishi-teki Kenkyu* [A Historical Study of the Constitution] (Revised Edition) (Tokyo, 1933), pp. 364-370.

[11] Osatake, *NKST*, II, 707-708.

[12] The list of lecture topics is given in *ibid.*, pp. 707-711.

[13] Colegrove, *op. cit.*, p. 1042.

and means of combatting this trend, I believe I have rendered an important service to my country, and I feel inwardly that I can die a happy man." [14]

On the way home, Ito and his party stopped off at Paris and later visited England, where they heard Herbert Spencer lecture on representative government. Ito returned to Japan in the fall of 1883, a little more than a year and a half after his departure from Japan.

Now that the period of preliminary investigation was over, Ito was put in charge of a newly-created bureau within the Imperial Household Ministry. This bureau was assigned the task of studying constitutional and administrative reform. The reason for placing it within the Imperial Household was to enable Ito and his assistants to work in secrecy and also to give the illusion that the drafting was being done under the personal supervision of the Emperor. Actually, according to Kaneko, little serious work on the constitution was done until 1886.[15] This delay may have been caused in part by the concentration of attention on preliminary matters. Owing to Ito's conviction that a constitution must be rooted in history, his assistants began a restudy of the history of their own country. Also in order to lay the ground work for the new structure, a number of institutional changes were made in the intervening years. In 1884 the nobility was rehabilitated, and five hundred patents of nobility were issued.[16] The following year the old *Dajokan* was abolished in favor of a cabinet, headed by Ito and composed of ministers who, in theory, were directly responsible to the Emperor. " Great stress," says one authority, " was laid by the oligarchy on the contention that by these changes true personal rule by the Emperor had been at last achieved, in order to discourage any popular attack on the regime." [17] The position of the Lord Keeper of the Privy Seal was created. New civil service regulations intended to develop an efficient bureaucracy that would be loyal to the state were also issued.

In 1886 Ito and his staff began the study of constitutional reform in earnest. The work was roughly allocated among three men, although in practice this arrangement was not strictly adhered to. Put in charge of the constitution and the Imperial House Law was

[14] Quoted in Asai, *op. cit.*, p. 407.
[15] Osatake, *NKST*, II, 717.
[16] McLaren, *Political History*, p. 183.
[17] Reischauer, *op. cit.*, pp. 71-72.

Inouye Kaoru. A fellow-clansman and trusted friend of Ito, Inouye had once lived in England and had held various important posts in the government. Ito Myoji, also of Choshu, concentrated his attention on the Law of the Houses. The third member, Kaneko Kentaro, who had attended Harvard Law School, was assigned to study election laws for the House of Representatives.

Ito wrote a memorandum indicating his conception of the scope of legislative power, the responsibility of the cabinet ministers and related matters.[18] In addition to Ito, Inouye depended on his Prussian adviser, Dr. Carl Friedrich Hermann Roessler, then teaching in the law school of the Tokyo Imperial University. Inouye would write questions in English, and Roessler would reply in English. Then the questions and answers were translated into Japanese for Ito's benefit. Since Roessler was no democrat, his advice no doubt accorded well with the predilections of Ito and Inouye. Roessler was opposed to popular rule; and it was his contention that the ministers should be responsible to the Emperor and not the Diet.[19]

On April 30, 1887 Roessler submitted to the group a draft of a constitution written in German. At Ito's request this was translated into Japanese.[20] In May, Inouye followed with two additional drafts of a constitution.[21] It was intended that these drafts would form the basis of further discussion.

About this time, Ito's new summer home in Natsushima, near Yokosuka, was completed. Since a secluded spot like Natsushima afforded greater secrecy, the group moved in June. Owing to the fact that Ito's new home was small, Ito Myoji, Inouye, and Kaneko stayed in a nearby town. But early in August a briefcase containing Roessler's draft was stolen. After this episode the three men moved into Ito's home for the sake of greater security.[22]

All through the summer of 1887 the staff continued its work, referring from time to time to the only two reference books

[18] Osatake, *NKST*, II, 719.

[19] Roessler's role in drafting the constitution is discussed in Suzuki Yasuzo, " Nihon Kempo Seitei ni Taisuru Heruman Resureru no Kiyo " [The Contributions of Hermann Roessler to the Establishment of the Japanese Constitution], *MBK*, May, 1935, pp. 46-71.

[20] A translation of Roessler's draft is reprinted in *MBZ*, IV, 490-496 under the title, *Nihon Kempo Soan*.

[21] For Inouye's drafts, see Suzuki, *Nihon Kensei Seiritsu Shi*, pp. 198-215.

[22] *Ito Hirobumi Den*, II, 578.

available in Ito's library, the *Spirit of the Laws* by Montesquieu and the *Federalist*.[23] Finally in September, a fourth draft based on the earlier drafts by Roessler and Inouye was completed. This draft was given to Roessler for his criticisms and suggestions.[24] Starting on October 15, the group began the task of revision. But before the revision was completed, Ito undertook a tour to Kyushu and to Okinawa. Early in 1888 discussions were resumed, and finally in April drafts of the constitution and Imperial House Law were finished.[25] Since no record of the proceedings is available we know very little in detail about the discussions which took place among the four, but we can be sure that there were some differences of opinion over phraseology. We get a glimpse of this in a letter which Ito sent to Inouye. " I have previously argued," wrote Ito, " about the phrase *gikai no shonin* [consent of the Diet]. In my opinion *sando* [approval] is the suitable word. But according to Mr. Roessler, ' concurrence ' and ' consent ' are greatly different in origin. That it so say, ' concurrence ' is used between those who are of equal authority, while ' consent ' implies recognition of the power of the sovereign, and does not apply to equal status. Accordingly, I supported that view in the end. . . ."[26]

With the draft of the constitution completed, there arose the question of the procedure to be used in ratification. Those in the democratic movement argued in favor of a constitutional convention, while many of the bureaucrats felt that approval by the Emperor was sufficient.[27] In the end it was presented to the newly-created Privy Council for ratification. Resigning as head of the cabinet, Ito became the president of the Privy Council. His three assistants were appointed secretaries of the Council. Included among the long list of appointments to the Privy Council were two names representing the political opposition, namely Okuma and Itagaki. The former, who by this time had been lured back into the government as foreign minister, accepted the appointment, but Itagaki declined. The inclusion of Okuma in the Privy Council, however, had no practical effect since he stayed away from the

[23] Osatake, *NKST*, II, 726.
[24] *Ito Hirobumi Den*, II, 579.
[25] *Ibid.*, p. 580.
[26] Quoted in *ibid.*, pp. 609-610.
[27] Harold S. Quigley, *Japanese Government and Politics* (New York: The Century Co., 1932), p. 41.

sessions. For one thing he was busy negotiating with the foreign powers for the revision of the unequal treaties and probably had little time to spare. But one suspects that a more fundamental reason for his boycotting the meetings was his dislike of Ito.[28]

Between May and December of 1888, the Privy Council met in forty-one sessions. Three special meetings were also called. All of the sessions except one were held in the presence of the Emperor. During these Council sessions, elaborate precautions were taken to prevent leakage of information. To make sure that the public was kept in the dark about the provisions of the proposed constitution, no one was allowed to take documents away from the conference room. Those wishing to give further study to the drafts were compelled to remain and work in the presence of a secretary. "This procedure," notes Professor Quigley, "was decided upon after Kaneko discovered that the deliberations of the American constitutional fathers had been in secret." [29]

It is difficult to appraise with any precision the role of the Privy Council in shaping the constitution into its final form, since not all of the documents have been published. We do know, however, that some changes were made. Chapter 3, Article 38 of the Ito draft provided, for instance, that " The Imperial Diet shall deliberate on bills submitted by the government." General Torio Koyata proposed that the Diet also be given power to initiate legislation. Very likely his suggestion was not prompted by liberal impulses, but rather by a realistic analysis of the political situation. He felt that if the Diet were denied such power, it would soon demand it. Torio's proposal was voted down, but later Ito, having given the matter further study, decided in favor of it. Another clause in the Ito draft provided that " Bills on the budget and other financial matters shall be presented to the House of Representatives first, and after passage shall be sent to the House of Peers. The House of Peers shall only deliberate on the bill as a whole and cannot remove or revise separate sections." After discussion in the Privy Council, this provision was revised to give both houses equal power.[30]

No doubt other suggestions were offered by the Privy Councillors.

[28] Cf., Colegrove, *op. cit.*, p. 1044.
[29] Quigley, *op. cit.*, p. 41.
[30] *Ito Hirobumi Den*, II, pp. 625-626.

But in view of the makeup of the Privy Council, it is reasonable to assume that no drastic changes were made in the draft prepared by Ito and his committee. Being composed entirely of conservative and reactionary bureaucrats, the Council could hardly be expected to seek a more liberal constitution than that envisaged by Ito.[31] Things having gone this far, only a successful drive to force the government to submit the draft to a constitutional convention for ratification would have produced a democratic constitution. But because, as we shall see in the next chapter, the democratic movement never fully recovered from its collapse in the mid-1880's, there was little likelihood of such a development.

[31] For a somewhat different interpretation, see Colegrove, *op cit.*, pp. 1044-1045.

CHAPTER XVI

THE FINAL PHASE

I.

THE local uprisings between the years 1883 and 1885 broke out after the leaders had repudiated the movement and the party machinery had been dismantled. Once the guiding hand of central leadership was withdrawn, the pressure of the rank and file erupted in pyrotechnic display, which for all its spectacular qualities, had no lasting effect. With grim efficiency, the government smashed the revolts, demonstrating again its ability to meet force with force. Thus with these attempts at direct action, the democratic movement virtually came to a close.

Hereafter time was on the side of the government. Business conditions began to improve, and the downward trend in the price of rice was reversed. This brought some measure of relief to the agricultural population and eased the tension in the countryside. At the same time, the government, taking advantage of the lull, set to work to draft a constitution which would provide an institutional basis for an absolute state.

Although political opposition after 1885 was no longer on an organized basis, anti-government sentiment still persisted in many quarters. The momentum built up through years of political agitation was not completely dissipated. Now that political activity within the framework of political parties was foiled, political opposition found expression in plots and movements which historically may be regarded as offshoots of the democratic movement.

One of the more curious of these offshoots was a conspiracy involving Oi Kentaro and some members of the radical wing of the *Jiyuto*, including a few women. Finding their efforts to establish a liberal regime in Japan blocked by government repression, this group turned its attention to Korea. Their plan was to assist the Progressive Party in Korea to establish a liberal regime in that country, and then use Korea as a base of operations for carrying

181

on agitation in Japan. Just as they were about to set sail from Osaka with arms and ammunition, the plot was discovered. On November 23, 1885 the police rounded up more than thirty conspirators.[1]

Another example of an offshoot was a case concerning the publication of anti-government newspapers in the United States. After the suppression of the democratic movement, a group of Japanese liberals fled to America and issued a mimeographed weekly paper in Oakland in the fall of 1888. In this publication they wrote articles attacking the policies of the Japanese government. These articles were not exactly to the liking of the Japanese government, but since the paper was printed outside of the country, it was helpless. So General Yamagata, then Home Minister, declared the paper to be detrimental to the peace of the country, and banned its sale in Japan. Later some of those who wrote for the paper were even brought to trial and fined in absentia. Other papers like *Dai Jukuseiki* (Nineteenth Century), *Jiyu* (Liberty), and *Kakumei* (Revolution) were published in the Bay Region. All of them were banned in Japan.[2]

Incidents like these, however, were of relatively little significance when compared to the movement which emerged under the leadership of Goto Shojiro. Eventually this movement, which came to be known as *Daido Danketsu* (Union at Large), attracted a fairly large following. It was large enough in scope to be legitimately regarded as a partial revival of the democratic movement.

But in order to follow the sequence of events leading up to the formation of Goto's *Daido Danketsu*, it is necessary to digress somewhat and take up the question of treaty revision. It will be recalled that Japan had been forced to conclude unequal treaties with the Western nations in the late 1850's. Since then at various intervals the Japanese had tried to persuade the Powers to modify these treaties, but without success. In 1886, Inouye Kaoru, in the capacity of foreign minister, initiated negotiations with foreign representatives for the purpose of drawing up new treaties. He proposed, among other things, that extraterritoriality be gradually eliminated and that in the transitional period a mixed court

---

[1] Uyehara, *op. cit.*, p. 99n; Norman, *Emergence*, p. 183.

[2] Ebihara Hachiro, " Soko Nihonjin Aikoku Domei Shimatsu " [The Case of the Japanese Patriotic League of San Francisco], *MBK*, No. 2 (May, 1934), pp. 102-109.

consisting of foreign as well as Japanese judges be established to try cases in which one of the parties was a foreigner.[3]

But before these negotiations were begun, the government launched a program of rapid Europeanization. The object was to convince the Western Powers that Japan was modern enough to deserve equal treaties. A large hall was built in Tokyo at government expense for the purpose of holding social gatherings along European lines. Dancing academies for teaching ballroom dancing were opened, and the study of foreign languages became popular. " The winter months of 1886-7," says McLaren, " were for Tokyo a season never to be forgotten. Among the lower orders the wearing of foreign articles of dress was advocated, and in every direction it was evident that ' foreign ways ' were to be adopted with all possible speed." [4]

Naturally such a policy of Europeanization under forced draft provoked criticisms and resistance. Conservative elements were outraged that the traditional Japanese civilization should be slighted in favor of a foreign civilization. To those with strong national and cultural pride, the slavish imitation of foreign customs amounted to an admission of inferiority.

In the meantime, the terms proposed by Inouye were prematurely revealed. When the public learned that foreign judges and prosecutors would participate in the work of Japanese courts, it immediately turned against the foreign minister. There was much talk about the infringement of Japanese sovereignty. Those of a more practical turn of mind were fearful of competition from foreigners. Under the existing treaties the foreigners were confined to treaty ports, but under the proposed arrangement they would be allowed to travel and reside freely in the interior and also to acquire real property.[5] Rural merchants and industrialists were not happy at the prospect of acquiring new competitors.

There was a wave of protests, and Inouye's policy of Europeanization and his attempts at treaty revision aroused much criticism. The Minister of Agriculture and Commerce, Tani Kanjo submitted a memorial denouncing the proposed arrangement. M. de Bois-

---

[3] For a summary of his proposals, see Ariga, " Diplomacy," in Stead, *op. cit.,* p. 208.

[4] *Political History,* p. 165.

[5] Cf., Francis Clifford Jones, *Extraterritoriality in Japan and the Diplomatic Relations Resulting in Its Abolition, 1853-1899* (New Haven, 1931), pp. 110-111.

sonade, the French jurist who was assisting in the revision of the
civil code also objected to the use of foreign judges in Japanese
courts. Somehow texts of the Tani memorial and the statement by
Boissonade leaked out. They were secretly printed and circulated.[6]
In the end Inouye was forced to resign and break off talks with the
foreign powers.

Taking advantage of this turn of events, some of the leaders of
the old *Jiyuto* and *Kaishinto* re-entered the political arena. Goto
started his *Daido Danketsu* which was more or less a league of
diverse elements brought together to oppose the government.
Urging everyone to put aside trifling differences and unite for a
common purpose, he succeeded in getting under his banner a
number of members of the old political parties.[7]

About this time Itagaki also came out of political retirement to
send out a call for delegates to present petitions to the government.
These petitions demanded the reduction of the land tax, the
revision of the treaties, and guarantees for the freedom of speech
and public assembly. In the fall of 1887 a series of political rallies
were held in Tokyo. Delegates from many prefectures assembled
in the capital. In one meeting it was resolved to send a delegation
bearing a petition to the Premier.[8] On October 12, 1887 a mass
meeting was called to discuss the question of merging the remnants
of the old *Jiyuto* and *Kaishinto*. From the press accounts, one
gathers that something of the enthusiasm which characterized the
democratic movement in its heyday was present. For instance, the
newspaper *Mezamashi* reported:

> The meeting was held at Iseiro the day before yesterday, the 10th. It
> was twice as large as the one held the other day. The crowd began to
> assemble about 9 a.m. and the numerous police officers who formed a
> barrier in front of the Iseiro took down the names of the spectators. Since
> they counted the people and admitted them [one by one], much time was
> required. In a short while there was a mountain of people in front, all
> pushing and trying to get in. Finally the police took some chairs and
> made a sort of barrier on a bridge a short distance away and about ten
> policemen maintained order. By noon the hall was full with no place to
> stand. Unable to get in, many went home. By the time the meeting began
> there were about 1,500 present. . . .

---

[6] Tokutomi, *Koshaku Yamagata Aritomo Den*, II, p. 960.

[7] Ukita, Itagaki and Okuma, " The History of Political Parties in Japan," *op. cit.*,
p. 159.

[8] Otsu, *op. cit.*, III, 28-29; Tokutomi, *op. cit.*, p. 963.

When the fifth speaker, Watanabe Kotaro mounted the rostrum and began his speech (on "I Read the Imperial Rescript of 1868") the police, in a loud voice, ordered the speaker to stop. The capacity crowd yelled, no, no, unjust. They threw bamboo sticks and lunch boxes, and the confusion was beyond description. The thirty-four policemen stationed outside the hall came in with their shoes on and pushed the crowd out in all directions. Moreover, many plain clothes men who had been hiding in the crowd until this time struck down the rioting spectators. The more violent ones were seized and taken to the police station.[9]

To counteract this renewed political activity, the police issued several regulations limiting the right to present petitions and to hold public meetings. At the same time, a much more drastic law was drafted by the Chief of the Metropolitan Police Bureau and several others under orders from General Yamagata, who was determined to put an end to the popular agitation. When Yamagata, as Minister of Home Affairs, ordered Mishima Tsuyo, the Police Inspector-General, to put the decree into effect, even the latter, who at various times had suppressed the democratic movement, hesitated. Yamagata's answer was, "If you are not strong enough, I can do it myself."[10] Mishima then gave secret instructions to the police to kill anyone who resisted. The army also took steps to meet an emergency situation. Squads of military police were sent out, and guards were posted at army installations like armories and arsenals. The Imperial Guard around the Palace was strengthened. Doctors were assembled at army hospitals, and army communications lines were strung.[11] General Yamagata made a personal inspection tour of Tokyo the night before the new law was put into effect. Indeed, it was as if martial law had been declared to put down an uprising.

Then on December 25, 1887 the notorious Peace Preservation Law was proclaimed. Under this law secret societies and assemblies were forbidden. The police were given authority to stop meetings and assemblies "whenever they deem such a course necessary." But the most important provision was article four which provided: "Any person residing or sojourning within a distance of three *ri* ($7\frac{1}{2}$ miles) radius around the Imperial Palace or around an Imperial place of resort, who plots or incites disturbances, or who

[9] This news item dated October 12, 1887 is reprinted in *SSMHS*, VI, 522.
[10] Tokutomi, *op cit.*, p. 969.
[11] *Ibid.*, p. 970.

is judged to be scheming something detrimental to public tranquility, may be ordered by the police, or local authorities, with the sanction of the Minister of State for Home Affairs, to leave the said district within a fixed number of days or hours." [12] The very same day, General Yamagata, acting under article four, authorized the forcible removal of more than five hundred persons, including practically all of the better known political figures and writers belonging to the opposition.[13] Thus in one diabolical stroke, the government cleared the capital of its political opponents.

Having thus struck a blow at its enemies, the government, in its usual opportunistic fashion, now extended a friendly hand to Okuma. In order to win over the large following which Okuma had, and also to placate hostile public opinion, the government offered Okuma the portfolio of foreign minister. The former leader of the *Kaishinto* accepted the position. He reopened treaty negotiations with the foreign powers, but was no more successful than Inouye.[14]

Even after the proclamation of the Peace Preservation Law, Goto continued his movement. He made several speaking tours through the northern prefectures and enlisted the support of many of the old *Jiyuto* members. In October, 1888 a big rally was held in Osaka at which thirty-two prefectures were represented.[15] Goto also started a party magazine called *Seiron* (Political Opinions) and attacked the government. In a period of fourteen months, the magazine was forced to suspend publication three times for carrying articles which displeased the Meiji bureaucracy.[16]

Although there were indications that the *Daido Danketsu* movement was slowly gaining strength, it was never strong enough to threaten the work on the constitution. As we saw in the last chapter, Ito and his associates were able to work without having to worry about political pressure from the outside. And in any case, Goto's movement proved to be rather short lived. Not many days after the promulgation of the constitution, he was lured into the government with an offer of the post of Minister of Communications. His disappointed followers who had been left in the lurch

[13] McLaren, *JGD*, pp. 502-503.
[13] Ukita, Itagaki, and Okuma, *op. cit.*, p. 160.
[14] *Ibid.*, pp. 160-161.
[15] Otsu, *op. cit.*, pp. 98-99.
[16] McLaren, *Political History*, pp. 184-185.

bitterly complained that he had used the *Daido Danketsu* movement as a stepping stone for furthering his personal career.[17] In accepting the position, Goto, of course, was following well established precedents. The history of the democratic movement could provide examples of men who conveniently forgot old quarrels and professed principles in their eagerness for political office.

II.

The draft constitution having been duly ratified by the Privy Council, there only remained the matter of official promulgation. In keeping with the fiction maintained throughout the Meiji era that the Emperor personally ruled, February 11, 1889 was chosen as the day for the historic ceremony. This, according to the official mythology, marked the anniversary of the accession of the Emperor Jimmu, the founder of the Imperial dynasty, to the throne in 660 B. C.

The promulgation ceremony took place in the Imperial Palace in the presence of high state officials, foreign diplomats and other prominent guests. A German doctor, Erwin Baelz, who witnessed the ceremony, has left an interesting account. After describing the arrangement of the guests in the Throne room, he says: " On either side of the throne a high dignitary now stepped forward, one of them Duke Sanjo, formerly imperial chancellor, each of them with a roll of parchment. The one Sanjo held was the constitution. The Emperor took the other document, opened it, and read it in a loud voice. It contained the decision to give the people voluntarily the promised constitution. Then the Emperor handed the charter itself to the prime minister, Kuroda, who received it with a deep reverence. Thereupon the Emperor nodded and left the hall, followed by the Emperess and suite. The whole business lasted about ten minutes." [18]

Meanwhile salutes were fired and bells were rung everywhere. A festive air filled the city, for the streets were gaily decorated with flags, bunting, and triumphal arches. The holiday crowd, dressed in their finery, mingled in the streets to watch the *dashi* or floats,

---

[17] Osatake, *NKST*, II, 813.

[18] *Awakening Japan: The Diary of a German Doctor: Erwin Baelz*, edited by Toku Baelz, and translated by Eden and Cedar Paul (New York, 1932), pp. 81-82.

which were built in the form of conplicated buildings or figures, and often accompained by bands and beautiful *geisha*.[19]

Actually there was little cause for the public to celebrate. " The Empire of Japan," said the constitution, " shall be reigned over and governed by a line of Emperors unbroken for ages eternal." " The Emperor is the head of the Empire, combining in himself the rights of sovereignty, and exercises them according to the provisions of the present Constitution." Drafted in secret, ratified by a small group of conservatives, and read, not to the public, but to a handful of high officials, the constitution did not alter in any significant way the structure of power in the Japanese state. Under it the majority of the people enjoyed no more political privileges than they had before. The authority of the Diet was circumscribed and the electorate was kept small by high property qualifications. Out of a population of some fifty millions, only 460,000 possessed the right to vote.

The muzzling of the press on the eve of the promulgation of the constitution foreshadowed the shape of events to come. Prior to the ceremony, the radical Tokyo newspapers were shut down, and others were warned not to criticise the constitution, at least for the time being. The hold of the oligarchy was intact and was to remain so. In fact one could say that its hold had been strengthened, for now the autocratic practices, which had been developed in the Meiji era, were " legitimatized " and sanctioned by the constitution.

Conclusion

THE history of Japanese politics in the twenty year period between the Restoration and the promulgation of the constitution in 1889 was strongly influenced by the character of the Meiji Restoration. The balance of political forces at the end of the Tokugawa era and their peculiar alignment encouraged the subsequent growth of a strong centralized state. The conjunction of two crises in the middle of the nineteenth century: the internal economic crisis and the external pressure of the Western powers enabled an anti-Tokugawa faction led by a small group of low ranking but able samurai to effect a political revolution.

[19] *Ibid.*, p. 82.

The symbols used in this movement, however, were traditionalist rather than revolutionary. The leaders of the Restoration gave their actions an aura of legitimacy by appealing to a remote past. The claim was put forward that the Shogun was an usurper and that the Emperor was merely being " restored " as the rightful head of the state. From the very beginning steps were taken to make the Emperor into an absolute monarch by reviving the ancient mythology which claimed for him divine origins. The Throne, it goes without saying, proved to be a useful tool for breaking down local loyalties and for creating a modern nation. Thus, in short, the scales were weighted in favor of the development of a regime in which power would be tightly held by a small group of men.

But, as has been shown in the foregoing pages, the group in power did not remain unchallenged. Some disaffected samurai, including a few who had been in the government, organized a popular movement to oppose those in control. From the point of view of the government this was a formidable movement because it had a more than rudimentary party organization and because one of the most important elements in it were the wealthier landowners and rural industrialists who had a firm grip on local government. Furthermore, one of the demands which the popular leaders made was the establishment of a national legislative assembly. The idea of an assembly had a fairly long history in Japan and it was difficult for the government to refuse these demands. In fact it was finally forced to call a Diet in 1890. The crucial issue, however, was the question of the amount of power which this assembly would have. If institutional arrangements which theorists like Ueki Emori had advocated had been put into effect, the balance of political power in the state would have been radically altered. The center of power would have shifted from the small group of ex-samurai to the newly-created Diet consisting chiefly of men from the opposition parties. Since the most prominent of these parties was the *Jiyuto*, an important consequence of this might have been a marked change in the tempo of industrialization and modernization, for the landowner-rural industrialists who were influential in the *Jiyuto* would have hardly favored voting large appropriations for subsidizing modern urban industries and for building up a huge military establishment. Also if, as Ueki proposed, universal suffrage had been adopted, the way would have been opened for small land-holders, tenant farmers, and industrial workers to have their interests represented in varying degrees in the government.

The fact is, however, that the democratic movement did not succeed in breaking the hold of the Meiji oligarchy; and it may be appropriate to present here some reflections as to why it ultimately failed. One of the most important reasons for its failure was the split within the *Jiyuto*. Such a split could have been avoided if the democratic movement had dealt adequately with the question of land reform. But this perhaps would have been asking for the impossible since the landowners who were powerful in the *Jiyuto* surely would have opposed such a move. A conclusion to be drawn from this is that the movement suffered from the lack of a more diversified basis of support. The fact that there existed no important groups of urban merchants and industrialists to join a movement of this kind resulted in serious weaknesses.

The second reason was inadequate leadership. Too often the leaders were willing to abandon the movement to take posts offered by the government. This may have been prompted in part by the persistence of class feeling which led the samurai to look upon themselves as forming a superior class best fitted for governing the nation.

Third, there was the matter of ideology. Although there were some theorists who had a precocious grasp of political theory, the movement was never able to produce an outstanding theorist of its own. In fact it could be said that the theorists for the democratic movement were men like John Stuart Mill, J. J. Rousseau, and Herbert Spencer. A practical consequence of this was the failure to produce new political symbols which could seriously compete with those available to the government, such as the Emperor. The advantage which the government enjoyed was that it could point to the Imperial court as an uniquely Japanese institution while those in the opposition could only appeal to universal concepts like natural rights. In a period of rising nationalism, this was an important factor.

This leads to the fourth reason, namely nationalism. Japan was modernized in a period when the Western powers were enlarging their colonial possessions by the use of military power. Like other Asiatic countries, Japan's sovereignty was impaired by the imposition of unequal treaties. The consequence of this was the growth of an exaggerated form of nationalism; and given their environment and history, the Japanese quickly learned the usefulness of armed might and began to emphasize military preparedness. Since the leaders of the democratic movement were themselves highly nationalistic, they were unwilling to oppose the principle of a strong state. They could only argue that an ingredient of national power was national unity and that the latter could be best obtained by providing wider representation for the various interests within the nation.

Finally, it is necessary to point to the remarkable ability of the Meiji leaders to grant concessions at the proper moment. Whenever popular pressure became too powerful to be suppressed, they would retreat without giving up the substance of power. They possessed the kind of suppleness which any regime wishing to remain in control must possess. Perhaps an explanation of this is to be found in the fact that these men were able to overthrow the Shogunate without having had to acquire a wide popular following. This left them unencumbered with commitments, thus enabling them to act freely as the occasion demanded.

There now remains the question of relating the lessons of an earlier age to the present. Here we tread on unfirm ground, and any remarks necessarily must be somewhat speculative. Comparisons can be misleading since a wide gulf separates the contemporary scene from the nineteenth century. Yet it is tempting to pose the question: " What are the prospects for democracy in contemporary Japan? "

Part Five:

EPILOGUE

PROSPECTS OF DEMOCRACY IN CONTEMPORARY JAPAN

I.

MORE than thirty years ago, Thorstein Veblen, fresh from his investigation of the effects of the industrial revolution in Germany, turned his attention to Japan. He saw, in his usual penetrating fashion, that Japan had many features in common with Germany. In an essay called " The Opportunity of Japan," [1] he developed the theme that although Japan had adopted new technology, its spiritual outlook, its ethical values, and its principles of conduct remained those of a past era. He felt that " this unique combination of a high-wrought spirit of feudalistic fealty and chivalric honor with the material efficiency given by the modern technology," [2] gave tremendous strength for war and aggrandizement. Subsequent history bore out many of Veblen's observations.[3] It is to his credit that he put his finger on one of the salient features of the development of modern Japan.

Historically, this gap between the material and non-material aspects of Japanese culture which Veblen noticed arose in part out of the Restoration settlement. As we have seen, already at the end of the Tokugawa period, there were present the beginnings of capitalistic enterprise. Scattered throughout the land were rural landowner-entrepreneurs who produced commodities, particularly textiles, under the " putting-out system " for sale in urban and other markets. At the same time, in the Western clans a start was being made in the development of large-scale industries, parti-

---

[1] Originally published in the *Journal of Race Development*, VI (1915-1916), it is reprinted in *Essays in Our Changing Order* (New York, 1934). Quotations are taken from the latter source.

[2] *Ibid.*, p. 251.

[3] See H. T. Oshima, " Veblen on Japan," *Social Research*, X (November, 1943), 487-494.

cularly those of a military nature, under state encouragement and aid. After the Restoration of 1868 the sundry restrictions, hitherto acting as a brake on rapid industrialization, were removed, and within a few decades capitalism became firmly established in Japan.

It has been the experience everywhere that the transformation of political and social institutions goes hand-in-hand with the rise of capitalism and the growth of industrialization. Werner Sombart emphasized what he called the " spirit " of capitalism which contained three elements: acquisition, competition, and rationality. The purpose of economic activity became acquisition, particularly in terms of money. Acquisition was to be achieved through competition in an environment free from outside interference. And finally long-range planning, exact calculation, in short, economic rationality, permeated the entire economic order.[4] In the social realm, hitherto submerged groups rose to prominence. Wealth became increasingly more important than social status. Individualism and self-help became virtues. In the political field, the hold of the feudal aristocracy was broken and new institutions of representative government, providing wider participation in the political process, emerged step-by-step.

It is significant that within broad outlines Japanese history in the latter half of the nineteenth century followed a similar course. Despite all the peculiar features of Japanese historical development, there was, as elsewhere, a rough correlation between industrialization and the demand for representative government. It was no historical accident that the supporters of the popular movement of the 1870's and 1880's found the ideas of Rousseau, Mill, Bentham, and Smiles congenial, and the slogans of " liberty and popular rights " meaningful. Where the Japanese democratic movement differed from its European predecessors was that it did not end in a complete victory for liberalism.

The failure of the democratic movement and the reaction which it provoked among the conservative groups led to an increasing divergence between the material aspects of Japanese civilization and the social and political theory. While industrialization was pushed forward along all fronts, the system of beliefs and values, in short what Professor R. M. MacIver has called the " social

---

[4] Werner Sombart's article on Capitalism in the *Encyclopedia of the Social Sciences.*

myth," [5] was pushed back, as it were, to an earlier age. We saw that as early as 1881, Ito Hirobumi shrewdly realized that if he acted quickly he could reverse the trend toward "republican" sentiments. The Constitution of 1889 proclaimed the fiction of rule by the Emperor and made certain that the legislature would remain an ineffectual branch of the government. The famous Imperial Rescript on Education, issued the following year in 1890, reinforced the element of Confucian thought present in the Japanese social myth and set the tone for its subsequent elaboration. [6]

A brief description of the cardinal points in the social myth may not be out of place here. We may note, first of all, that according to the interpretation prevailing before V-J Day, the fountainhead of Japanese history was to be found in the ancient past when the Sun Goddess, Amaterasu-o-Mikami, commanded her grandson to become the ruler of Japan. The Japanese state, therefore, was believed to be divine in origin, and its fundamental character (kokutai) unique, immutable, and eternal. [7] In the beginning was the Emperor and in time his descendants became his subjects. Hence the relationship between ruler and subject was fixed for all time. "Sovereigns of other countries," wrote Tokutomi Iichiro,

---

[5] By "myths" Professor MacIver means the "value-impregnated beliefs and notions" that men have. In his view it is the myth system that holds together society. R. M. MacIver, *The Web of Government* (New York, 1947), pp. 4 ff., and Chapter III.

[6] For instance, the Rescript contains the following passage: "Ye, Our Subjects, be filial to your parents, affectionate to your brothers and sisters; as husbands and wives be harmonious, as friends true; bear yourselves in modesty and moderation. . . ." In 1912, Yoshikawa Akimasa, who was Minister of Education in 1890 wrote: "At the time of the Restoration the late Emperor declared it would be the guiding principle of his government to introduce Western civilization into the country. . . . Consequently every institution in Japan was Westernized and the atmosphere of the 'new civilization' was felt in almost every stratum of society. . . . The excessive Westernization of Japan very naturally aroused strong opposition among conservative people, especially scholars of the Japanese and Chinese classics, who thought it dangerous for the moral standard of this Empire to see this process carried even into the moral teachings of the people." Quoted in Robert King Hall, *Shushin: The Ethics of a Defeated Nation* (New York, 1949), pp. 36-37. See also Ienaga Saburo, "Kyoiku Chokugo Seiritsu no Shiso-teki Kosatsu" [A Study of the Ideological Background of the Imperial Rescript on Education], *Shigaku Zasshi*, LVI, No. 12 (December, 1946).

[7] The term usually used to describe the fundamental character of the state is "kokutai." The *Kokutai no Hongi* [Basic Principles of Kokutai], published by the Ministry of Education in 1937 may be regarded as an official explanation of kokutai. An English translation of this work under the above title has been made by John Gauntlett (Harvard University Press, Cambridge 1949).

a well-known journalist, " are like hats. One can change them at
any time. The Emperor of Japan is like the head. If one cuts off
the head of an individual he dies. In other countries the sovereign
exists because the people exist. In Japan the people exist because
the sovereign exists." [8]

Another way of expressing the connection between the ruler and
the subject was to regard the Japanese nation as a family of
families. The Emperor was looked upon as the patriarch and his
subjects as his children. The relationship between the Emperor
and his subjects, therefore, came to be expressed more in terms of
father and son than in terms of ruler and ruled. This had the effect
of equating political obligation with filial piety. It was professed
that no conflict existed between filial piety and loyalty to the state.
It was the solemn duty of every son to put the welfare of his
family above his personal interest. Since the state was merely a
large family, the individual naturally was expected to sacrifice his
interests for the good of the state. The *Shimmin-no-michi* (The
Way of the Subjects), an official publication of the Ministry of
Education stated the matter in this way: " Now in our country
filial piety exists because of loyalty; loyalty is the root. Within our
families we are offspring of our parents; both parents and offspring
are subjects. Filial piety as found in our families must be transformed into loyalty without alteration. Loyalty and filial piety
are one." [9]

Thus every citizen was supposed to be linked to the sovereign by
the sentiment of loyalty and filial piety. This did not imply,
however, that all citizens were of equal status in the eyes of the
ruler. On the contrary, just as in a human being, the brain is more
important than the little toe, so in the state there is inequality,
and hence hierarchy. Attacking the idea of equality and freedom
found in the West as " false notions," a Japanese writer said: " The
equality and freedom which Japan considers, and, moreover, tries
to realize is the true equality and freedom resting on just principles
of nature (tenchi no kodo). That is to say, by the recognition of
man's inequality, each individual is given his appropriate place.
Human beings, who to begin with are unequal, are thus enabled to

[8] Tokutomi Iichiro, *Showa Kokumin Tokuhon* [The Showa National Reader],
(Tokyo, 1939), p. 68.
[9] This quotation is taken from the 6th edition published in 1943, pp. 47-48.

avoid the misfortunes arising from this inequality; and each person is permitted to fully manifest his talents and ability." [10]

It should be apparent that the Japanese social myth outlined above was basically incompatible with democratic ideals.[11] The idea of an Emperor holding sovereign power as an inheritance from the Sun Goddess could not be made to harmonize with the doctrine of popular soverignty. Equality, a basic underlying theme of democracy, clashed head on with the belief in hierarchy.

The history of Europe reveals, however, that at one time a social myth in many respects similar to the Japanese social myth prevailed.[12] But under the impact of the Renaissance, the Reformation, and later the various revolutionary movements it was destroyed and replaced by a new myth. In his essay, Veblen expressed the view that what he called the "Spirit of Old Japan," or medievalism would have to give way in the face of changing conditions in the field of business and technology. "Ideals, ethical values, principles (habits of thought) induced by the conditions of life in the past," he said, "must presently give place to a different range of ideals, values, and principles, so soon as the range of habituation to which they owe their force has ceased to be operative." [13] In another place he said that industrialization required a high rate of literacy for securing "matter-of-fact information," and an exacting system of communications and a "materialistic" habit of mind. "So, e. g., the spread of such matter-of-fact information and such mechanistic conceptions must unavoidably act to dissipate all substantial belief in that *opéra bouffe* mythology that makes up the state religion and supplies the foundation of the Japanese faith in the Emperor's divine pedigree and occult virtues. . . ." [14]

What Veblen could not foresee was that under certain circum-

[10] Nakaoka Hiroo, *Nihon-teki Sekaikan Josetsu* [An Introduction to the Japanese World-View], (Tokyo, 1944), p. 200.

[11] It should be noted that the old social myth has not been completely eradicated by defeat. For a recent discussion on this point see Robert King Hall, *op. cit.*, pp. 237 ff.

[12] The parallels between the European and Japanese social myths are brought out in Frederick Watkins, "Aspects of Constitutional Democracy," in *Japan's Prospect* edited by Douglas Haring (Harvard University Press, Cambridge, 1946), pp. 305-331.

[13] *Essays in Our Changing Order*, p. 256.

[14] *Ibid.*, pp. 261-262.

stances the system of communications and education which he thought would result in the decline of the " belief in that *opéra bouffe* mythology " could be used to perpetuate that very myth. Once the state became firmly committed to a certain type of social myth, it could preserve it through centralized control of the educational system, rigid censorship, thought control and propaganda. This meant, of course, the insistence on strict orthodoxy and the denial of such values as freedom of expression.

The difficulty, however, was that the freedom to investigate and to express oneself could not be easily denied. The number of books banned every year was symptomatic of the constant tug-of-war between the insistance on orthodoxy, on the one hand, and the desire to express heretical views, on the other.[15] Because the content of the myth was so obviously puerile, it was sometimes difficult even for the government to defend it. In 1940 Professor Tsuda Sokichi, of Waseda University, who was given to publishing new interpretations of ancient mythology from time to time, was brought into court on the charge of having impaired the dignity of the Imperial house. The court held that Tsuda had not violated the law. The judges found that when it came to tales about ancient Japanese history, " there are not a few which we, on the basis of every day experience, cannot accept as resting on facts. There are many instances where to interpret these tales as accounts of historical happenings would do violence to our present-day reasoning process and knowledge. Therefore, the interpretation of these tales must be a problem which confronts all people who wish to read and understand the ancient documents. It goes without saying that the feeling of respect for the Imperial house and the love of country, which our people have, have been long nurtured by our history and are firmly established. Hence they are not the kind to be easily shaken by doubts as to [the authenticity] of ancient records." [16]

There is in the foregoing statement by the court a hint of the need to accommodate the social myth to the scientific method. In freer societies there is constantly going on a reinterpretation of the

[15] See John Paul Reed, *Kokutai, A Study of Certain Sacred and Secular Aspects of Japanese Nationalism* (Chicago, 1940), pp. 106-7.

[16] Seki Yuki, *Tokugawa, Meiji, Taisho, Showa Chomei Saibanroku* [Accounts of Prominent Court Trials in the Tokugawa, Meiji, Taisho, Showa Eras], (Tokyo, 1948), p. 362.

social myth to bring it more or less in line with technological and institutional change.[17] This, as we know, was not permitted in Japan. The problem of determining the results flowing from rigidities introduced into the myth system is a difficult one. We can infer, however, that in all likelihood it impeded social integration and contributed to political instability.

II.

It has sometimes been observed that in Japan the concept of " public " has not been fully developed.[18] In Japan there are no " public servants "; instead there are the Emperor's officials. The idea of " public welfare " would not enter the heads of most people. In fact the common word for " public " is *ko* and it occurs in such compounds as " koan " (public peace) and " koen " (public garden or park), but the primary meaning of *ko* is " prince " or " duke." It would appear, thus, that in the Japanese mind " public " was at one time associated with " prince."

We saw earlier that the nation was conceived to be a big family and that political obligation was expressed in terms of filial piety. To the average Japanese individual there existed his " iye " or " house," and his nation — a big family — but no " society " in the real sense. " A ' house ' in the family system," wrote Hani Setsuko, " is in itself a world, which essentially hinges on the moral idea that places the foremost value on the vertical relations between the members of the family." [19] In this " world " the male head was a dominant figure, and a code of behavior governed the relation of the other members of the family to the head and to each other. An important part of this code were the " externals of performance," such as acts of obeisance, and the use of honorific language.[20] Ideally, the family in its relations with other families maintained a united front. Thus, as Mrs. Hani put it, the house " stands for a family community, where vertical relations predominate over all

[17] Cf., MacIver, *op. cit.*, pp. 5-6; 51-58.
[18] E. g., Oshima Shotoku, *Demokurashii to Kokumin Sei* [Democracy and Japanese National Character], (Tokyo, 1949), especially Chapter 6; Oshima Yasumasa, " ' Iye ' no Mondai " [The Problem of " House "], *Tembo*, April, 1946, pp. 17-29.
[19] Hani Setsuko, *The Japanese Family System* (Tokyo, 1948), p. 9.
[20] Cf., Kawashima Takenori, *Nihon Shakai no Kazoku-teki Kosei* [The Family Structure of Japanese Society], (Tokyo, 1949), Chapter 1.

the other relations, it is essentially exclusive and isolated in character, which is contrary to the idea of modern society." [21]

An individual brought up under such a system knew, in general, where he fitted in, and what his privileges and obligations were insofar as his family was concerned. By extension, he also knew what his obligations were vis-à-vis the state. But once he stepped beyond the confines of the family and state and ventured out into " society " there were no " guide lines," as it were, for him to follow. Professor Kawashima Takenori, of the Law College of Tokyo University, expressed it thus: " To people accustomed to this type [i. e., Japanese] of family life, society outside of the family appears as a human relationship ' without order,' and without an intrinsically necessary tie. People are mutual enemies, or, if not that, they are in no way bound together. Under such circumstances, individuals cannot respect each other as human beings; there can be no social morality; and what is known as morality can exist only within the family." [22] But, says Professor Kawashima, people inevitably form associations outside of the family. In such instances, however, the " individual feels isolated and insecure." [23] In the end he seeks the protection of some individual and there is established, as a result, a kind of father-son relationship. Associations thus took on a family pattern.

Certain consequences flowed from this. The cement binding together an association was not common interests or common principles. Rather the ties between leaders and followers were such " external " factors as love of wine, the ability to play chess, or the fact of having been born in the same village, town, or prefecture. The behavior of an individual was not governed by his analysis of the choices open to him and his conviction that a particular course of action was morally right. Instead it was blind obedience to the persons in positions of authority, and hence there could be no sense of individual responsibility.[24] Moreover, the expression of individual opinion or criticism was discouraged. Groups became shot

[21] Hani, *op. cit.*, p. 9.

[22] Kawashima, *op. cit.*, p. 16.

[23] *Ibid.*, p. 17.

[24] This lack of a sense of personal responsibility is clearly brought out in Maruyama Saneo. " Gunkoku Shihaisha no Seishin Keitai " [The Spiritual Makeupon of the Leaders of a Militaristic National], *Choryu* [Current], May, 1949, pp. 15-37. Professor Maruyama, of the Tokyo University, makes use of the documents of the International Military Tribunal for the Far East to illustrate his ideas.

through with factions and cliques, with each clique closing ranks in the face of external criticism. And unless each individual attached himself to one faction or another, and thereby secured the protection and support of some powerful leader, he could not look forward to advancement.[25]

At this point we are reminded of the remark that the veteran parliamentarian, Ozaki Yukio, once made. Speaking of political parties in Japan, he said:

Here in the Orient we have had the conception of a faction; but none of a public party. A political party is an association of people having for its exclusive object the discussion of public affairs of state and the enforcement of their views thereon. But when political parties are transplanted into the East, they at once partake of the nature of faction, pursuing private and personal interests instead of the interests of the state—as witnessed by the fact of their joining hands by turns with the clan cliques or using the construction of railways, ports, and harbours, schools, etc. as means for extending party influence. Besides, the customs and usages of feudal times are so deeply impressed upon the minds of men here that even the idea of political parties, as soon as it enters the brains of our countrymen, germinates and grows according to feudal notions. Such being the case, even political parties . . . are really affairs of personal connections and sentiments, the relations between the leader and the members of a party being similar to those which subsisted between a feudal lord and his liegemen, or to those between a "boss" of gamblers and his followers in this country. A politician scrupulous enough to join or desert a party for the sake of principle is denounced as a political traitor or renegade.[26]

Ozaki was correct in attributing the tendency toward factionalism to "feudal notions." The Tokugawa heritage was scarcely conducive to the growth of political and other associations based on democratic principles. The technique of social control utilized by the Tokugawa rulers included, among other things, the enforcement of groups responsibility through the *gonin-gumi*. Under the Tokugawa political system each individual was in effect a detective and a policeman, and those who reported infractions of regulations were rewarded, while those who failed to do so were punished.[27] The Tokugawa rulers, moreover, strictly forbade what they called "toto" (factions, cabals), which in our terminology would be political associations. This meant that any attempt to form politi-

[25] Cf., Kawashima, *op. cit.*, pp. 19-21.

[26] Ozaki Yukio, *The Voice of Japanese Democracy*, translated by J. E. De Becker (Yokohama, 1918), pp. 93-94.

[27] Tokutomi Iichiro, *Kinsei Nihon Kokumin Shi: Tokugawa Bakufu Joki*, II, 507.

cal groups had to be done in secret. When seen against such a background, the nation-wide spread of political associations in the early years of the Meiji era, which have been described in detail in the preceding chapters, seems all the more remarkable.

III.

One of our major themes has been that the family served as a prototype for social organization in modern Japan. The nation, as we noted, was likened to a big family, and social groups within the nation tended to take on a family-like structure. Yet over the years the family itself has been undergoing slow but unmistakable change. This fact it likely to have, in the long run, far-reaching effects.

The evolution of the family, like any other institution, was affected by the character of the Restoration settlement. Broadly speaking, in the Tokugawa period there were two types of family system: one prevailing among the samurai class and the other among the plebeian class. To be sure they were not mutually exclusive, since there was a tendency for social inferiors to ape their social betters. At the same time, the samurai class had begun to disintegrate through intermarriage, adoption and the like. Nevertheless, one might say that among the samurai families, the Confucian influence was stronger, the authority of the head of the family was greater, and the relations between the individual members were more formalized than among plebeian families. Among the latter, the family atmosphere was less austere, and the relationship of the members freer and more natural in the sense that there was more display of spontaneous human affection. The samurai, to whom the externals of performance were more important than the spirit in which it was done, thought family life among the commoners was undisciplined, unaffected by rules of propriety and hence " animal-like." That the two types of family organization were in conflict is evidenced by the presence, in Tokugawa literature, of the persistent theme involving the clash of " giri " (obligation), representing the " pull " of the Confucian social code, and " ninjo " (human feeling), representing the more human qualities of affection and sympathy.[28]

[28] Kawashima Takenori, " Nihon no Iye " [The Japanese Family] in *Toyo no Iye*

After the Meiji Restoration the legal distinctions between classes were abolished. A fluid state of affairs obtained in the early years of the Meiji era; and family organization, if allowed to take its natural course of development, very likely would have moved away from Confucian ideals and become more like families in the Western world. In fact demands were made by those democratically inclined that the traditional system of adoption known as the *yoshi seido* be abolished since it impeded man's natural freedom. One writer opposed the system on the ground that an adopted person had dual restraints put on him — one by his real parents, and the other by his adopted parents. " Now," continued this writer, " an adopted person is a human being and was born into this free world with human rights. Yet he suffers restraints and is oppressed by both families. . . ." [29] Another writer thought that the system was unnatural because " one cannot get something out of nothing." He argued that it was a violation of natural principles for a childless couple to acquire a child through adoption since nature intended that they should have no children.[30]

Instead of trying to guide family organization into more democratic paths, the Meiji government took steps to impose the samurai-type of family structure on the entire population. For instance, a decree issued in 1873 by the *Dajokan* stated that the commoners should follow the system of primogeniture prevailing among the nobility. " Although no decrees have been issued as yet, with respect to the rights of family succession among commoners, there is no reason why in terms of moral codes a different system of family succession should obtain between the upper and lower classes. Procedure among the commoners should be the same as that among the samurai." [31] The civil code adopted in 1898 contained many provisions which harked back to the feudal period.

An even more effective method of inculcating Confucian ideas on family organization was the indoctrination program carried on in the schools. To combat the spread of democratic ideas, Motoda Eifu, a bureaucrat and Confucian scholar wrote, in 1879, a book

to Kanryo [The Oriental Family and Bureaucracy], edited by the Toyo Bunka Kenkyu Kai (Tokyo, 1948), pp. 125-135.

[29] Aoyama Michio, *Nihon Kazoku Seido no Kenkyu* [A Study of the Japanese Family System], (Tokyo, 1947), p. 142.

[30] *Ibid.*, p. 140.

[31] *Ibid.*, p. 169.

called *Kyogaku Daishi* [Great Principles of Education]. In one passage he said: " The essence of education is to make clear benevolence, justice, reverence, and wisdom, cultivate learning and talent, and thereby serve humanity. . . . Although at one time we took the best features of the West and succeeded in getting in new things, the serious defect was to relegate benevolence, justice, reverence and wisdom to a secondary position. The thing to fear of blindly seeking after Western customs is that in the end the great principles governing the relations between ruler and subject, and father and son will be forgotten. . . . For moral guidance Confucius is the most important. People should cultivate sincerity and moral conduct, and after that they should pursue the various subjects of learning to the best of their ability." [32]

It must be said that, on the whole, those who set out to encourage the spread of Confucian family ethics succeeded in their immediate objectives. What they did not foresee was that with the passage of time this type of ethical family code forcibly carried over from a past age would become increasingly incompatible with living realities, thus giving rise to tensions and unresolved conflicts. Speaking of the peculiar nature of disputes in Japan between parents and children, Professor Nakagawa Zennosuke noted: " There is, on the one hand, the Confucian idea of filial behavior which makes filial piety the basis of all action, while, on the other hand, there exists the rather strong individualistic economic life. A great many of the causes [of disputes between parents and children] can be found in the fact that it is not so easy as it used to be to reconcile the two." [33]

As this quotation suggests, undoubtedly the Japanese family system has been undergoing change owing to the impact of capitalism and industrialization. In the absence of large-scale sociological studies, it is not possible to treat the matter of change statistically; but it cannot be disputed that the family has been breaking down. Of the various long range factors contributing to the transformation of the family, urbanization is probably one of the most important.

Census figures show that, as one might expect, the rural areas have a higher birth rate than the cities. Yet the overall rural

[32] Kawashima, " Nihon no Iye," *op. cit.*, p. 127.
[33] Tamaki Hajime, *Kazoku Ron* [On the Family], (Tokyo, 1947), p. 124.

population has remained relatively stationary. This is brought out by Professor Ueda's figures which show that in the 37-year period between 1888 and 1925 there was an estimated population increase of a little over nineteen and a half millions. Of this increase, 16,683,000 were living in towns and cities with 10,000 population or more.[34] In 1930 one-third of the male population of Tokyo between the ages of 15 and 24 had migrated to Tokyo within the preceding five-year period.[35]

Owing to the prevalence of the system of primogeniture, it was generally the second and third sons who migrated to the cities. There they lived away from their families in dormitories and boarding houses. A survey made in 1920 in Tokyo revealed, for instance, that 72 percent of the men in the 15-19 age bracket and 69 percent of the 20-24 bracket were not living with their families.[36] In order to provide amusement for this large group of young men freed from direct parental supervision there sprang up in Tokyo in the 1920's a large number of bars, cafes, taxi dance halls, and other places of amusement. The well-known phenomena of the "mobo" and "moga" or the emancipated "modern boy" and "modern girl" were also a reflection of the cityward movement of young men and women.

Economic independence, city life, sophisticated education—these were not conducive to the perpetuation of the old Confucian family system. More and more the young wished to choose their own mates, and to pursue their own careers. Moreover with the acquisition of a new set of values, the old customs became absurd if not irksome. The brilliant novelist and satirist, Natsume Soseki, caught some of this conflict in his novel, *Kokoro*. After graduation from a university, the young hero returns home to his parents, who are extremely pleased at their son's achievement. Then, says the hero:

To celebrate my graduation, my parents began to talk about inviting our neighbors to a dinner at which we should have sekihan [mixture of rice and red beans served on happy occasions]. It was the very thing that I had been secretly dreading since my arrival. I at once objected to it, saying, "Please don't make a fuss about my graduation."

[34] Ueda Teijiro, *Nihon Jinko Seisaku* [Japanese Population Policy], (Tokyo. 1937), p. 277.
[35] *Ibid.*, p. 282.
[36] Toda Teizo, *Iye to Kazoku Seido* [House and Family System], (Tokyo, 1944), pp. 186-191.

I hated country guests. Their only purpose in coming was to drink and eat. They were mostly the kind of people who looked forward to some event which would make them foregather at somebody's house. . . . But I could hardly say to my father and mother that they should not make merry with such vulgar people. So I only repeated that I did not care for such extravagance.

" It is not so extravagant, as you think. Your graduation is an event which will never occur in your life again. It is reasonable to celebrate it. You must not refuse," my mother said, who seemed to regard my graduation in the same light as my marriage.

" Of course we can do without it. But you know how people talk," said my father, who disliked other people's backbiting. It was true that these foolish country-people made plenty of ill-natured remarks against people who did not do what they expected.

" The country is different from Tokyo, and very troublesome," he observed again.

" Besides it will affect your father's honor," my mother added.[37]

Other examples from Japanese literature could be easily supplied. Indeed it would be no exaggeration to say that one of the most persistent themes of modern literature is the problem of the individual and the family, and it attests to the severe strains which the family system has been undergoing during the past decades.

Undoubtedly, the disruption of the family has been accelerated by the war and defeat. The evacuation of cities owing to bombing and the resultant scattering of families, the severe shortage of housing, and the post-war inflation all have contributed to the weakening of family ties.[38] Thus the emancipation of the individual from his family, which has been one of the underlying trends in Japanese society, is bound to continue in the coming years.

We have dealt at length with the Japanese family system because it seems to provide a clue to the riddle of democracy in post-war Japan. We have observed how the family pattern imposed itself on associations in Japan, and how in the case of the political party it impeded its effective working. As Professor Kawashima says, " Japanese society is made up of families and family-type organizations; and the dominant family principle is directly opposed to democratic principles. . . . Indeed, the principle of family-type organization is even now strongly obstructing the democratization

[37] Natsume Soseki, *Kokoro* [Heart], translated by Ineko Sato (Tokyo, 1941), pp. 97-98.
[38] Oshima Yasumasa, *ibid.*, p. 25.

of social life, and without its ' denial ' our democratization cannot succeed." [39]

If it is true, however, that the family itself is disintegrating, then can we not expect that the imposition of the family pattern on group life will gradually cease? This in turn should clear the way for the rebuilding of political and other associations along more democratic lines. In other words, the disintegration of the family, itself a negative factor, can contribute to positive political reconstruction.

There are already some indications that the development of new types of associations is in the offing. No one would have predicted during the war years, for example, that the end of hostilities would see the rapid revival of labor unions. Yet this has happened much to the astonishment of American observers. Labor union membership jumped from 5,300 in October, 1945 to 6,910,000 members in March, 1949.[40] A recently published survey of the labor movement in post-war Japan, while critical of the various weaknesses in the labor unions, comes to the conclusion that " Of the various democratic organizations encouraged as a definite part of the occupation policy, labor unions are far and away the most dynamic and articulate organs of expression for any important segment of the society." [41] In another passage the same article notes that although there is danger that the labor movement might prove to be of service to totalitarian extremists, " most informed observers discount this possibility." " They point," it continues, " to the increasingly democratic practices in evidence at union meetings and the vigorous forensics displayed at conventions; the unions do, on the whole, give articulate expression to the aspirations of their memberships." [42]

Much the same thing has taken place in the field of agricultural cooperatives in Japan. The first law governing cooperatives was passed in 1900, and by 1940 there were 15,101 cooperatives. Like other associations, cooperatives came increasingly under the domination of the government and during the war served " as the instrumentality through which agricultural prices and production were con-

[39] Kawashima, *Nihon Shakai no Kazoku-teki Kosei*, p. 22.
[40] William T. Moran, " Labor Unions in Postwar Japan," *Far Eastern Survey*, XVIII, No. 21 (October 19, 1949), p. 242.
[41] *Ibid.*, p. 248.
[42] *Ibid.*

trolled, food collections and rationing activities were accomplished, and rural capital was obtained in support of national policy." [43] After the end of the war a program of decentralization was put into effect by the Occupation authorities, thus making it possible to carry on operations within a new framework. In a report prepared by John L. Cooper, of the Natural Resources Section of SCAP, it is stated: "The readiness and thoroughness with which her farmers have organized and proceeded with operations under the new cooperative laws strike the casual observer as phenomenal. Certainly the formation within one year of more than 30,000 associations embracing eight million members and representing 99 percent of the nation's farm households has few parallels." [44] Commenting on the magnitude of the difficulties that had to be overcome, the report continues, "New cooperative associations had to be formed, officers chosen by secret ballot with emphasis on avoidance of prewar leadership, and business conducted under the new procedures. Initiative rested in the local people and not in national authority." [45] The report concludes with the statement: "It was no easy task to replace a system completely dominated by central authority, with over 30,000 individual cooperatives run by their own membership. The transition has been achieved and the new organizations are effectively functioning. It is generally felt that the cooperatives are making a notable contribution to the maintenance of democratic principles throughout the nation." [46]

It is important to note that in the case of both labor unions and agricultural cooperatives, the institutional framework was already at hand. The history of unions and cooperatives alike goes back to the turn of the 20th century. The Japanese, therefore, are not without previous experience in these matters. In the case of parliamentary procedures, this is even more apparent. The continuity of the Japanese Diet since its inception in 1890 has not been broken. Even during the war the Diet as an institution was not abolished. The very fact that the government felt it necessary to handpick the members of the House of Representatives would seem

[43] John L. Cooper, *Development of Agricultural Cooperatives in Japan*, Natural Resources Section, SCAP (Tokyo, 1949) (mimeographed), p. 3.
[44] *Ibid.*, p. 10.
[45] *Ibid.*
[46] *Ibid.*, p. 15.

to indicate that the Diet was not a completely innocuous and impotent organization.

A similar situation obtains with respect to the operation of political parties, electoral processes, and parliamentary procedures. The accumulation of decades of experience means that energies, which otherwise would have gone into the creation of new institutions and the learning of novel techniques, can be devoted to the perfecting of institutions and techniques already at hand.

In fact a careful survey would probably reveal that "forerunners" of many of the reforms inaugurated by the Occupation authorities can be found in Japanese history. Agitation for woman suffrage began, for example, as early as 1884.[47] In the 1880's proposals were made for land reform by Oi Kentaro. This was followed by other proposals which showed the influence of the writings of Henry George.[48] The reform, if not the abolition, of the Privy Council was a favorite topic of discussion among political scientists in the 1920's.

It is in the matter of a liberal tradition that contemporary Japan suffers rather obvious weaknesses. Yet here again it should be emphasized that there have been liberal periods in Japan's past. The truism that every generation writes its own history is borne out by the prominent place given to the Meiji democratic movement in post-war Japanese historical publications. One might also point to the ground work laid in the 1920's by liberal intellectuals like Yoshino Sakuzo and Kawai Eijiro, whose works had wide influence. It is no accident that the collected works of Yoshino were recently published [49] and that the writings of Kawai are being reprinted.

One of the serious obstacles to the smooth functioning of constitutional government the world over has been the existence of sharp cleavages within the population along cultural, religious, or racial lines. Wherever sharp divisions occur stable government through discussion and compromise is made well-nigh impossible. Japan is

[47] Material regarding the early movement for woman suffrage is brought together in *Meiji Bunka Zenshu*, XXI, 427-457.

[48] In 1906 Miyazaki Tamizo advocated the equal distribution of land and he also organized the Association for the Restoration of Land, Chitoshi Yanaga, *Japan Since Perry* (New York, 1949), p. 239. Miyazaki's book is reprinted in the *Meiji Bunka Zenshu*, XXI, 301-327.

[49] *Yoshino Sakuzo Hakase Minshu Shugi Ronshu*, 8 vols. (Tokyo, 1948).

remarkably free of such divisions. Earlier there existed a small group of outcasts known as Eta but the process of assimilation has been going on until today they represent no real problem. For centuries the Japanese have enjoyed a cultural unity. There have arisen, moreover, no religious issues to split the nation into warring camps in modern times. These are unspectacular features; but they are real assets for the growth of effective parliamentary government.

Related to the problem of cultural, religious and racial unity is that of social and economic groupings within the country. It is Professor C. J. Friedrich's view that cultural and economic divisions are the most formidable cleavages in modern times.[50] Since no detailed studies of long-term trends in social stratification in Japan are available, it is difficult to arrive at a clear picture. It is fairly evident, however, that although the middle classes—and particularly the business class—did not grow to be as powerful as their counterparts in Western Europe, they still exist. The nature of Japanese capitalism was such that there were, on the one hand, a few powerful *zaibatsu* firms closely linked with the government, and, on the other hand, a large number of small individually-owned enterprises, which eventually came under the economic domination of the *zaibatsu*. Some idea of the extent of these individually-owned enterprises may be obtained from the fact that in 1947 there were a total of 3,277,124 establishments (including agriculture, forestry, fisheries, mining, construction, manufacturing, utilities, commerce, finance, transportation and communication, personal service, professional services, government, and other). Of these, 967,174 were engaged in manufacturing, and 776,275 of these enterprises employed from one to four persons, while only 362 employed more than 1,000 persons. Commerce presents much the same picture. There were listed 1,012,633 establishements engaged in commerce, and 949,715 of them employed four persons or less.[51]

The matter may also be approached from the point of view of the composition of the total labor force. In 1947 the total labor force

[50] Carl J. Friedrich, *Constitutional Government and Democracy* (Boston, 1941), p. 162.

[51] Ministry of Finance, *Statistical Year-Book of Finance and Economy of Japan, 1948* (Tokyo, 1948), pp. 584-585.

came to 16,944,918 persons. This total was divided into the following classifications: [52]

Officers of companies and organizations 6%
Owners of enterprises & family employees 29%
Regularly employed white collar and manual workers .. 56%
Temporary employees and day laborers 9%

Incidentally, one ought to make a further distinction in the category, " Regularly employed white collar and manual workers." It is a characteristic of modern capitalism that it gives rise to a fairly large number of specially trained individuals providing a variety of services. The successful operation of industry on a mass-production basis could not be achieved without chemists, engineers, accountants, personnel managers, and a host of other technicians and specialized workers. Moreover, if it is to keep going, a productive industrial machine requires an auxiliary sales organization, with its army of salesmen, clerks and the like. Thus, it can be said that a capitalistic society produces many individuals whose education and function set them apart from the proletariat. In fact such individuals generally identify themselves with the middle class, and their aspiration is to acquire property and, if possible, become owners of enterprises. Not everyone, of course, could achieve such goals; but even a cursory examination of the biographies of Japanese businessmen indicates that it was not altogether impossible.

When one includes the more than 3 million farmers tilling their own land, the number of those possessing property and engaged in their own enterprises is not small. In the past many of these people supported Japanese fascism, and fears have been expressed in some quarters that they might join a neo-fascist movement in the future.[53] To discuss this question in detail would take us too far afield. The point to be noted here is that under certain conditions they could become supporters of democratic parties. One might add parenthetically that one of these conditions would involve the problem of whether the Japanese economic system could be made productive enough to give a sense of economic security to a large

[52] Chuo Rodo Gakuen, *Rodo Nenkan* [Labor Year-book], 1949 (Tokyo, 1949), p. 38.

[53] For instance, Okamoto Seiichi, " Nihon Fascism no Hokai to Saiken " [The Decay and Revival of Japanese Fascism], *Sekai Hyoron* [World Review], III, No. 11 (November, 1948), pp. 22-30.

number of people. This, in turn, is related to the question of the balance between population growth and the supply of natural resources, and also to the question of future trends in world trade. If these factors should operate in such a way as to lead to a prolonged decline in the standard of living, the possibilities of democratic government would be greatly reduced.

The final consideration to be made in this analysis of the democratic potentials in Japan is attachment to the idea of equality. In modern times, equality has become an integral part of democracy as a social philosophy. To most liberals, equality does not necessarily imply the acceptance of the dogma that all men are of equal capacity, or that the world's goods must be distributed equally. It does involve, however, the acceptance of the principle that every individual must be given equality of opportunity to achieve the position that is commensurate with his ability.[54]

As we have seen, equality was not a characteristic feature of the Japanese social myth. On the contrary, as defined by the dominant ideology, the state was a vast organism. It followed from this that hierarchy was to be an inherent feature. Yet it appears that very few, if any, were willing to accept their social station in life as something permanently fixed. Such an attitude was in keeping with the forces shaping the modern world. Industrialization, the disappearance of the old samurai class, new mobility, urbanization, insecurity of status and livelihood—all of these were antagonistic to the principle of a rigidly stratified society.

No thoroughgoing study of the problem of social mobility in Japan exists. Such a study, when made, would throw a great deal of light on political change and subsidiary problems. Until more information is available, we can only give a few examples which seem to illustrate certain trends.

Every society has its own mechanisms for selecting new leaders and moving individuals up and down the social ladder. An obvious mechanism in Japan was the educational system. A degree from a leading university like the old Tokyo Imperial University was a key that opened many doors to desirable positions in government, business, and the professions. The demand for education, therefore, was tremendous. But since educational facilities were severely limited, relatively few could be accommodated. To be included

---

[54] Francis Wilson, *Elements of Modern Politics* (New York, 1936), p. 233.

among these few it was necessary to pass a series of competitive examinations. So difficult were the examinations and so severe the competition that it gave rise to the rather descriptive term " shiken jigoku " or " examination hell." Hugh L. Keenleyside and A. F. Thomas make the following observation in their *History of Japanese Education and Present Educational System:* [55]

> But in the middle schools the student is just starting on the steepest incline of the rocky pathway to education success. Having left the elementary school he feels it is incumbent to strive for academic success. To this end he is pushed on by his family and friends. The chances are heavily against him; it will not do merely to pass the examinations; he must pass among the highest or his possible career is ended. For boys just entering adolescence the responsibility and the strain are often too severe. . . . In probably the majority of the cases the student realizes that his parents have made tremendous sacrifices to give him this opportunity, and that their hopes for the future of the family (a very serious consideration in Japan) are largely centered in him. . . . It is impossible to withhold admiration for the spirit with which the average Japanese boy tackles his problem. But it is a problem which he ought not be asked to. solve at that age. As proof of this it may be added that many give way under the strain and not a few commit suicide in despair.

The very fact that young students were willing to go to such extremes testifies to the widespread desire for social success. The actual number of people who achieved their ambitions, however, is probably relatively small. A survey made before the war of a group of men who left the rural areas shows, for example, that some 5.8 percent of individuals coming from the lower classes succeeded in becoming government officials, teachers, company officials or doctors.[56] It would not be surprising if a careful study should reveal that the existing system was regarded by many as being too rigid to permit a sufficient number of talented individuals to rise, and hence was a cause of considerable dissatisfaction. In this connection, we should note that a book published in 1932 on the communist influence in education considered the type of young school teacher most likely to embrace communism. According to this account, he would be a young man who had been in adverse circumstances for a long time and had been unable to enter normal

[55] Tokyo, 1937, p. 198.
[56] Nojiri Shigeo, *Nomin Rison no Jissho-teki Kenkyu* [Field Studies on Departure from the Rural Areas], (Tokyo, 1942), p. 329. See also Otabashi Sadahisa, " Tomin no Shokugyo Keifu " [Occupational Genealogy of City Dwellers], *Rodo Mondai Kenkyu* [Studies of Labor Problems], February, 1948.

school. Accordingly, he studied on his own, and finally secured a license to teach by passing a competitive examination. His ambition was to secure a license to teach in secondary schools, but that was not easily realized. Meanwhile, his colleagues who possessed diplomas from normal schools won promotions, while he stayed in the lower ranks of the teaching hierarchy. " This " warns the book, " is something to which the authorities must give considerable attention." [57]

If our hypothesis about the widespread attachment to the idea of equality is correct, it would mean that a basic value or goal of democracy is already present. We cannot jump to the conclusion, however, that the emergence of political democracy is thereby automatically guaranteed. The problem of translating this and other democratic values into institutional structures remains. At this point we return to one of our main themes. The decline of the Japanese family should make possible the development of new associations for the individual, organized along democratic lines. Modern society is a multi-group society, and under certain conditions this multiplicity of associations can stand as a barrier to the growth of a leviathan state. If there can be maintained a shifting balance between various rival groups, we would have a modern version of the classical doctrine of the separation of powers.[58] The proliferation of groups, which is characteristic of modern life, brings in its train, on the other hand, a host of new problems. The demands of conflicting groups must be overcome. But, as Professor MacIver has pointed out, the reconciliation of diversity and unity is an age old problem of politics.[59] Modern political history suggests that a democratic state can provide a framework wherein not only diversity will be recognized, but methods of compromise and accommodation also will be provided.

Here we see one of the basic differences between democracy and the Japanese social myth. The latter postulated a specious unity which served as a facade for deep seated maladjustments and conflict. It seems almost certain, moreover, that some of these maladjustments arose from the divergence between the social myth and the social, economic, and political changes taking place. A

[57] Hashimoto Keiichiro, *Kyoiku Sekka to Sono Taisaku* [Communist Influences in Education and Counter Measures], (Tokyo, 1932), p. 87.
[58] Friedrich, *op. cit.*, pp. 182-183.
[59] MacIver, *op. cit.*, p. 438.

consequence of the successful democratization of Japan, therefore, should be a better integrated and more stable society. After all true stability can only be achieved by recognizing the existence of differences of views and conflict and providing for their peaceful solution.

In the foregoing analysis the factors favorable to the democratization of Japan have been purposely emphasized. The author does not wish to imply, however, that he believes that the emergence of a democratic Japan is a foregone conclusion. On the contrary, he is in sympathy with many of the books and articles that have appeared since the end of the war describing the numerous obstacles that exist. Occasionally, however, there is in these publications an assumption, implicit or explicit, that the Japanese are incapable of becoming democratic, for historical, cultural, or other reasons. With this assumption it is difficult to agree. The history of the democratic movement in the Meiji era shows conclusively that modernization was accompanied by the assertion that the masses of the people should have the right to bring the institutions of government under their control and thereby be able to run their own affairs. Not only did the democratic movement fail in the Meiji era; the realization that it might have succeeded provoked a reaction among the power-holders, who deliberately took steps to strengthen and elaborate the old social myths.

It is of crucial importance that we recognize this fact and that American policy in Japan take it into account. If the divergence which Veblen noted between technology and " spiritual outlook " was largely the product of deliberate policy, then, by the same token, it ought to be possible to overcome it by deliberate policy. There is evidence that Japanese conservatives preferred surrender to prolonging the war because of fear that the latter course would lead to the destruction of the social myth.[60] Moreover, in con-

---

[60] According to Kido Koichi, Konoye Fumimaro made the following remarks in a conference of Senior Statesmen in 1944:

" During the past few decades there has been present leftist ideology in one section of the Army. At present some have made connections with the armed forces, the bureaucracy, and the people, and are planning a leftist revolution. This is of greater danger than defeat in war. I personally fear a leftist revolution even more than defeat. This is because the Imperial Household and the *kokutai* (fundamental character of the state) can be preserved even in defeat, but not so in case of a revolution." Kyokuto Kokusai Gunji Saiban Kenkyu Kai [Society for the Study of the International Military Tribunal for the Far East], editor, *Kido Nikki* [The Kido Diary], (Tokyo, 1947), p. 128.

nection with the new constitution, a great debate took place as to whether the fundamental character of the Japanese state was changed by it.[61]

This should serve as a warning that in this instance history may well repeat itself. Such an eventuality would be tragic, for, as many Japanese observers point out, one of the most urgent tasks confronting the Japanese nation today is to complete the process of modernization begun in the Meiji era.

[61] Cf., *Shin Kempo no Kenkyu* [A Study of the New Constitution] edited by Kokka Gakkai (Tokyo, 1947), pp. 13-14.

A NOTE ON JAPANESE SOURCES

THERE has been a growing interest in Meiji studies among Japanese scholars during the past two decades. This interest has arisen in part from the conviction that the political patterns evolved in the formative Meiji era left their indelible imprint on the structure and practice of government in recent Japan. Thanks to the labors of scholars like Yoshino, Osatake, Tsuchiya, and Suzuki, our knowledge of the politics of this important period has been immeasurably enriched.

As one might expect, in the earlier years considerable attention was paid to the collection and publication of basic source materials. A group which included the late Professor Yoshino Sakuzo and Dr. Osatake Takeki set to work to bring together the more important documents and other primary materials. The product of their efforts was the *Meiji Bunka Zenshu* [Collected Works on Meiji Culture], Tokyo, 1930, in 24 volumes. This collection, containing reprints of books, pamphlets, and magazine and newspaper articles, constitutes a mine of information on almost every aspect of Meiji culture. Included in each volume are valuable bibliographical notes written by specialists and a chronological list of books published on the subject during the Meiji period. For students of political science the volumes on Meiji political history (volumes 2 and 3), constitutional history (volume 4), the democratic movement (volume 5), diplomacy (volume 6), politics (volume 7), law (volume 8), thought (volume 15), and social questions (volume 21) are of particular interest.

The contemporary newspapers are an important source of information. Unfortunately, files of Meiji newspapers are virtually non-existent in this country. For this reason, the *Shimbun Shusei Meiji Hennen Shi* [A Chronological Meiji History Compiled from Newspapers], Tokyo, 1935, consisting of 14 volumes plus an index volume and edited by Nakayama Yasumasa is especially welcome. As the title indicates, this is a compilation of clippings from Meiji newspapers arranged in a chronological order. Since the editor has included news items, dispatches from rural correspondents, editorials, and even cartoons, it provides us with a survey of Meiji civilization as it appeared to contemporaries. For the present study, however, the usefulness of the work was somewhat diminished by the fact that the editor has drawn heavily from the *Tokyo Nichi-Nichi*, a pro-government paper. A similar compilation, although on a much smaller scale, is *Meiji Shonen no Seso* [Aspects of Life in the Early Meiji Period], Tokyo, 1927, edited by Yokose Yau. For anyone studying the introduction of socialist ideas into Japan, this is an important work.

The various learned journals are rich in material, which so far has not been tapped to any extent by Western scholars. For those interested in Meiji studies, the *Meiji Bunka Kenkyu* [Studies in Meiji Culture], and the *Meiji Seiji Shi Kenkyu* [Studies in Meiji Political History] may be recommended. Another excellent journal, which unfortunately is now hard to obtain, is the *Shinkyu Jidai* [The Old and New Period]. The leading political science journal is the *Kokka Gakkai Zasshi* [Journal of the Political Science Association]. It carries relatively few articles on Meiji politics, but those that do appear in this journal are generally first rate.

In the field of history, the *Rekishi Gaku Kenkyu* [Studies in Historical Science] is a rewarding journal because it carries a fairly high proportion of articles on Japanese history. Two post war magazines, the *Nihon Rekishi* [Japanese History] and *Rekishi Hyoron* [Historical Review] show promise of becoming stimulating publications. For those interested in economic history, there are at least three leading periodicals. Both the *Shakai Keizai Shigaku* [Social and Economic History] and the *Keizai Shi Kenkyu* [Studies in Economic History] carry numerous articles on local economic history. The third journal, *Keizai Gaku Ronshu* [Studies on Economics] is interested, on the whole, in economic studies of a more theoretical and technical nature.

Then there are two well known magazines, the *Chuo Koron* [Central Review] and *Kaizo* [Reconstruction], which correspond roughly to *Harper's Magazine* and *Atlantic Monthly*. Considering that they are magazines for general circulation, they carry a surprising number of specialized articles by recognized authorities. The fact, however, that there exists no handy index to which one may turn detracts from their usefulness. About the only way to get at the material is to examine each volume laboriously.

Given the present state of Japanese studies in this country, the large body of monographic material and general works written by Japanese scholars is likely to remain an important source of both information and interpretations. It is only in recent years that Western students have begun to delve into Japanese sources, and consequently American scholarship on Japan has lagged behind. Our library facilities, moreover, are far from complete; and although the total number of Japanese books found in the various American libraries is much larger than is generally supposed, the materials are scattered and there still exist numerous gaps. Until our libraries become more adequate, and until more basic studies on Japanese politics have been completed by Western scholars, it is difficult to see how we can discard the convenient crutch of Japanese secondary sources.

Of the general works on Meiji political history, one of the most helpful is the 12th volume of the *Sogo Nihon Shi Taikei* [A Synthesis of Japanese History], Tokyo, 1934. This volume on the Meiji period was written by Fujii Jintaro and Moriya Hidesuke, both of whom were engaged in the editing of Restoration materials for the Ministry of Education. The great bulk of the work appears to be based on documents as well as on private papers of Meiji statesmen. Next there is the old but often quoted *Meiji Seishi* [Meiji Political History] by Sashihara Yasuzo which is conveniently reprinted in the second and third volumes of the *Meiji Bunka Zenshu*. This is a straight forward political history in which the narrative is arranged chronologically.

A work which is indispensable for certain aspects of Meiji political development is the *Jiyuto Shi* [A History of the Liberal Party], Tokyo, 1910, 2 volumes. It was written by Uda Tomoi and Wada Saburo under the supervision of Itagaki Taisuke. The title gives the impression that it is a history of a political party, but actually it is almost a general political history of the Meiji era. Naturally the *Jiyuto Shi* contains much data on the *Jiyuto*, but it is also rich in letters and other documentary materials. In this connection, those interested in party development should consult, in addition to the *Jiyuto Shi*, the *Jiyu Minken Undo Shi* [A History of the Democratic Movement], Tokyo, 1947, edited by Suzuki Yasuzo. This book is a reprint of a series of articles which appeared in a Tosa newspaper between July and December of 1899. Finally, it should be mentioned that Suzuki's article, "Risshisha no 'Nihon Kempo Mikomi An'" [Risshisha's Draft of a Japanese Constitution] in *Kokka Gakkai Zasshi*, volume 53 (1939) throws new light on the nature of the *Risshisha*.

There are several excellent studies on constitutional history. Many of the basic documents are collected together in *Nihon Kensei Kiso Shiryo* [Basic Historical Materials on Japanese Constitutional Government], Tokyo, 1939, and edited by the Gikai Seijisha. A standard work on the subject is Osatake Takeki's *Nihon Kensei Shi Taiko* [An Outline of Japanese Constitutional History], Tokyo, 1938, 2 volumes. Being an indefatigable researcher the late Dr. Osatake published a great deal, but as a social scientist he had shortcomings. Because of his familiarity with primary sources, he unearthed much new material. We owe, for instance, most of our information on early assemblies to his digging in early Meiji newspapers.

An old but still valuable work is the *Dai Nihon Kensei Shi* [Comprehensive Constitutional History of Japan], Tokyo, 1929 by Otsu Junichiro. The first three volumes of this ten volume work deal with the early Meiji era. The *Dai Nihon Kensei Shi*, like so many Japanese secondary works, contains lengthy extracts and quotations from other books and from documents. It is therefore a very valuable source of material which otherwise would not be available in this country.

Another scholar who has written a great deal on constitutional history is Suzuki Yasuzo. His *Nihon Kensei Seiritsu Shi* [History of the Establishment of Japanese Constitutional Government], Tokyo, 1933 as well as his *Kempo no Rekishi-teki Kenkyu* [A Historical Study of the Constitution], Revised Edition, Tokyo, 1933 are critical studies representing the approach of a Japanese liberal. Among his magazine articles, the "Nihon Kempo Seitei ni Taisuru Heruman Resureru no Kiyo" [The Contributions of Hermann Roessler to the Establishment of the Japanese Constitution], *Meiji Bunka Kenkyu*, May, 1935, and "Kempo Seitei Ron no Hassei" [The Genesis of the Argument for the Establishment of the Constitution]. *Chuo Koron*, volume 56, March, 1941 present revealing interpretations.

Two other books may be mentioned in passing. In *Meiji Rikken Shiso ni Okeru Eikoku Gikai Seido no Eikyo* [The Influence of the

British Parliamentary System on Meiji Constitutional Thought],
Tokyo, 1939, Professor Asai Kiyoshi brings together material which
is of value to those interested in Western influences on Japan. The
significance of the *Meiji Kensei Keizai Shiron* [Historical Essays on
Meiji Constitutional Government and National Economy], Tokyo,
1919, edited by the Kokka Gakkai lies in the fact that many of the
contributors were active participants in Meiji politics.

A field related to constitutional government which may be
pursued with profit is Meiji thought. No entirely satisfactory work
appears to have been written on this subject. Okamoto Keiji's
Meiji Taisho Shiso Shi [History of Meiji-Taisho Thought], Tokyo,
1929, does not dig into the subject very deeply. The *Meiji Shoki
Shakai Keizai Shiso Shi* [A History of Social-Economic Thought in
the Early Meiji Era], Tokyo, 1937 by Kada Tetsuji is worth consulting, especially for his references. A recent study by Ono Hisato,
Meiji Ishin Zengo ni Okeru Seiji Shiso no Tenkai [The Development
of Political Thought in the Restoration Period], Tokyo, 1944 is
well balanced, especially when one considers that it was published
during the war. A book whose interpretations are worthless, but
which is nevertheless useful as a guide to the sources is *Dai Nihon
Seiji Shiso Shi* [Comprehensive History of Japanese Political
Thought], Tokyo, 1939, 2 volumes by Sato Seikatsu.

In the *Meiji Shakai Shiso Kenkyu* [A Study of Meiji Social
Thought], Tokyo, 1932 by Shimoide Junkichi, a number of articles
which the author had previously published have been brought
together. His studies on the influence of Mill and Spencer are
especially good. Then there are two shorter studies based on the
technique of studying opinion as found in Meiji newspapers. In
" Jiyu Minken Ron no Shakai-teki Genkai " [The Social Limits of
Japanese Democratic Thought] in *Kokka Gakkai Zasshi*, volume
53, August, 1939, Hayashi Shigeru shows in detail the attitude of
Japanese liberals towards socialism. Professor Oka Yoshitake's
article, " Meiji Shoki no Jiyu Minken Ronja no Me ni Eijitaru Toji
no Kokusai Josei " [The International Situation as It was Viewed
by Those in the Democratic Movement in the Early Years of the
Meiji Era] in *Seiji Oyobi Seiji Shi Kenkyu* [Studies in Politics and
Political History], Tokyo, 1935 edited by Royama Masamichi
reveals the nationalistic tendencies in Meiji thought.

Biographies of leading Meiji statesmen can be used to advantage by students of politics. There is a biography of the last Shogun written by Shibuzawa Eiichi under the title *Tokugawa Keiki Ko Den* [The Biography of Prince Tokugawa Keiki], Tokyo, 1917. Of the eight volumes, four are devoted to the biography, three to documents, and one is an index volume. Two particularly useful biographies are those of Yamagata Aritomo and Ito Hirobumi. On Yamagata we have the *Koshaku Yamagata Aritomo Den* [Biography of Prince Yamagata Aritomo], Tokyo, 1933, a 3-volume work totalling several thousand pages. This was written by the well known author, Tokutomi Iichiro (pen name Soho). Because Tokutomi wrote this biography under the auspices of a society formed to honor Yamagata, he was given access to letters·and other documentary material. Fortunately for us, Tokutomi generally permitted these documents to tell the story, hence the biography can be used as a convenient source of documents which show the political attitudes of leading Meiji statesmen. Much the same thing can be said of the *Ito Hirobumi Den* [The Biography of Ito Hirobumi], Tokyo, 1940, 3 volumes, published by the Shunbo Ko Tsuisho Kai.

With regard to economic history, the literature is very extensive, but on the whole there are not many general works. On pre-Meiji industrial development a certain amount of data has been published in connection with the "manufacture" controversy. A summary of the recent literature on this subject as well as references to the older publications may be found in Hatori Takuya, "Bunsan Manufakucha Ron Hihan" [A Critique of the Theory of Dispersed Manufacture] in *Rekishi Gaku Kenkyu*, No. 127, May, 1947. A recent work which is valuable because it attempts to synthesize the earlier theories and because it presents a considerable amount of new documentary material is *Nihon Kinsei Sangyo no Seisei* [The Formation of Modern Japanese Industry], Tokyo, 1948, by Fujita Goro.

A few studies which throw some light on the economic decline of the Tokugawa regime may be mentioned. The *Hoken Shakai Hokai Katei no Kenkyu* [A Study of the Process of Decay of the Feudal Society], Tokyo, 1927 by Tsuchiya Takao is valuable because of its treatment by regions. The *Bakumatsu Keizai Shi Kenkyu* [Studies on the Economic History of the Late Tokugawa Era], edited by the Nihon Keizai Shi Kenkyujo, Tokyo, 1935, and

Bakumatsu no Shin Seisaku [New Policies at the End of the Tokugawa Period], edited by Honjo Eijiro, Tokyo, 1935 are symposiums with contributions by leading authorities.

On Meiji economic history, one of the basic collections is *Meiji Zenki Zaisei Keizai Shiryo*, 20 volumes, Tokyo, 1931 edited by Tsuchiya Takao and Ouchi Hyoei. In volume 18 may be found the *Kogyo Iken* [Opinions on Industry] which is a government report giving the industrial picture in every prefecture. For those interested in Japanese capitalism, there is the well known group study published under the title *Nihon Shihonshugi Hattatsu Shi Koza* [Lectures on the Development of Japanese Capitalism], Tokyo, 1933-1935 (reviewed in *Pacific Affairs*, March, 1934, pp. 71-76). This work as a whole suffers from dependence on Marxist concepts and terminology. Some of the brochures have been censored so severely that they are virtually unintelligible. Other interpretive works that deal with the subject of Japanese capitalism are Hirano Yoshitaro's *Nihon Shihonshugi Shakai no Kiko* [The Mechanism of Japanese Capitalistic Society], Tokyo, 1934, and *Nihon Shihonshugi Hattatsu Shi Gaisetsu* [An Outline History of the Development of Japanese Capitalism] by Tsuchiya Takao and Okazaki Saburo, Tokyo, 1937. Hirano Yoshitaro also has written a provocative article on the economic aspects of the democratic movement. Originally published in the December, 1933 issue of *Kaizo*, it is reprinted in his *Buruja Minshushugi Kakumei* [The Bourgeois-Democratic Revolution], Tokyo, 1948 under the title "Jiyu Minken."

Because of its importance in Japanese economic life, no one studying Meiji Japan can afford to ignore agriculture and agriculturalists. On Tokugawa agrarian problems, Honjo Eijiro's *Kinsei Noson Mondai Shiron* [Historical Essays on Modern Agricultural Problems], Tokyo, 1925 is a straight forward account whose value is enhanced by the fact that the author explains many of the special terms found in Tokugawa documents. On Meiji agriculture, perhaps the most useful work is a recent book by Ono Takeo, one of the leading authorities on the subject. The title is *Noson Shi* [History of Japanese Agriculture], and it forms volume 9 in the series, *Gendai Nihon Bummei Shi* [History of Contemporary Japanese Civilization], Tokyo, 1941. For the subject of the land tax and related problems, Ono Michio's account in *Kinsei Noson*

Keizai Shiron [History of Japanese Agricultural Economics in Modern Times], volume 59 in *Keizaigaku Zenshu* [Collected Works on Economics], Tokyo, 1933 provides a good introduction. Some illuminating passages on tenancy and tenant farmers may be found in *Sanju Sannen no Yume* [The Thirty-three Year Dream] by Miyazaki Torazo, Tokyo, 1902.

There exist several good studies on the peasant revolts which broke out in the early 1880's. The most complete account of the Iida uprising seems to be that contained in Kobayashi Hirobito, *Ina Nomin Sodo Shi* [History of Peasant Revolts in Ina], Tokyo, 1933. The revolt which has aroused the greatest interest among Japanese investigators is the Chichibu revolt. An indispensable study based on field work is the article " Chichibu Sodo " [The Chichibu Uprising] by the well known socialist, Sakai Toshihiko in the *Kaizo*, volume 10, October, 1928. Hirano Yoshitaro's article, " Chichibu Jiken " [The Chichibu Incident], which was originally published in the *Rekishi Kagaku* [Historical Science], December, 1934, and reprinted in *Buruja Minshushugi Kakumei*, makes good use of contemporary newspapers.

Obviously the foregoing list of titles does not even begin to cover the extensive literature on the subject of Meiji Japan. This list represents only those works which the author has found to be helpful either because they contained essential factual information, or because they presented interpretations that stimulated further thinking about the problems involved. It is hoped that this bibliographical guide will provide some signposts for those wishing to explore the field of Meiji politics through the medium of Japanese sources.

WORKS CONSULTED

I. Books in Western Languages

Allen, George C. *A Short Economic History of Modern Japan, 1867-1937.* London. 1946.

Anesaki, Masaharu. *A History of Japanese Religion with Special Reference to the Social and Moral Life of the Nation.* London. 1930.

Baba, Tatsui. *The Political Condition of Japan, Showing the Despotism and Incompetency of the Cabinet and the Aims of the Popular Parties.* Philadelphia. 1888.

Baelz, Toku (editor). *Awakening Japan: The Diary of a German Doctor: Erwin Baelz.* Translated by Eden and Cedar Paul. New York. 1932.

Barret, F. *L'Evolution du Capitalisme Japonais.* Volume 1. Paris. 1945.

Britton Roswell S. *The Chinese Periodical Press.* Shanghai. 1933.

Clarkson Jesse D. and Cochran Thomas C. (editors). *War as a Social Institution.* New York. 1941.

Commerical Reports of Her Majesty's Consuls in Japan, 1881. London. 1882.

Dennett, Tyler. *Americans in Eastern Asia.* New York. 1941.

The First Japanese Embassy to the United States of America. Translated by Miyoshi Shigehiko. Tokyo. 1920.

Friedrich, Carl J. *Constitutional Government and Democracy.* Boston. 1941.

Fukuzawa, Yukichi. *The Autobiography of Fukuzawa Yukichi.* Translated by Kiyooka Eiichi. Tokyo. 1934.

Hamada, Genji. *Prince Ito.* Tokyo. 1936.

Haring, Douglas G. *Japan's Prospect.* Cambridge. 1946.

Hummel, Arthur W. (editor). *Eminent Chinese of the Ch'ing Period.* 2 Volumes. Washington. 1944.

Idditi, Smimasa. *The Life of Marquis Shigenobu Okuma.* Tokyo. 1940.

Jones, Francis Clifford. *Extraterritoriality in Japan and the Diplomatic Relations Resulting in Its Abolition, 1853-1889.* New Haven. 1931.

Key, V. O., Jr. *Politics, Parties, and Pressure Groups.* Second Edition. New York. 1947.

Kuno, Yoshi S. *Japanese Expansion on the Asiatic Continent.* 2 Volumes. Berkeley. 1937, 1940.

Lattimore, Owen. *Solution in Asia.* Boston. 1945.

MacIver, R .M. *The Web of Government.* New York. 1947.

McLaren, W. W. *A Political History of Japan During the Meiji Era, 1867-1912.* London. 1916.

———— (editor). *Japanese Government Documents.* Transactions of the Asiatic Society of Japan. Volume 42, May, 1914. Tokyo.

Mayet, Paul. *Agricultural Insurance in Organic Connection with Savings-Banks, Land-Credit, and the Commutation of Debts.* Translated by Arthur Lloyd. London. 1893.

Mitsui, The House of, A Record of Three Centuries. Tokyo. 1937.

Mounsey, Augustus H. *The Satsuma Rebellion.* London. 1879.

Murdoch, James. *A History of Japan.* Volume 3. London. 1926.

Norman, E. Herbert. *Feudal Background of Japanese Politics.* (In Mimeograph). Secretariat Paper No. 9 for the Ninth Conference of the Institute of Pacific Relations. New York. 1945.

———. *Japan's Emergence as a Modern State.* New York. 1940.

———. *Soldier and Peasant in Japan: The Origins of Conscription.* New York. 1943.

Okuma, Shigenobu (editor). *Fifty Years of New Japan.* 2 Volumes. English Edition edited by Marcus B. Huish. London. 1910.

Orchard, John E. *Japan's Economic Position.* New York. 1930.

Paske-Smith, M. *Western Barbarians in Japan and Formosa, 1603-1868.* Kobe. 1930.

Pooley, A. M. *Japan At the Cross Roads.* London. 1917.

Quigley, Harold S. *Japanese Government and Politics.* New York. 1932.

The Recent Economic Development of Japan. Compiled by the Bank of Japan. Tokyo. 1915.

Reischauer, Robert Karl. *Japan, Government and Politics.* New York. 1939.

Sansom, George B. *Japan, A Short Cultural History.* Revised Edition. New York. 1943.

Schumpeter, E. B. (editor). *The Industrialization of Japan and Manchukuo.* New York. 1940.

Stead, Alfred (editor). *Japan by the Japanese. A Survey by its Highest Authorities.* London. 1904.

Swisher, Carl Brent. *The Growth of Constitutional Power in the United States.* Chicago. 1946.

Takekoshi, Yosaburo. *The Economic Aspects of the History of the Civilization of Japan.* 3 Volumes. New York. 1930.

Takizawa, Matsuyo. *The Penetration of Money Economy in Japan.* New York. 1927.

Uyehara, George Etsujiro. *The Political Development of Japan.* London. 1910.

II. Books in Japanese

Asai, Kiyoshi. *Meiji Rikken Shiso ni Okeru Eikoku Gikai Seido no Eikyo* [The Influence of the British Parliamentary System on Meiji Constitutional Thought]. Tokyo. 1939.

Baba, Tsunego. *Nihon Seito Shi* [History of Japanese Political Parties] in *Dai Shiso Ensaikuropijiya* [The Great Thought Encyclopedia]. Volume 17. Tokyo. 1928.

Bakumatsu Keizaishi Kenkyu [Studies on the Economic History of the Late Tokugawa Era]. Edited by the Nihon Keizaishi Kenkyujo. Tokyo. 1935.

Fujii, Jintaro and Moriya, Hidesuke. *Sogo Nihon Shi Taikei: Meiji Jidai Shi* [A Synthesis of Japanese History: The Meiji Period]. Tokyo. 1934.

Fujita, Goro. *Nihon Kindai Sangyo no Seisei* [The Formation of Modern Japanese Industry]. Tokyo. 1948.

Hani, Goro and Izu, Kimio. *Meiji Ishin ni Okeru Seido Jo no Henkaku* [Institutional Changes in the Meiji Restoration] in *Nihon Shihonshugi Hattatsu Shi Koza* [Lectures on the Development of Japanese Capitalism]. Tokyo. 1933-1935.

Hattori, Shiso. *Meiji Ishin Shi Kenkyu* [A Study of the Meiji Restoration]. Tokyo. 1933.

Hattori, Shiso and Shinobu, Seisaburo. *Nihon Manufakucha Shiron* [Historical Essays on Japanese Manufacture]. Tokyo. 1947.

Hirano, Yoshitaro. *Buruja Minshushugi Kakumei* [The Bourgeois-Democratic Revolution]. Tokyo. 1948.

————. *Gikai Oyobi Hosei Shi* [History of the Diet and Legislation] in *Nihon Shihonshugi Hattatsu Shi Koza.*

————. *Meiji Ishin ni Okeru Seiji-teki Shihai Keitai* [The Form of Political Control in the Meiji Restoration] in *Nihon Shihonshugi Hattatsu Shi Koza.*

————. *Nihon Shihonshugi Shakai no Kiko* [The Mechanism of Japanese Capitalistic Society]. Tokyo. 1934.

Hirose, Bin. *Nihon Sosho Sakuin* [A Bibliography of Japanese Collected Works]. Tokyo. 1939.

Homma, Hisao. *Meiji Bungaku Shi* [History of Meiji Literature]. Volume 10 in *Nihon Bungaku Zenshu* [Collected Works of Japanese Literature]. Tokyo. 1935.

Honda, Masanobu [?]. *Hon-Sa-Roku* [The Record of Honda, Sado-no-Kami]. Reprinted in *Nihon Keizai Taiten* [A Cyclopedia of Japanese Political Economy]. Edited by Takimoto Seiichi. Volume 3. Tokyo. 1928.

Honjo, Eijiro. *Bakumatsu no Shin Seisaku* [New Policies at the End of the Tokugawa Period]. Tokyo. 1935.

————. *Kinsei Noson Mondai Shiron* [Historical Essays on Modern Agricultural Problems]. Tokyo. 1925.

Inaoka, Susumu. *Nomin no Jotai Oyobi Nomin Undo Shoshi* [A Short History of the Condition of the Peasantry and Agricultural Movements] in *Nihon Shihonshugi Hattatsu Shi Koza.*

Ishikawa, Kyokuzan. *Nihon Shakaishugi Shi* [A History of Japanese Socialism]. Reprinted in *Meiji Bunka Zenshu* [Collected Works on Meiji Culture]. Edited by Yoshino Sakuzo. Volume 21. Tokyo. 1930.

Itagaki, Taisuke. *Jiyuto Shi* [History of the Liberal Party]. 2 Volumes. Tokyo. 1910.

Ito Hirobumi Den [The Biography of Ito Hirobumi]. 3 Volumes. Published by the Shunbo Ko Tsuisho Kai. Tokyo. 1940.

Kada, Tetsuji. *Meiji Shoki Shakai Keizai Shiso Shi* [A History of Social-Economic Thought in the Early Meiji Era]. Tokyo. 1937.

Kato, Hiroyuki. *Jinken Shinsetsu* [A New Theory of Human Rights]. Reprinted in *Meiji Bunka Zenshu*. Volume 5.

————. *Shinsei Tai-i* [Principles of True Government]. Reprinted in *Meiji Kaikaki Bungaku Shu* [A Collection of Literary Works on Period of the Meiji Enlightenment]. Volume 1 in *Gendai Nihon Bungaku Zenshu* [Collected Works on Modern Japanese Literature]. Tokyo. 1931.

Kazahaya, Yasoji, *Zaisei Shi* [History of Public Finance], in *Nihon Shihonshugi Hattatsu Shi Koza*.

Kobayashi, Hirobito. *Ina Nomin Sodo Shi* [History of Peasant Revolts in Ina]. Tokyo. 1933.

Kokkai Kaisetsu Ronja Higi Tanbun Sho [A Record of the Secret Deliberations of the Advocates of the Establishment of a National Assembly]. Reprinted in *Meiji Bunka Zenshu*. Volume 22.

Meiji Bunka Kenkyu Ronso. Edited by the Meiji Bunka Kenkyu Kai. Tokyo. 1934.

Meiji Kensei Keizai Shiron [Historical Essays on Meiji Constitutional Government and National Economy]. Edited by the Kokka Gakkai. Tokyo. 1919.

Miura, Hiroyuki. *Nihon Shi no Kenkyu* [Studies in Japanese History]. Volume 2. Tokyo. 1930.

Miyazaki, Torazo. *Sanju Sannen no Yume* [The Thirty-three Year Dream]. Tokyo. 1902.

Nakae, Chomin. *Fude Nao Ari, Shita Nao Ari* [I Still Have My Pen and My Tongue]. Tokyo. 1922.

————. *Ichinen Yuhan* [One Year and a Half]. Reprinted in *Shakai Bungaku Shu* [Collection of Social Literature]. Volume 39 in *Gendai Nihon Bungaku Zenshu*.

Nakayama, Yasumasa (editor). *Shimbun Shusei Meiji Hennen Shi* [A Chronological Meiji History Compiled from Newspapers]. 15 Volumes. Tokyo. 1935.

Nakazawa, Benjiro. *Nihon Beika Hendo Shi* [A History of Price Fluctuations of Rice in Japan]. Tokyo. 1933.

Nihon Keizai Shi [A History of Japanese Economy]. Volume 39 in *Keizaigaku Zenshu* [Collected Works on Economics]. Tokyo. 1930.

Nihon Kensei Kiso Shiryo [Basic Historical Materials on Japanese Constitutional Government]. Edited by the Gikai Seijisha. Tokyo. 1939.

Okabe, Fukuzo (editor). *Kozuke Jimbutsu Shi* [Accounts of Men from Kozuke]. 2 Volumes. Tokyo. 1924.

Okamoto, Keiji. *Meiji Taisho Shiso Shi* [History of Meiji-Taisho Thought]. Tokyo. 1929.

Ono, Hisato. *Meiji Ishin Zengo ni Okeru Seiji Shiso no Tenkai* [The Development of Political Thought in the Restoration Period]. Tokyo. 1944.

Ono, Michio, and Tsuchiya, Takao. *Kinsei Noson Keizai Shiron* [A History of Japanese Agricultural Economics in Modern Times]. Volume 59 in *Keizaigaku Zenshu*. Tokyo. 1933.

Ono, Takeo. *Noson Shi* [A History of Japanese Agriculture]. Volume 9 in *Gendai Nihon Bummei Shi* [History of Contemporary Japanese Civilization]. Tokyo. 1941.

Osatake, Takeki. *Nihon Kensei Shi* [Japanese Constitutional History]. Tokyo. 1930.

———. *Nihon Kensei Shi Taiko* [An Outline of Japanese Constitutional History]. 2 Volumes. Tokyo. 1938.

Otsu, Junichiro. *Dai Nihon Kensei Shi* [A Comprehensive Constitutional History of Japan]. Volumes 2 and 3. Tokyo. 1929.

Royama, Masamichi (editor). *Seiji Oyobi Seiji Shi Kenkyu* [Studies in Politics and Political History]. Tokyo. 1935.

Sakai, Kunio. *Ijin Ansatsu Shi* [History of Assassinations of Great Men]. Tokyo. 1937.

Sampei, Takako. *Nihon Mengyo Hattatsu Shi* [A History of the Development of the Japanese Cotton Industry]. Tokyo. 1941.

Sanshi Yokan. [Essentials of Silk Thread]. Edited by the Dai Nihon Sanshi Kai. Tokyo. 1926.

Sashihara, Yasuzo. *Meiji Seishi* [Meiji Political History]. Reprinted in *Meiji Bunka Zenshu.* Volumes 2 and 3.

Sato, Seikatsu. *Dai Nihon Seiji Shiso Shi* [Comprehensive History of Japanese Political Thought]. 2 Volumes. Tokyo. 1939.

Shibuzawa, Eiichi. *Tokugawa Keiki Ko Den* [The Biography of Prince Tokugawa Keiki]. Volume 1. Tokyo. 1917.

Shimoide, Junkichi. *Meiji Shakai Shiso Kenkyu* [Studies in Meiji Social Thought]. Tokyo. 1932.

Shirayanagi, Shuko. *Meiji Taisho Kokumin Shi: Kensei Juritsu Hen* [Popular History of the Meiji and Taisho Periods: The Establishment of Constitutional Government]. Tokyo. 1940.

Shiseki Kaidai [A Bibliography of History]. Tokyo. 1936.

Sumitani, Etsuji. *Nihon Keizaigaku Shi no Issetsu* [An Act in the History of Japanese Economics]. Tokyo. 1934.

Suzuki, Yasuzo (editor). *Jiyu Minken Undo Shi* [A History of the Democratic Moverment]. Tokyo. 1947.

———. *Kempo no Rekishi-teki Kenkyu* [A Historical Study of the Constitution]. Revised Edition. Tokyo. 1933.

———. *Nihon Kensei Seiritsu Shi* [History of the Establishment of Japanese Constitutional Government]. Tokyo. 1933.

Takimoto, Seiichi. *Nihon Keizai Shiso Shi* [A History of Japanese Economic Thought]. In Volume 15 of the Dai Shiso Ensaikuropijiya.

Tanaka, Sogoro. *Iwasaki Yataro.* Tokyo. 1940.

Toda, Shintaro. *Nihon Shihonshugi to Nihon Nogyo no Hatten* [Japanese Capitalism and the Development of Japanese Agriculture]. Tokyo. 1947.

Tokutomi, Iichiro. *Kinsei Nihon Kokumin Shi: Tokugawa Bakufu Joki* [A History of the Japanese People in Modern Times: The Early Part of the Tokugawa Bakufu]. Volume 2. Tokyo. 1924.

———. *Koshaku Yamagata Aritomo Den* [The Biography of Prince Yamagata Aritomo]. 3 Volumes. Tokyo. 1933.

Tsuchiya, Takao. *Hoken Shakai Hokai Katei no Kenkyu* [A Study of the Process of Decay of the Feudal Society]. Tokyo. 1927.

Tsuchiya, Takao and Okazaki, Saburo. *Nihon Shihonshugi Hattatsu Shi Gaisetsu* [An Outline History of the Development of Japanese Capitalism]. Tokyo. 1937.

Tsuchiya, Takao and Ouchi, Hyoei (editors). *Meiji Zenki Zaisei Keizai Shiryo* [Collection of Materials on Finance and Economy in the Early Meiji Period]. 20 Volumes. Tokyo. 1931.

Ueki, Emori. *Ikkyoku Gi-in Ron* [An Essay on Unicameral Assemblies]. Reprinted in *Meiji Bunka Zenshu*. Volume 7.

————. Kokkai Soshiki: *Kokumin Dai Kaigi* [The Organization of the National Assembly: People's Convention]. Reprinted in *Meiji Bunka Zenshu*. Volume 7.

————. *Minken Jiyu Ron* [On Popular Rights and Liberty]. Reprinted in *Meiji Bunka Zenshu*. Volume 5.

————. *Tempu Jinken Ben* [*In Defense of Natural Rights*]. Reprinted in *Meiji Bunka Zenshu*. Volume 5.

Uesugi, Shigejiro. *Meiji Kempo no Seiritsu* [The Establishment of the Meiji Constitution] in *Shin Nihon Shi Koza* [Lectures on New Japanese History]. Tokyo. 1948.

Watanabe, Shinichi. *Nihon Noson Jinko Ron* [On the Japanese Agricultural Population]. Tokyo. 1934.

Yamada, Seitaro. *Nihon Shihonshugi Bunseki* [An Analysis of Japanese Capitalism]. Tokyo. 1934.

Yokose, Yau (editor). *Meiji Shonen no Seso* [Aspects of Life in the Early Meiji Era]. Tokyo. 1927.

III. Periodical Articles in English

Abel, Theodore. "The Pattern of a Successful Political Movement." *American Sociological Review*. Volume 2. 1937.

Blakemore, Thomas L. "Post-war Developments in Japanese Law." *Wisconsin Law Review*. July, 1947.

Borton, Hugh. "Peasant Uprisings in Japan of the Tokugawa Period." *Transactions of the Asiatic Society of Japan*. Volume 16. May, 1938.

Brinton, Crane. "The Manipulation of Economic Unrest." *The Tasks of Economic History*. Supplement 8. 1948.

Colegrove, Kenneth. "The Japanese Constitution." *The American Political Science Review*. Volume 31. December, 1937.

Gilmartin, William M. and Ladejinsky, W. J. "The Promise of Agrarian Reform in Japan." *Foreign Affairs*. Volume 26. January, 1948.

van Gulik, R. H. "Kakkaron." *Monumenta Serica*. Volume 4. 1939-1940.

Honjo, Eijiro. "The Importance of ' Goyokin ' or Forced Loans in the Meiji Restoration." *Kyoto University Economic Review*. Volume 18. July, 1933.

Horie, Yasuzo. "The Development of the Domestic Market." *Kyoto University Economic Review*. Volume 15. January, 1940.

————. "Government Industries in the Early Years of the Meiji Era." *Kyoto University Economic Review*. Volume 14. January, 1939.

Hummel, Arthur W. " Some American Pioneers in Chinese Studies." *Notes on Far Eastern Studies in America.* No. 9. June, 1941.

Ike, Nobutaka. " Landownership and Taxation in the Westernization of Japan." *The Journal of Economic History.* Volume 7. November, 1947.

———. " Triumph of the Peace Party in Japan in 1873." *The Far Eastern Quarterly.* Volume 2. May, 1942.

———. " Western Influences on the Meiji Restoration." *The Pacific Historical Review.* Volume 17. February, 1948.

Pollard, Robert. " The Dynamics of Japanese Imperialism." *The Pacific Historical Review.* Volume 8. March, 1939.

Satow, E. M. " The Revival of Pure Shin-tau." *Transactions of the Asiatic Society of Japan.* Volume 3. 1888. Appendix.

Sawada, Sho. " Financial Difficulties of the Edo Bakufu." Translated by Hugh Borton. *Harvard Journal of Asiatic Studies.* Volume 1. November, 1936.

Shiomi, Saburo. " On the Revision of the Land Tax." *Kyoto University Economic Review.* Volume 4. 1929.

Simmons, D. B. and Wigmore, John H. " Notes on Land Tenure and Local Institutions in Old Japan." *Transactions of the Asiatic Society of Japan.* Volume 19. 1891.

Smith, N. Skene. " Materials on Japanese Social and Economic History: Tokugawa Japan." *Transactions of the Asiatic Society of Japan.* Second Series. Volume 14. 1937.

Smith, Thomas C. " The Introduction of Western Industry During the Last Years of the Tokugawa Period." *Harvard Journal of Asiatic Studies.* Volume 11. June, 1948.

Stifler, Susan Reed. " Elijah Coleman Bridgman, The First American Sinologist." *Notes on Far Eastern Studies in America.* No. 10. January, 1942.

Tsuchiya, Takao. " Economic History of Japan." *Transactions of the Asiatic Society of Japan.* Second Series. Volume 15. 1937.

Tsuru, Shigeto. " Economic Fluctuations in Japan, 1868-1895." *The Review of Economic Statistics.* Volume 23. 1941.

IV. PERIODICAL ARTICLES IN JAPANESE

Asano, Kenshin. " Sada Kaiseki no Hakurai Hin Haiseki ni Tsuite " [On Sada Kaiseki's Boycott Movement Against Imported Goods]. *Shakai Keizai Shigaku* [Social and Economic History]. Volume 8, No. 11. February, 1939.

Baba, Tsunego. " Hogaki no Seito to Sono Shikin " [Early Political Parties and Their Finances]. *Chuo Koron* [Central Review]. Volume 44, No. 10. October, 1929.

Ebihara, Hachiro. " Soko Nihonjin Aikoku Domei Shimatsu " [The Case of the Japanese Patriotic League of San Francisco]. *Meiji Bunka Kenkyu* [Studies in Meiji Culture]. No. 2. May, 1934.

Hatori, Takuya. " Bunsan Manufakucha Ron Hihan " [A Critique of the Theory of Dispersed Manufacture]. *Rekishi Gaku Kenkyu* [Studies in Historical Science]. No. 127. May, 1947.

Hayashi, Shigeru. " Jiyu Minken Ron no Shakai-teki Genkai " [The Social Limits of Japanese Democratic Thought]. *Kokka Gakkai Zasshi* [Journal of the Political Science Association]. Volume 53, No. 8. August, 1939.

————. " Ueki Emori no Kempo Shian to Iwayuru Risshisha An no Kiso " [Ueki Emori's Private Draft of a Constitution and the Drafting of the So-called Risshisha Draft]. *Kokka Gakkai Zasshi* [Journal of the Political Science Association]. Volume 51, No. 9. September, 1937.

Irimajiri, Koshu. " Tosa Han Higashi Chiho ni Kansuru Sho-Shiryo " [Various Historical Materials on the Eastern Areas of the Tosa Clan]. *Shakai Keizai Shigaku* [Social and Economic History]. Volume 7, No. 9. December, 1937.

Ishii, Takashi. " Bakumatsu Isseiso Keitai no Bunseki " [An Analysis of the Form of Political Struggle at the End of the Tokugawa Period]. *Rekishi Gaku Kenkyu* [Studies in Historical Science]. Volume 1, No. 1. November, 1933.

————. " Bakumatsu Kaiko ni Yoru Kokunai Keizai no Konran to Bakufu no Boeki Tosei Keikaku " [Internal Economic Disorder due to Opening the Country and the Bakufu's Foreign Trade Control Plan]. *Rekishi Gaku Kenkyu* [Studies in Historical Science]. Volume 4, No. 1, May, 1935.

————. " Bunkyu Nenkan ni Okeru Gaikoku Boeki no Hatten to Bakufu no Yokuatsu Seisaku " [The Development of Foreign Trade in the Bunkyu Era and the Suppression Policy of the Shogunate]. *Shakai Keizai Shigaku* [Social and Economic History]. Volume 5, No. 4. July, 1935.

Kaji, Ryuichi. " Nakae Chomin." *Tembo* [View]. October, 1946.

Kajinishi, Mitsumi. " Nihon Shihonshugi Seiritsu Shi " [A History of the Establishment of Japanese Capitalism]. *Yuibutsu Shikan* [Historical Materialism]. Volume 1. November, 1947.

Kimura, Takeshi. " Meiji Bungaku ni Arawaretaru Jiyu " [Liberty as Revealed in Meiji Literature]. *Soken* [Foundation]. Volume 1, No. 5. May, 1946.

Kobayashi, Yoshimasa. " Bakumatsu Girudo no Tokushitsu ni Kansuru Ikkosatsu " [A Study Concerning the Special Characteristics of the Guilds at the End of the Tokugawa Period]. *Kaizo* [Reconstruction]. Volume 15, No. 10. October, 1933.

Konishi, Shiro. " Bakumatsu no Shishi to Kane " [Money and the Loyalists at the End of the Tokugawa Era]. *Nihon Rekishi* [Japanese History]. No. 11. March, 1948.

Matsuyoshi, Sadao. " Tosa Han no Chomin Goshi ni Tsuite " [On the Merchant Goshi of the Tosa Clan]. *Keizai Shi Kenkyu* [Studies in Economic History]. Volume 1, No. 5. March, 1930.

————. " Tosa Han no Gokurashi Kaiage ni Tsuite " [On the Purchase of

Paper by the Tosa Clan]. *Keizai Shi Kenkyu* [Studies in Economic History]. Volume 1, No. 1 and 2. November, 1929 and December, 1929.

Nishida, Nagahisa. " Meiji no Shimbun " [Meiji Newspapers]. *Kokumin no Rekishi*. Volume 1, No. 10. November-December, 1947.

Nishioka, Toranosuke. " Nihon Nogyo ni Okeru Jikyu Keizai Seikatsu no Shi-teki Tenkai " [The Historical Evolution of the Self-Sufficient Farm Economy in Japan]. *Rekishi Gaku Kenkyu* [Studies in Historical Science]. No. 125. August, 1946.

Nomura, Motonosuke. " Tanaka Shozo Kun to Watakushi " [Mr. Tanaka Shozo and I]. *Meiji Bunka Kenkyu* [Studies in Meiji Culture]. December, 1934.

Ono, Takeo. " Hyakusho Ikki Ya, Kinno Gun Ya " [Peasant Revolts or Pro-Emperor Armies?]. *Shakai Keizai Shigaku* [Social and Economic History]. Volume 6, No. 4. July, 1936.

———. " Meiji Ishin to Nomin Kaikyu no Kakumei Shiso " [The Meiji Restoration and the Revolutionary Thought of the Agricultural Class]. *Shakai Gaku Zasshi* [Journal of Sociology]. No. 63. July, 1929.

Osatake, Takeki. " Chiho Minkai " [Local Popular Assemblies]. *Meiji Seiji Shi Kenkyu* [Studies in Meiji Political History]. No. 2, May, 1936.

———. " Han Gi-in to Chiho Minkai " [Clan Assemblies and Local Popular Assemblies]. *Meiji Bunka Kenkyu* [Studies in Meiji Culture]. No. 4. December, 1934.

———. " Ito An Izen no Kempo Soan " [Draft Constitutions Before Ito's Draft]. *Meiji Bunka Kenkyu* [Studies in Meiji Culture]. No. 1. February, 1934.

———. " Seito Shi no Issetsu " [An Episode in the History of Political Parties]. *Meiji Bunka Kenkyu* [Studies in Meiji Culture]. No. 2. May, 1934.

Ozaki, Hiromichi. " Kinsei Shakaito no Genin wo Ronzuru " [On the Origins of Modern Socialist Parties]. Reprinted in *Meiji Bunka Zenshu* Volume 21.

Ozeki, Tsugio. " Waga Kuni Kirisuto Kyo Bunka Shi E no Ichi Tembo " [A View of the Trend Towards a Christian Culture in Our Country]. *Rekishi Gaku Kenkyu* [Studies in Historical Science]. Volume 4, No. 1. May, 1935.

Sakai, Toshihiko. " Chichibu Sodo " [The Chichibu Revolt]. *Kaizo* [Reconstruction]. Volume 10, No. 10. October, 1928.

Sekiguchi, Tai. " Meiji Jurokunen no Chiho Junsatsushi " [A Local Administrative Inspector in 1883]. *Toshi Mondai* [Municipal Problems]. Volume 29, No. 5. November, 1939.

Shimomura, Fujio. " Kinsei Noson no Kaikyu Kosei: Choshu Han no Baai " [Class Structure in Modern Farm Villages: The Example of Choshu Clan]. *Rekishi Gaku Kenkyu* [Studies in Historical Science]. Volume 3, No. 2. December, 1934.

Shiota, Yasumi. " Meiji Shonen ni Okeru Keisatsu to Rikugun no Bunka "

[The Differentiation of the Police and Army in the Early Years of the Meiji Era]. *Rekishi Gaku Kenkyu* [Studies in Historical Science]. Volume 4, No. 5. September, 1935.

Suwa, Jiro. " Yugo to Itagaki Haku Sono Ta " [Hugo and Count Itagaki and Others]. *Denki* [Biography]. Volume 2, No. 7. July, 1935.

Suzuki, Yasuzo. " Genron Jiyu Ron no Kaiko " [Looking Back on the Demand for Freedom of Speech]. *Kaizo* [Reconstruction]. Volume 16, No. 2. February, 1934.

————. " Kempo Seitei Ron no Hassei " [The Genesis of the Argument for the Establishment of the Constitution]. *Chuo Koron* [Central Review]. Volume 56, No. 3. March, 1941.

————. " Nihon Kempo Seitei ni Taisuru Heruman Resureru no Kiyo " [The Contributions of Hermann Roessler to the Establishment of the Japanese Constitution]. *Meiji Bunka Kenkyu* [Studies in Meiji Culture]. No. 5. May, 1935.

————. " Rikken Seiji E no Kato " [The Transition to Constitutional Government]. *Chuo Koron* [Central Review]. Volume 56, No. 5. May, 1941.

————. " Risshisha no ' Nihon Kempo Mikomi An ' " [Risshisha's Draft of a Japanese Constitution]. *Kokka Gakkai Zasshi* [Journal of the Political Science Association]. Volume 53, No. 11. November, 1939.

————. " Tairiku Shinshutsu no Hitsuzensei to Joyaku Kaisei " [The Inevitability of the Continental Advance and Treaty Revision]. *Chuo Koron* [Central Review]. Volume 56, No. 4. April, 1941.

Takahashi, Shingo. " Meiji Juyonen no Seihen ni Tsuite " [On the Political Crisis of 1881]. *Waseda Seiji Keizai Gaku Zasshi* [Waseda Journal of Politics and Economics]. No. 61. October, 1938.

Tanaka, Sogoro. " Shakaito Ko " [On the Rickshamen's Party]. *Rodo Hyoron* [Labor Review]. Volume 2, No. 4. April, 1947.

Toyama, Shigeki. " Jiyu Minken Undo ni Okeru Shizoku-teki Yoso " [The Shizoku Elements in the Democratic Movement]. *Rekishi Hyoron* [Historical Review]. Volume 2, No. 3. May, 1947.

Tsuchiya, Takao. " Bakumatsu Doran no Keizai-teki Bunseki " [An Economic Analysis of the Unrest During the Later Tokugawa Period]. *Chuo Koron* [Central Review]. Volume 47, No. 10. October, 1932.

————. " Ishin Henkaku no Keizai-teki Urazuke " [Economic Support for the Meiji Revolution]. *Chuo Koron* [Central Review]. Volume 55, No. 9. September, 1940.

————. " Ishin Shi Kenkyu no Chushin Ronten " [The Central Point of Dispute in the Study of Restoration History]. *Kaizo* [Reconstruction]. Volume 16, No. 1. January, 1934.

————. " Nihon Manufakucha Zusetsu " [Illustrations on Japanese Manufacture]. *Rekishi Gaku Kenkyu* [Studies in Historical Science]. Volume 1, No. 4. February, 1934.

————. " Nihon Zaibatsu Shiron, Josetsu " [Historical Essays on the Japanese Zaibatsu, An Introduction]. *Chuo Koron* [Central Review]. Volume 61, No. 7. July, 1946.

———. " Sonno Tobaku Undo to Shomin Kaikyu " [The Pro-Emperor Anti-Tokugawa Movement and the Common People]. *Chuo Koron* [Central Review]. Volume 52, No. 9. September, 1937.

———. " Takinogawa Kashima Bosekisho no Soritsu Keiei Jotai " [The Establishment and Management of the Kashima Cotton Spinning Mill at Takinogawa]. *Keizaigaku Ronshu* [Studies in Economics] Volume 3, No. 10. October, 1933.

———. " Tokugawa Jidai no Manufakucha " [Manufacture in the Tokugawa Period]. *Kaizo* [Reconstruction]. Volume 15, No. 9. September, 1933.

Uchida, Shigetaka. " Meiji Shoki no Seiji Shiso to O-Bei Shiso " [Political Thought in the Early Meiji Period and European Thought]. *Waseda Seiji Keizai Gaku Zasshi* [Waseda Journal of Politics and Economics]. No. 61. October, 1938.

Watanabe, Kuriyama. " Meiji Juyonen Seihen ni Tsuite " [On the Political Crisis of 1881]. *Meiji Bunka Kenkyu* [Studies in Meiji Culture]. No. 2. May, 1934.

Yada, Soun. " Keikan Monogatari " [Tale of Police Officers]. *Chuo Koron* [Central Review]. Volume 44, No. 1. January, 1929.

Yagizawa, Zenji. " Meiji Shoki no Defureshion to Nogyo Kyoko " [Deflation in the Early Meiji Era and the Agricultural Panic]. *Shakai Keizai Shigaku* [Social and Economic History]. Volume 2, No. 3. June, 1932.

———. " Seinan Senekigo no Infureshion " [Inflation After the Satsuma Rebellion]. *Keizai Shi Kenkyu* [Studies in Economic History]. Volume 7. July, 1932.

Yamamoto, Fumio. " Meiji Shin Seifu no Shimbun Seisaku " [The Newspaper Policy of the New Meiji Government]. *Rekishi Gaku Kenkyu* [Studies in Historical Science]. Volume 9, No. 3. March, 1939.

Yanagida, Sen. " Angaido Shujin Komuro Nobusuke." *Meiji Bunka Kenkyu* [Studies in Meiji Culture]. No. 2. May, 1934.

Yanagigawa, Noboru. " Kiryu Orimono Gyo ni Okeru Maegashi Seido " [The Domestic System in the Kiryu Textile Industries]. *Keizaigaku Ronshu* [Studies in Economics]. Volume 1, No. 8. November, 1931. Volume 2, No. 2. February, 1932.

Yoshino, Sakuzo. " Gneist, Stein to Ito Hirobumi " [Gneist, Stein and Ito Hirobumi]. *Kaizo* [Reconstruction]. Volume 15, No. 2. February, 1933.

———. " Minken Undo Danatsu Sokumen Shi " [A Sidelight on the Suppression of the Democratic Movement]. *Chuo Koron* [Central Review]. Volume 44, No. 10. October, 1929.

INDEX

A

Hashimoto, Sanai, 28
Hatamoto, 31
Hatori, T., 12n
Hattori, S., 12n, 21n, 64n
Hayashi, S., 119n, 130n, 132n, 134n-135n
Hibi, S., 161-162
High Treason Case, 108
Hirano, Y., 14n, 77n, 80n, 82n-83n, 146n, 162n, 164n
Hirano, Yataro, 106
Hirata, Atsutane, 20
Hirata, Tosuke, 174
Hirose, B., 26n
Hiroshima, 88n
History of Japanese Education and Present Educational System, 215
Hizen, 17, 49, 96
Hokkaido Affair, 95*ff*, 102*ff*
Homma family, 19n
Homma, H., 121n-122n, 125n
Honda, Masanobu, 9
Honjo, E., 17n, 23n, 35n, 150n
Horie, Y., 73n-74n, 75, 75n
Hugo, Victor and Itagaki, 121
Hummel, Arthur, 28n, 37n

I

Ibaraki, 103, 157, 161
Ichinen Yuhan, 126
Idditti, S., 48n, 50n, 94n
Ienaga, S., 197n
Iida Incident, 165*ff*, 167
Ike, N., 50n, 77n
Imperial court, 5-6, 25, 33, 42
Imperial Guard, 89, 92, 185
Imperial House Law, 176, 178
Imperial Household Property, 173, 175
Imperial Rescript of 1881, 98, 101, 138, 171
    on Education, 197
Ina, 22
Inaoka, S., 145n
Indigo, 20
Industrial production, 12
Industrialists, 11, 13-14, 16
Industrialization, 74, 76, 85, 189, 196, 206
Inflation, 79-82, 139*ff*
Inouye, Kaoru, 152, 171, 173, 177-178, 182-184
Inouye, Momonosuke, 161
Irimajiri, K., 63n
Ishii, T., 15n-16n
Ishikawa, 147
Ishikawa, K., 109n, 114n, 149n
Itagaki, Taisuke, 32, 50, 50n, 52, 52n, 53, 55-56, 56n, 59-60, 60n, 61, 61n, 65, 65n, 66, 66n, 68, 69n, 85, 87, 88n,

89, 92, 101, 101n, 102, 104-105, 106n, 113, 125, 151n, 157n-158n, 161n, 178, 184
Itagaki, goes abroad, 151*ff*
Ito, Hirobumi, 94-96, 98, 117, 152, 171, 173*ff*, 174n, 178-179, 197
Ito, Jintaro, 109
Ito, Myoji, 172, 174, 177
Iwakura Mission, 51-52
Iwakura, Tomomi, 5-6, 36, 42, 49, 51-52, 94, 98, 125, 128, 152, 172-173
Iwasaki, Yataro, 75, 97-98, 109, 154
Iye, 201.
Izu, K., 85n

J

Jacobin Clubs, 69
Japan Railway Co., 75
Japanese nation, 198
Jingo, Empress, 48
Jinken Shinsetsu, 116
Jinrikisha, 107
Jiyu, 155, 182
Jiyu minken undo, xiii
Jiyu no Uta, 106
Jiyuto, 101, 104, 106-109, 115, 138, 148, 153, 155, 158, 163, 168, 181, 184, 189-190
    contributions to, 157
    dissolution of, 159-160
    membership of, 103, 120, 151, 158
    program of, 102
Jokai Haran, 121
Jones, F. C., 183n
Joryu no Minken Setsu, 59

K

Kada, T., 109n, 149n-150n
Kagoshima, 54
Kaientai, 64
Kainan Gisha, 61
Kaji, R., 124n
Kajin no Kigyu, 123
Kajinishi, M., 13n
Kakumei, 182
Kamata, battle of, 22-23
Kanagawa, 147, 157, 167
Kaneko, Kentaro, 115, 176-177
Kanno, Wataro, 74n
Kashima, Mampei, 16n
Kataoka, Kenkichi, 66, 88-89
Kato, Hiroyuki, 58-59, 114-116, 118
Kawahara, J., 130n
Kawaii, Eijiro, 211
Kawashima, Tadanosuke, 122
Kawashima, Takenori, 201n, 202, 202n-204n, 208, 209n
Kazahaya, Y., 73n

9

Mito, 18, 22
Mitsubishi, 75, 96-98, 104, 108, 152, 154-155
Mitsui, 23, 75, 84, 152
Mitsukuri, Genpo, 27, 37
Mitsukuri, Shogo, 26
Miura, Hiroyuki, 91, 91n
Miura, Kamekichi, 108
Miyajima, Seiichiro, 42
Miyazaki, Muryu, 122
Miyazaki, T., 143n
Miyazaki, Tamizo, 211n
Miyoshi, S., 29n
Mizuno, Tadakuni, 41
Modernization, 53, 76, 217-218
Money economy, 11, 63
Money lenders, 10, 19-20, 163
Monopolies, 14, 21, 74
Montesquieu, 178
Moran, W. T., 209n
Mori, Arinori, 38-39, 113
Mori, of Choshu, 31
Mori, Shigeru, 50
Moriya, H., 4n, 33n, 35n, 37n-39n, 90n, 95n-96n,
Mosse, Albert, 174
Motoda, Eifu, 205
Motooka, Keiji, 38
Mounsey, A., 48n
Muirhead, William, 28
Muragaki, Norimasa, 29
Muramatsu, Aizo, 166-167
Murdoch, J., 3n, 8n, 17n, 32n
Mutsu, Munemitsu, 125
Mythology, interpretation of, 200

N

Nabeshima, Kanso, 149
Nagano, 69, 71, 73, 89, 163, 165, 167
Nagasaki, 25, 28, 37
Nagoya, 68, 166
Nakae, Chomin, 124*ff*
Nakagawa, Zennosuke, 206
Nakajima, Nobuyuki, 102
Nakamura, Masanao, 112
Nakaoka, H., 199n
Nakayama, Y., 68n
Nakazawa, B., 77n
National isolation, abandonment of, 24
Nationalism, 135, 190
Nationalist scholars, 20-22
Natsume, Soseki, 207, 208n
Natsushima, 177
Natural calamities, 143, 146*ff*
Natural rights, 61, 116, 135-137
Natural selection, 116
New landlords, 19

Nihon Keizaishi Kenkyujo, 63n
Niigata, 146
Nijo castle, 34
Ninjo, 204
Nishi, A., presents draft of constitution, 33
Nishida, N., 90n
Nishikawa, Tsutetsu, 122
Nishioka, T., 19n
Nojiri, S., 215n
Nomura, M., 92n
Norman, E. H., 9n, 14n-15n, 18n, 19, 22n-23n, 27n, 30n, 48n, 54n, 64n-65n, 66, 66n, 74n, 77n, 81n, 85n, 91n-92n, 104, 104n, 107n, 144n, 151n, 182n
Numa, Morikazu, 159

O

Oi, Kentaro, 128, 181, 211
Oishi, Masami, 152-153
Okabe, F., 16n
Okada, Setsu, 29
Okamoto, S., 213n
Okayama, 70, 87
Oki, 52
Okubo, Ichio, 30
Okubo, M., 19n
Okubo, Toshimichi, 48n, 52, 65
Okuma, Shigenobu, 52, 75, 94-95, 97-98, 104-105, 154, 159, 178, 186
Okumiya, Kenji, 108-110
On Liberty, 112
Onken Chakujitsu, 105
Ono, 23
Ono, Azuma, 94
Ono, H., 173n
Ono, M., 76n, 77n-79n, 128n, 145n
Ono, Takeo, 20n, 71n, 73n, 76n, 78n-82n, 139n, 143, 145n, 146n, 163n
Opening the country, economic consequences, 72
Orchard, J. E., 72, 72n
Oriental Socialist Party, see *Toyo Shakaito*
Osaka, 6, 11, 30, 63, 73, 87
Osatake, Takeki, 23, 28n-29n, 38n, 39, 39n-41n, 42, 56n, 62n, 66n, 87n, 89n, 93n, 96, 105n, 115n, 152n-153n, 174n-178n, 187n
Oshima, H., 195n
Oshima, S., 201n
Oshima, Y., 201n, 208n
Otabashi, S., 215n
Otokai, 104
Otsu, J., 101n-102n, 159n, 184n, 186n
Ouchi, Hyoei, 82n
Ozaki, Yukio, 159, 203, 203n